Also by Susan Manion MacDonald

published by New World Publishing

BALANCE, nature's way to heal your body

SYMPTOMS:
The Language of the Soul

A Gift of Transformation

SUSAN MANION MACDONALD

#1 Best Selling Author of BALANCE

BALBOA.
PRESS
A DIVISION OF HAY HOUSE

First Edition

Neither the publisher nor the authors are engaged in rendering professional advice or services to the individual reader. The ideas, procedures, and suggestions contained in this book are not intended as a substitute for consulting with your physician. All matters regarding your health require medical supervision. Neither the author nor the publisher shall be liable or responsible for any loss or damage allegedly arising from any information or suggestion in this book.

While the author has made every effort to provide accurate telephone numbers and Internet addresses at the time of publication, neither the publisher nor the author assumes any responsibility for errors, or for changes that occur after publications.

Balboa Press books may be ordered through booksellers or by contacting:

Balboa Press
A Division of Hay House
1663 Liberty Drive
Bloomington, IN 47403
www.balboapress.com
1-(877) 407-4847

Because of the dynamic nature of the Internet, any web addresses or links contained in this book may have changed since publication and may no longer be valid. The views expressed in this work are solely those of the author and do not necessarily reflect the views of the publisher, and the publisher hereby disclaims any responsibility for them.

The author of this book does not dispense medical advice or prescribe the use of any technique as a form of treatment for physical, emotional, or medical problems without the advice of a physician, either directly or indirectly. The intent of the author is only to offer information of a general nature to help you in your quest for emotional and spiritual well-being. In the event you use any of the information in this book for yourself, which is your constitutional right, the author and the publisher assume no responsibility for your actions.

Any people depicted in stock imagery provided by Thinkstock are models, and such images are being used for illustrative purposes only.
Certain stock imagery © Thinkstock.

ISBN: 978-1-4525-5402-0 (hc)
ISBN: 978-1-4525-5400-6 (sc)
ISBN: 978-1-4525-5401-3 (e)
Library of Congress Control Number: 2012911183

Printed in the United States of America

Balboa Press rev. date: 8/11/2012

Table of Contents

Dedication

I am grateful to God; this book is God's work and I feel as a Prophet bringing it forth to the world. Thank you God!

Thank you to my wonderful husband James, for supporting the shift to authentic self and the joy we share.

To my children Tammy, Charlene, Dan and grandchildren Benji, Katie, Adam, Carl, Gia, Brady and Noah, great grandchildren Tyler, Faith, Brooklyn, Jayden Gavin and Madison, thank you. Each of you is a gift in my life that I get to open over and over. Thank you for the part you each play in helping me learn who I am. "I am that, I am."

Special thanks to the many students who have come for guidance and taught me a great deal in return. You have always been worth it!

To all who have come before me transforming and transporting knowledge and wisdom-blessings!

Foreword

Susan Manion MacDonald is on an intriguing journey of self-discovery, and fortunately we get to go along for the ride too. This exciting ride commenced for Susan in 2002 when she was diagnosed with Stage 4 Lymphatic Cancer from which she eventually healed herself using natural methods. This experience led to the writing of her first book 'BALANCE: Nature's way to heal your body' which became a bestseller in her native Canada.

Now she is continuing her never-ending journey toward that ultimate State of Perfection which we're all striving for, and this leg of her journey has guided her deep into herself to finally discover and fall in love with her Real Self, which is her God-Self. This stage of her journey has spawned another extremely informative and indeed inspiring book which Susan has written titled 'SYMPTOMS: The Language of The Soul'. Having recently read the manuscript for this book, I honestly believe that it will assist a great number of people in expanding their awareness of who they really are, of their Divine Heritage. This in turn will assist them in learning to really love and unconditionally accept who they are. As I have taught for years, you MUST love yourself FIRST before you can start to love anyone else; and when you finally learn to unconditionally love YOU, your Real, your AUTHENTIC self; negative emotions which ultimately lead to dis-ease will be eliminated.

Unfortunately, when anything goes wrong in a person's life we tend to immediately endeavor to deal with 'The Symptom'. But what Susan quite correctly highlights in her book, is that Symptoms do not just occur out of the blue, so to speak; there are Causes for all Symptoms. Now, whilst The Symptoms are usually clearly visible, The Causes are not for they are buried deep within the mind as 'Sickly Thoughts' and 'Destructive Emotions'. These thoughts and emotions must be flushed out and dealt with adequately before The Symptom can be eliminated and the patient finally cured. As James Allen put it in his book 'As a Man Thinketh' "The body is the servant of the mind . . . . it obeys the mind" . . . . yes it does! As a Metaphysician, I know that literally everything that happens to us in all aspects of our life, including from a health perspective, always commences simply as a thought in the human mind. Susan deals extensively with this most important aspect of healing in this book.

As stated already, emotions play a big role in our overall health. But all emotions are preceded by thoughts, so we must learn to control our thoughts thus not allowing toxic emotions to destroy our physical body, which they most definitely will if not discovered and adequately dealt with. The ultimate treatment to ensure excellent health at all times is daily contact with The Great Physician, The God WITHIN through meditation and the use of positive affirmations.

I feel greatly honored and indeed privileged to have been asked by Susan to write this forward. Having read the book, I honestly believe, that anyone who reads her new book, with a completely 'Open Mind', and then fully digests her wisdom and very practical solutions, will indeed experience excellent health. They will of course, also learn who they really are, which is an Awesomely Talented, Very Special and Unique 'Child of God'

D. Paul Reilly, Ph.D., President, CorporateMotivation.org

Preface

In 2002, when I was diagnosed with terminal cancer it, was hard to comprehend. I decided to live and it took years to know what that meant. Cancer, as other disease, is an acknowledgment from the Soul that one is not living life. Living is doing, while living life is BEing present daily to self.

It took me approximately a month following the diagnosis, to strengthen cells, balance nutrients and remove toxins, as well as to start listening to my intuition: gut feeling. Mentally shutting down the lists, judging self and others as well as letting go of the mind talk took longer. I felt alone at times as conventional medicine kept directing me back to death; their only known response. The flow of the beginning of the journey was easily transformed into my first book, *BALANCE, nature's way to heal your body.*

In 2005 I opened a natural health business to teach what I had learned, so others could have the opportunity to also transform. Symptoms of different types started to show up again in my life, as well as with the students I worked with. Utilizing all the tools and knowledge in my repertoire it was not a difficult shift to the emotional connection. Students reversed illness and disease as if, some would say, by magic. When change and wellness did not occur the understanding was clear that emotional feelings were not dealt with, worth not strengthened, good enough not believed, nor love of self acknowledged.

Symptoms: The Language of the Soul was formed from the heart while in the magic of wellness felt by others and self.

Acknowledgements

Maggie Lawrence what a great gift of generosity to move this book forward, thank you!

Bev Jones for pre-editing and transforming the words that will help touch lives.

Francis Mitchell for guidance and understanding, when more editing was required as well as editing my Introduction and first Chapter.

Karen Lee, you came to me at the right moment in time to freshen up the grammar and complete the editing. Thank you!

Dianna, the knowledge you possess energetically, spiritually, and soulfully were a blessing in turning this book into a positive life message for others. Thank you!

D. Paul Reilly, Ph.D. for you insights and the foreword for this book you have become a special friend in my life.

Gil Collicott, artist and friend for the amazing drawing of the cover for this book that touches my Soul. You are blessed!

Introduction

The intention of this book is to share the discovery and the excitement of how one can transform illness and disease. The latter terms are simply names applied by scientists, physicians, and pharmaceutical companies to one or more symptoms of the physical Body.

Science has proven that renewal occurs in practically every cell of the Body. Therefore, if the liver has the ability to renew itself every six weeks, why is it renewed with the same cancer? Eczema is another example of rogue cells that can be still present after thirty days, the length of time for the skin to renew itself. Simply put, research has demonstrated that renewal of the physical Body comprises only twenty percent of the healing process, while blocked emotional feelings make up the difference; that is to say, a whopping eighty percent.

Symptoms are presented as physical manifestations within an organ, gland, or structure of the Body that represent a specific trapped emotional feeling. Over time if one does not pay attention to one's instincts, additional symptoms, or the deepening of symptoms already present, will occur. Symptoms are the language of the Soul. Simply put, they are the authentic you, speaking up to change one's life—towards living and being rather than merely doing!

The physical Body does not stand alone and separate in one's life; the chief administrator is one's Soul, and energy source is one's Spirit. Surrounding the Body is an Energy Field, which acts similar to the white protein that surrounds the egg yolk; its primary purpose being to protect and nourish one's physical form. The Spirit and the Soul connect the human Body to God and the Universe.

Throughout this book, the use of "God" will play a role in the explanations and truth. Readers may choose to think of this term in many varied ways: as the "Source", "Buddha", "Allah" or other titles used in different cultures or religious communities. The term I have chosen to use is "God."

Trapped emotional feelings create static within the Energy Field weakening the field's ability to protect the Body. Toxins are then able to filter through; mal-absorption of nutrients occur, which in turn, decreases cellular and organ abilities leading to illness, or disease (symptoms) then develop.

Most natural health practitioners operate within a framework of oneness. The appropriate choice of practitioner will be able to facilitate wellness from one to eighteen months, even if diagnosed with terminal cancer. If symptoms do not disappear or new ones appear, then perhaps the choice of practitioner was not the best one; personal responsibility may not have been taken; or a prescribed protocol was not followed.

Not everyone wants to be healed, in part due to a fear of success or, even a fear of failure . . . or low self worth. Death can also occur when one loves another more than self or, one is unable to forgive or accept forgiveness . . . healing cannot occur without these.

The Soul guides one back to living life more fully, involving a mode of language that includes discomfort or pain. The increased emphasis on symptoms depends on the ability to BE in the present and to recognize those important connections.

Symptoms: The Language of the Soul has a summary at the end of each chapter to assist those unable to find the common threads presented, or are unable to complete the book in its entirety due to illness and disease.

Listen and BE present to that which one truly is in this life; BE the gift the world needs today. Understand that at every moment an answer is always available if one only asks the right question. *When the student is ready, the teacher will come.* Build a bridge for others to follow. Everyone passes on to future generations both thoughts and feelings; let those that follow walk in a path of wellness in joy, peace, harmony and love.

My youngest daughter Charlene surprised me a number of years ago at a YMCA Convention in Geneva Park, Ontario, where she was asked to make a presentation. Charlene gave a great speech and the profoundness of her ability to see, as well as to listen, touched my Soul. The Bridge Builder (below) is a poem Charlene incorporated into her presentation that bears repeating and sharing.

The Bridge Builder
by Will Allen Dromgoole

An old man, going a lone highway,
Came, at the evening, cold and gray,
To a chasm, vast, and deep, and wide,
Through which was flowing a sullen tide.

The old man crossed in the twilight dim;
The sullen stream had no fears for him;
But he turned, when safe on the other side,
And built a bridge to span the tide,
"Old man," said a fellow pilgrim, near,
"You are wasting strength with building here;
Your journey will end with the ending day;
You never again must pass this way;
You have crossed the chasm, deep and wide-
Why build you a bridge at the eventide?"

The builder lifted his old gray head:
"Good friend, in the path I have come," he said,
"There followeth after me today,
A youth, whose feet must pass this way.

This chasm, that has been naught to me,
To that fair-haired youth may a pitfall be.
He, too, must cross in the twilight dim;
Good friend, I am building the bridge for him."

I want to build a bridge for others to follow a simple path to wellness, joy, peace, harmony and love. Awareness slows down life to allow emotional feelings to be released. Failure is not a bad thing, as it can be a powerful lesson of love and guidance towards success, with practise. Awareness is the wisdom necessary to live life!

Disease is a variety of symptoms-a powerful message from the Soul, propelled by the Spirit to produce awareness.

CHAPTER 1

A Gift of Transformation

In December 2002, after learning I had been diagnosed with terminal cancer, the journey to discover my authentic self began. At that time, I had no comprehension of the path that would lead to locating my true self.

"People often try to hide who they truly are by trying to be normal and fit in with the crowd. To be honest with others about who you are in this world, you must first be honest with yourself." Madisyn Taylor

A diagnosis of any disease or illness can cause a person who is not living authentically to his or her true self, to become fearful. I believe that a person does not become ill or acquire a disease if he or she is living life authentically in the present.

One can ask, *"How does an individual discover one's authentic self?"* A fun way to start would be to have a look in one's closet and ask these questions:

- "Does this item connect with me in a positive way?"
- "Is it romantic, powerful, or relaxing?"
- "Did the price or someone else's opinion influence my decision to purchase it?"

My first husband did not like green. At sixteen, I was naive enough to agree to not wear green during the eight years we spent together. I like green in certain shades, yet chose to go against my true self to avoid conflict: Low self-worth played a factor in this decision.

This is one example of how a spouse, parent or friend can negatively influence what we wear, what we do, or what we choose, including a quality of life that has been lost as a child, thereby creating a pathway for the inability to speak-up for oneself. One cannot really love someone deeply unless we trust that person and more specifically, trust oneself. To learn to love self first is being true to one's authentic self. Trust is heart felt and connected to chakra energy, green reflects the heart, in context of energy life force. (See Chapter 3 for more chakra information.)

A few items of clothing may have been bought to hide one's self, for example, the clothes are too large, are lacking in color, or are old-fashioned. Remember: if old-fashioned is romantic or powerful, then it is okay! Think of how it feels when an item is worn; for example, by being my authentic self when I need to feel physically and emotionally comfortable, I wear a pair of worn turquoise shoes I love. I do not care if they match my outfit or what others might say.

The above clothes example is a way of beginning with the basics of discovering one's true self. We can then move forward to look at our profession. For example, some individuals work in a specific profession because it is generational; their parents were a doctor or lawyer and expect their chosen profession to be followed by their children, to the point in some scenarios of having a trust fund blocked if they choose otherwise. A lack of worth can also play a part in the profession that we choose, believing there are no other choices.

When I was growing up, my father suggested I had two career choices; secretary, or mother. I believed there were other options, although they were limited at that time due to my lack of self worth and need for approval. It was not until I got the cancer at fifty-two that I began to realize life is not simply based on luck and that we have the power to guide our own destiny.

To live life authentically, I found we need to have a relationship with self. How can that be possible when we may not recognize who self is? To recognize self, it is necessary to know the difference between unconditional love and enabling behaviors.

Unconditional love is about freedom of choice without fear of punishment. It is learning and accepting that one has the same freedom of choice as others. When I can free myself from judging others or even judging myself, then I am practicing unconditional love.

Enabling refers to a third party taking responsibility or blame for another person. This third party may try to solve another person's problems or accommodate another person's troubling conduct. Often this is done with good intentions; however, it is operating from a base of fear or insecurity. An example of this is when one sees that a friend has a problem and decides to solve the problem for them, instead of giving them knowledge to solve the problem on their own. Another example would be when one makes a call to their spouse's workplace on their behalf because he or she is having difficulty going into work that day. If the spouse is making a choice to avoid work, they need to take responsibility for that choice, and not be enabled to avoid doing so.

At different times through the years, I have enabled a friend, sibling, child and husband without recognizing the symptoms. My diagnosis of cancer helped me realize what I had been unknowingly doing. I realize now that when we enable other people, it takes away their ability to grow their own wings and fly. Keeping another person too close does not give love in the best way; rather this behavior reduces love within oneself and limits another's ability to love self in a healthy way. Weak boundaries, low self-worth, or lack of assertiveness can be reasons why we take such steps to enable others.

It is time to put one's self first without guilt. It is time to connect with one's Spirit and Soul, to shift the negative self-talk, and to assertively communicate thoughts and feelings to others. It is time to live life with meaning, purpose and passion, as well as to shine one's light in the world.

Affirmations are a wonderful way to develop a stronger self, once one has become aware of any negative talk that is being self projected. Seeking to look into one's own eyes in a mirror, and voice an affirmation is a connection with Soul, and it is powerful.

"When you fashion a life where the decisions you make and the actions you take are considered, deliberate and in harmony with what's important to you, you are living an authentic life." Suzanne Zoglio

There are natural health modalities and organizations available to help one learn to ground self and connect with the Universe. They provide guidance as we do the inner work by ourselves. Learning to BE vulnerable takes time and is part of a relationship with self. It is necessary at times to connect with others to embrace this concept of self.

Dr. Ryke Geerd Hamer's healing modality, *German New Medicine* presents insight on how to find and strengthen one's authentic self. Dr. Hamer discovered that every disease originates from a shock or trauma that catches one completely by surprise. The moment the unexpected conflict occurs, the shock strikes a specific area in the brain causing a lesion, referred to as the *Hamer Focus* (HH-Hamerscher Herd). The lesion is visible on a brain scan as a set of sharp concentric rings. A Magnetic Resonance Imaging (MRI) is used to locate the mark. Resolving the inner conflict will reverse the effect of the shock, thereby dissolving the lesion. It is possible to maintain this mind and emotional conflict going on in the background for years, with the physical Body experiencing this struggle in many ways via symptoms it is experiencing.

In 2009, I refined Dr. Hamer's process, using Energy Response Testing, similar to Applied Kinesiology and Muscle Response Testing. Rather than the high cost and time required for MRIs, Energy Response Testing, with the permission of the student, identifies the trauma using simple questions and answers. I realized during my research that each individual experienced a trauma approximately four years prior to the onset of a disease. The current trauma in one's life will allow another event to surface that had been emotionally put away years earlier. When combined with physical toxins, these buried emotional feelings can actually create disease. I have subsequently named this process *"The Fourth Principal"*; the area of the Body affected by symptoms is in relationship to the buried emotional feelings. Such feelings that are held in the physical Body too long will create a frequency or vibration weakness in the human Energy Field and protection is no longer an option. The organs or glands and their specific emotional feeling are identified in Chapter 2.

The diagnosis of terminal cancer I received in 2002 was due to a trauma that occurred in my life in 1998. I began to receive signals from my Soul via symptoms, from that point on. Most of the symptoms I ignored as simply a progression towards old age, and I approached the remainder of the symptoms with conventional medicine—without resolve. Low self-worth and the constant need for approval brought about during childhood created a major conflict between my Spirit (mind) and my Soul (heart). The first book I wrote, *"BALANCE nature's way to heal your body"*, discusses a lot of what occurred in my life, including an incident when I left home at sixteen. I averted death from cancer by going within and resolving this conflict, while removing toxins, strengthening cells and adding nutrients. Forgiving self and others were also part of the resolution process. The end result has been discovering my authentic self and who I am meant to BE.

During my journey the cancer was resolved, cells were strengthened and vitality returned. My physical Body has actually strengthened to a point where allergies endured since the 1970s also disappeared, while today at age sixty-two, I feel like a twenty-year-old. Despite these positive advances, I had not resolved all past emotional feelings, so other symptoms continued. This again was the Soul reflecting the need for me to be more authentic . . . to BE completely authentic.

In the fall of 2005 my eldest daughter decided it was time to resolve a conflict from her past. She went to the police about a childhood molestation she had experienced at the hands of one of my former male partners. He had molested her between the ages of six and ten. The court case was difficult as we had to testify. He was found guilty, put under house arrest and his name was placed on a list of sexual predators for future reference by law enforcement.

What I did not realize at the time was that the trauma of the court case had brought up past buried emotional feelings within me, and they were starting to affect me physically. Symptoms started to occur that were an indication that the human vibration of my Body was not in harmony with self or the earth. Remember, symptoms have a cause and that cause is a trapped emotional feeling. The Soul has two ways to get one's attention in order to facilitate change. The first and least invasive or dangerous way is with meditation, and connecting to one's authentic self; intuition is a part of this process; the second is through physical symptoms. I still had not learned the first way, to the extent that I was really not listening closely enough to what my Body was saying.

A lump below my Thyroid area that had formed during the process of cancer and had subsequently disappeared now re-appeared. Physically, this was due to a blockage created by a sluggish spleen not allowing the Body to dispose of dead cells; not digesting protein. Instead of debris from the Body flowing along the appropriate path, it was backing up within the lymph system and creating a lump at the neck area. Eventually, the physical pressure caused a lesion in the skin, with a mass of dead cells to form outside the Body. The emotional feeling connected to the base of the neck is about not speaking up: In this case sooner, and to the spleen about abandonment; although this was not learned by self until 2009.

In December of 2006 I decided to go to Sedona, Arizona for spiritual enhancement training and to begin the process of being authentic to self, using vision with passion to find the money to finance this course. The course was to begin on January ninth and end late in the evening of January fourteenth.

Prior to booking a flight, I received an unusual email from The Gerson Institute in San Diego, CA, asking if I would be interested in participating in a project on natural healing at a new residence they recently opened. There were only three positions available and nine hundred possible applicants (members). I had purchased a couple of booklets years prior from The Gerson Institute and my name was put on their membership list. Life is no accident.

The moment I read the email, it became apparent this was where I needed to go, to gain knowledge to resolve what was happening with the mass on my neck, and learn more about natural health to support the students I was teaching. Two years prior I had begun my own natural health business and any new information that could come my way would be valuable. I was chosen due to being authentic to self and center with both feelings and thoughts in harmony. The program started the day following the completion of the course in Sedona; January fifteenth at nine in the morning. The shuttle in Sedona was unable to deliver me to the airport in time to catch an earlier flight arrive in time, so we settled on noon as an arrival time.

During the spiritual training I remained authentically visualized, prayed to God and held that passion, I could shift the arrival time and start the Gerson course with the other participants. The class finished at ten in the evening on the fourteenth and I went back to my room to pack. My roommate stayed for the social, so I asked her to keep an ear open; confident someone would get me to Phoenix airport in time to catch the early flight. She called me about fifteen minutes later, quite astonished, and stated that a man named Dan was driving there at three in the morning and would like company. I changed my flight at the airport, called The Gerson Institute to arrange an earlier pickup and off I went.

Manifesting both events to occur in my life was a marvelous experience that taught me a great deal about my authentic self at the level of the Spirit and Soul level. Sedona and the Gerson Residence in San Diego also touched my Soul and empowered my Spirit. I met Charlotte Gerson who was then in her eighties; a woman with clarity, as well as youthful energy after years of daily following the Gerson Protocol. Gerson has two facilities now; San Diego is a teaching facility, while Mexico is a healing facility. The most profound thing I learned was how to strengthen the liver. A gentleman from Australia who was also there became the reason I purchased a Vespa Scooter in April 2007 for my birthday. He excited my Soul to the possibilities.

Being present and learning who I really am, along with being present with my desires, have been paramount in the lessons that I have been learning. To be authentic, I need to be present in my own life, not live in the past or wish for the future to change my life. Life only changes in the present. When one stands up for whom one is, one does not fall for anything. However, until old emotional feelings are resolved, to hold onto one's authentic self is a real challenge.

"It is not enough to take steps which may someday lead to a goal; each step must be itself a goal and a step likewise." *Goethe*

It took until 2012 to learn to be truly authentic to my emotional feelings; to let them out and BE vulnerable was the most valuable part of those lessons since 2005. In late 2007 when my first book was printed and placed in my hands, the fear of success that had been buried since childhood manifested physical symptoms that were a cause for concern. A blocked lymph node in the jaw area grew rapidly and radiation was required. After each radiation treatment I was extremely nauseated and later learned from research that the enzyme amylase resides in the mouth. Radiation destroys this enzyme as well as the mineral zinc in the Body and without those nausea is manifested. The process also gave me insight into what most refer to as "morning sickness." When a woman is pregnant, the baby utilizes much of the amylase during the first trimester, resulting in nausea. Amylase a simple digestive enzyme for protein will resolve the nausea.

My husband, James also learned a lesson as well from this process. We travelled to New York on a bus tour within days of the last radiation treatment. There Wayne Dyer was presenting a seminar we attended and I gave him a copy of my book during a break. That night I could not sleep and spat up burning phlegm continuously. James wanted to take me to the hospital however, I refused. I understood what was happening, however, did not know how to stop it at that moment. Authentically, I knew going to the hospital would do nothing to help and might actually add to the toxic burden. The bus was heading home that day and I intuitively knew I would be fine.

James, "on the other hand" found it difficult to resist taking me to the hospital as he had not learned to be authentic to his self and believed if I died in New York that others would blame him. We had a long discussion and with inner work he has since resolved the need for approval of others, as we both now make decisions based on our hearts.

On Sunday when we arrived home James called my Naturopath as I could not be understood with a blistered swollen mouth. We determined after a discussion and Energy Response Testing that the radiation had shut down my detoxification pathways. Energy Balance Harmony (See this process in Appendix C) rectified that and the spitting of toxic liquid stopped immediately.

I learned through the same Naturopath, Dr. Hayhoe about a way to remove the radiation using a bath. (See directions in Appendix A). After radiation has done its job, it needed to be removed or it stays in the Body for one's life, as Protein can stop absorbing, cells become weak, while toxins are created. X-rays absorbed while travelling by plane can also build-up over time creating illness or disease. The radiation bath is a tool I now present often to students. The bath relieves the Body of toxic radiation and increases immune response and oxygen levels.

Why did the detoxification pathways block emotionally? Nothing in life is an accident, they are all lessons; this lesson was about ego. I *"felt"* that Wayne Dyer's ego showed up at the seminar when I was taking a photo of him. The fear I held was that success would create ego in me and thus hurt others. The need for approval in my life subconsciously tried to stop that perceived hurt and I blocked some of my life systems to prevent success. It seems so absurd we can do this to ourselves. The Soul, our authentic self, wants us to BE in the present and our emotional feelings which have been held over years diminish the qualities of which one can BE. Symptoms are the Soul's language, and if one does not meditate and listen to instinct, physical symptoms are the only method left to pass the message on.

I have had many lessons and wonder when it will stop, until I realized that once a person goes within on a daily basis, listening to one's Soul, there will always be lessons. The lessons will not be attached to symptoms relating to illness or disease unless we stop listening. We have a built in GPS; relax, let it guide and enjoy the ride.

James and I are learning wonderful things about our authentic selves. It has taken awhile to learn the lessons and at times we still go back to old habits that seem friendlier. What is great is that we now get it!

A few more examples might help here. James has always had an issue with money, wanting it, yet putting up roadblocks up to stop the inward flow. We live in a wonderful bungalow in an affluent neighborhood; I chose the home and location due to its easy access to downtown, as well as the comfortable open concept of the home, not the neighborhood. It has taken James a number of years to accept living on what he calls this side of the tracks.

James came from a poor family, which during his childhood was judged by some and that judgment stuck to his persona. Subconsciously, he has always been trying to get back to poverty, his former perceived level of worth. James is a wonderful man, full of knowledge, love and laughter, yet he had gotten stuck finding his authentic self. Incidents occurred, such as parking and hitting a curb and blowing a tire just as he thought of the negative power of money. To negate money, cost him two hundred dollars for a new tire. To value money, we believe this would not have occurred.

Working on our emotional, spiritual and subconscious self has dramatically shifted our energy, and it's the sustainability of that energy with which we both still struggle. Holding a positive intention in life brings riches, if we choose to live authentically in the present.

In 2008 the natural health centre we operated out of our home expanded to the point of requiring new employees and more space. We placed a bid on a wonderful Victorian home with five bedrooms, two baths, a dining area, a double kitchen and a double living room. At first sight, my Soul spoke instinctively to me this was the right place and the right time. I did not quibble and quickly offered the full asking price. In previous experiences this would not have occurred, as the price would have been negotiated and a feeling of anxiousness would prevail as one's inner self held conflicting responses. However, on this day I was present authentically and trusted instinct.

On the day we were to get the loan for the centre, it fell through as another buyer had the funds was stepping in within four hours. James and I used our tools to unblock energy that we had negatively manifested around money. Once energy protocols were complete, the phone immediately rang and a name of a mortgage broker given to us by the bank. The broker lived a few houses from us, yet we had no idea she existed until then. God works in mysterious ways. Paperwork whizzed back and forth; papers were signed and we were able to purchase the building for the centre.

Do not leave life to fate, stand up for the person we've become; BE present in one's life and one too will achieve greatness-we all have that ability.

What happened next brought us back to old habits. I had been taught very early by my father that we should work hard in life, and enjoy fun later-if there was time left over. Not a good policy in life, yet something I had grown accustomed to. Opening our expanded centre triggered past life actions and I forgot to balance my personal life with my professional and have fun in both. Instead I spent many hours at work. Not saying "No" to students who wanted assistance at late hours, etc. I reverted back to what the cancer lesson taught me; cancer was my "No."

I did not get cancer again, however I did experience illness, as a virus in my liver created severe pain while I was in Newfoundland delivering lectures. I chose not to go to the hospital and the Universe presented another plan. I write more about this in the section on the Soul, so I will leave it at that for now.

Business fell away as I was not able to BE present or physically able to give the students what was of value. It was a hard year. Balance in my life was difficult with fear being present on numerous occasions, thus creating joint pain and arthritic symptoms. Fear shuts down the energy going to and from the kidneys, raises or lowers blood pressure, and reduces absorption of magnesium as well as vitamin D. A calcium and magnesium imbalance due to mal-absorption of magnesium creates stiffness in limbs and joints. I talk about this further in Chapter 5.

Clearing emotional feelings is usually an easy process, however, in this case it was during the night while sleeping that the fear arose in dreams, and consequently, I would waken with difficulty in opening and closing my hands. Within minutes this was resolved with Energy Balance Harmony; however, once I was asleep the fear would occur again. I tried different natural health modalities to see if this could be resolved. I would have one or two nights reprieve and then the fear would start creating the symptoms again.

God responded again with the right path as I opted to become a Doctor of Acupuncture. I began the program and immediately knew it was where I was meant to be. The second month proved enlightening on a personal level.

The five elements (fire, earth, metal, water and wood) are used when setting up an acupuncture needling protocol. As a demo, the teacher had a few individuals from the class sit in front of the room while the remainder did an analysis using questions, along with a visual aid. A description of one's parents is also required. I was blessed to be chosen for the demos-again, no accident. My father fit the criteria of wood, which is associated with the liver and gall bladder. It seems ironic that my father died at age fifty-six at a time when his liver was no longer able to process. My mom was indicative of earth element (spleen and stomach).

The teacher mentioned to the class that they were not noticing something important. The teacher had noticed that when I responded, I would look at him for approval. That is when I realized all my life I have searched for approval. I often excelled in most things, even to the point of becoming an enabler for fear of not being approved of and losing love. That was the emotional feeling that was stuck and was attached to the night fears. Once out of Pandora's Box, resolving the conflict was easy. The answer is always present to one's self; it is simply whether or not the person is present to the answer.

Whether one has cancer, heart disease, diabetes, MS, or something else, it is imperative to resolve the emotional feelings, stand authentically as self, and then strengthens the physical, which will transform the Body's ability to heal. Instead of overcoming illness, use the positive principle of allowing wellness. A relief of symptoms indicates that there is progress. For the disease to continue, one must to realize they have not authentically found self. Remember, our thoughts and feelings form reality by creating a vibration of energy that affects life; when we shift our thoughts and feelings, then reality shifts, allowing this to happen. If one feels an urgency to have this occur, one is not allowing, instead they are trying to control. Disease is control!

The more a person lives in the truth, the more one's emotional feelings will assist one to see clearly. To forgive the past is vital in healing. Trusting the process is a prominent part of that. Remember, forgiveness does not establish a relationship; behavioral change and trust do that. Forgiveness does not excuse anything. Forgiveness is a process that shifts one's life from remaining a victim to being able to experience love, to be loving, and to be a lover! There is no illness when love, as well as respect of self is present.

Take this moment in time to learn who one really is! Connect with one's Soul by looking in the mirror directly into one's eyes. Sit in meditation and listen to one's inner self. Once the mind is quiet, the heart will identify who one really is. Ask questions, BE present and pay attention to what one likes, how one reacts and what makes one joyful, loved, and at peace. Remember one's childhood likes and dislikes around six or seven years old, as they can help identify what one really wants to do in life. Everyday, one is given the answer to all the questions one has. Pay attention to life! When the student is ready, the teacher will come. Build a relationship with self, one is worth it. Living life is only possible in present time.

Transformations:
Lewis is a student of mine who is currently living his dream. He met me at the Amherst Home Show in May of 2007 where we both had

booths. His health had become a major issue over a six month period after his mother passed away in 2006 from congestive heart failure.

He gained over twenty pounds and was diagnosed with gout and had increased stomach problems. Lewis came to our centre for a Live Blood Analysis, consultation and ionic footbaths. These symptoms indicated a potential for a heart attack or stroke if lifestyle changes were not imminent. He started a program at the centre to detoxify; emotionally and physically; his health improved so much by August, 2008 that he applied to the Canadian Armed Forces to become a part-time Reservist. At age fifty-two he was sworn in and completed CAF Basic Military Qualifications with other recruits half his age or less: ages sixteen to thirty. This was a personal dream he never thought was possible at his age.

Currently at age fifty-three, he weighs one hundred and sixty-eight pounds, can do thirty-three pushups in one minute and run one kilometer in five minutes and fifteen seconds. He no longer has gout or takes any medication. Lewis was recently evaluated by his personal insurance and scored Health Style #2; in twenty years of writing policies, the insurance consultant had only ever had healthy twenty to twenty-five year olds approved at the HS2 level. Ten years ago he was a HS3. Lewis is living his life authentically and works full-time as an investment councilor.

Pat, who is sixty-five years of age, has suffered for a number of years with a lot of arthritis and allergies as well as had a couple of bad falls. She was unable to stay in bed at nights due to unbearable pain in her hips and lower back, while her sleep was almost nil making it difficult to function during the daytime.

Seeing a chiropractor weekly helped some, however with little long term relief. I asked Pat to be a participant as a case study in my acupuncture certification program and she accepted. After a few weeks of acupuncture she noticed a marked difference and finally, there was full relief as she was able to sleep through the night. She now feels alive with ambition and energy, and has a sense of happiness again, being able to go for a walk and climb stairs pain-free. Her digestion has improved as well and the spider veins in her legs are disappearing.

Removing emotional and physical toxins were a part of the protocol and the entire process has given Pat the ability to understand the need to BE authentic to self.

Judy lived an active, and busy life working long hours and travelling often. During that time she began to experience tingling and itching all over her body; directly under the skin. She referred to this as "creepy crawlers" all over her Body, so much so that it became difficult, even unbearable, to sleep. Judy tried lotions, tub soaks, pills for nerves and visits to the medical community, yet the itching continued. She had a consultation with me and a series of ionic footbaths; it was unbelievable yet at the time she was ready to consider anything! After only one footbath she noticed that her symptoms were slightly less severe, and by the fourth session were completely gone. She was amazed! Judy's Body had been experiencing symptoms of emotional and environmental toxins and the liver was unable to do its job. The lymph system which resides directly under the skin was unable to remove chemicals due to a weakened liver, therefore causing the itch from the inside as the buildup progressed. Judy is living her life authentically today.

Carroll was diagnosed with high blood pressure in 2006 and was on medication. Even with the medication his blood pressure continued to rise and the medication was increased. In 2008 he began ionic footbaths at our center, while receiving guidance on other aspects of his health. After several visits his blood pressure started to come down while he was gradually able to decrease and eventually discontinue his medication. Carroll is living an authentic life, medication free.

These wonderful students took responsibility for their Body, listened, released and took actions that promoted natural healing. I thank each of them and the thousands of others I have worked with for their grace and trust, while celebrating their success. Thank you!

Aubrey Hepburn was a famous actress from the past, well known for starring in "Breakfast at Tiffany's". The following is a poem Audrey kept and read to her children. It encompasses what one would imagine back then of her authentic self.

Time Tested Beauty Tips

For attractive lips, speak words of kindness.

For lovely eyes, seek out the good in people.

For a slim figure, share your food with the hungry.

For beautiful hair, let a child run his or her fingers through it once a day.

For poise, walk with the knowledge you'll never walk alone.

People, even more than things, have to be restored, renewed, revived, reclaimed, and redeemed; Never throw out anybody.

Remember, if you ever need a helping hand, you'll find one at the end of your arm.

As you grow older, you will discover that you have two hands, one for helping yourself, the other for helping others.

The beauty of a woman is not in the clothes she wears, the figure that she carries, or the way she combs her hair. The beauty of a woman must be seen from in her eyes, because that is the doorway to her heart, the place where love resides.

The beauty of a woman is not in a facial mole, but true beauty in a woman is reflected in her soul. It is the caring that she lovingly gives, the passion that she shows, and the beauty of a woman with passing years only grows!

By Sam Levenson

Summary of Chapter 1

1. Discover one's likes and dislikes;

2. Love who one is and who one wants to BE;

3. Visualize destiny and let fate fade away;

4. Clear past emotional feelings to BE present today in life;

5. Choose to forgive. It is about you, not them;

6. Connect with one's Soul via meditation, look into one's eyes and affirm who one is.

CHAPTER 2

Soul Peace

Anything in life is possible. The Soul never says NO, it never judges, and is there to guide when one is present to life. One needs to stop doing and start BEing. Soul energy is one's light and meaning to life.

In June 2009, symptoms materialized which indicated that my Soul had made a decision to depart my Body. I received this message by way of a deep dread that overcame me following a number of days of illness. Even when diagnosed with cancer in 2002, this dread was not present. As previously mentioned in Chapter 1, while in Newfoundland lecturing, a virus had settled in my liver. Severe pain emulated from the liver capsule, and laryngitis plus fatigue added to this combination. A wonderful Homeopathic doctor, who was formerly a nurse, helped with the pain; however, the fatigue was still present. James and our daughter Charlene met me at the airport since I did not have the strength to drive home.

A few days following my homecoming, I mentioned to James that there was something else wrong which needed urgent and immediate intervention. The dread was paralyzing.

We contacted two colleagues who work with Universal Energy. As the Universe works, they were both available at the time, and over a number of hours applied their shared knowledge to strengthen my life energy.

I drifted in and out of consciousness during this process. Later that evening, they returned and I noticed them in my garden digging weeds.

Soon they came in and transformed my home, utilizing a process called "Feng Shui." They made wonderful suggestions to enhance my Soul, and the re-beautification was pretty amazing.

Balance is important in one's life and when opening a new natural health centre in 2008, I had put my personal life on hold, while building the business. In May of 2009, I had picked up a cold, the first one in seven years. The start of a cold indicates congestion and/ or grief in one's life, an overabundance of mucous can indicate thymus and spleen involvement. This was the first message I recognized from my Soul, however, still in my busy world ignored the message and did not slow down.

Friends who had noticed the weeds, household clutter, dying plants, etc. recognized that my Soul needed to be nourished. They stepped in as comrades and colleagues to help. Since that day, I have kept a balance with personal and professional paths of my life. A life mission includes balance in both paths, not as separate entities, as ones life flows freely inside and out, connecting with the Soul and God via the heart.

"Your work is to find the myth (blueprint) you were meant to live." Carl Jong

The Soul holds its individual divine plan. To understand the complexity of the Universe, it is necessary to love one's self and then others. When life is looked at through the mind, it works only at the Spirit level, which has the ability to be higher or lower depending on the heart/Soul connection. This connection also affects the Energy Field, and its ability to protect the Body. If affected by emotional feelings at the Soul level, the Energy Field will in turn create a pathway of illness or disease on one level, and the certainty of the Spirit leaving on another. The Spirit will also leave the physical Body when "will" has been diminished. This can happen when the mind diverts the physical Body from purpose. Stories that light one up are clues to one's blueprint on earth.

The Soul crosses the threshold of the Universe and enters the Body a few days prior to birth. The heart/Soul connection is designed to guide human life. The Spirit arrives during conception and utilizes the mind connection. The mind is meant to store while maintaining knowledge, it is not meant to guide human life. The Soul is positioned to be the driver of the whole entity that makes up one's self.

> **"Silence is the bridge between this world and the world beyond. It is the bridge between head and heart. Dwelling in Silence leads to quieting the body and the mind. It encourages you to embrace and fully participate in the present moment and it opens the door for you to contact your own truth."**
> **The Personal Transformation and Courage Institute**

Life circumstances create opportunities for the loss of Soul qualities. Individuals can move the Soul to the backseat or in some cases the trunk, allowing the Spirit to take over as the driver in life events. This is living a life of doing, not being. To do and BE is a life in balance. The loss of qualities can occur anytime after the Soul is present, such as from mental or physical abuse directed at the birth mother while pregnant. This creates imbalance at all energy levels. To BE true to one's authentic self, it is vital to restore the quality or qualities one has lost on one's journey. Symptoms become the Soul's method of garnering attention when one has not activated one's intuitive side.

Five main qualities or gifts

1. **Assimilation** is the absorption of life experiences. Without this quality, joy is not present; the gift opened is not yet received.
2. **Inspiration** is the act of inspiring others by showing the way. It is the ignition necessary to transform energy into being and doing.
3. **Expression** involves communication by putting thoughts and emotional feelings into words or pictures. It is speaking one's truth on all levels and being authentic.
4. **Free Will** (non-attachment even to life) is the ability to let go and enjoy a carefree life even in the midst of struggle.

5. **Action** is about cause and effect; it is an act of Will. This should precipitate a heart connection and shift the focus of action to approach life in terms of vibration and desire.

Other essential qualities

1. **Intuition:** the curious plus enthusiastic path for presence and purpose;
2. **Confidence:** the ability to stand for one's self and to BE grounded in the present;
3. **Forgiveness:** to understand that this process is about one's self not about others;
4. **Integrity:** an honest portrayal of self;
5. **Truth:** trust in God and self;
6. **Joyfulness:** happiness from within, not relying on material things;
7. **Love of God, self and then others:** to feel, see, and hear on each of those levels;
8. **Acceptance:** the ability to see oneness. The complete positive connection of each individual on earth;
9. **Hope:** the realization that all is within one. What others say are just words;
10. **Courage:** to walk through the fear to clarity and personal power in the present;
11. **Wisdom:** the ability to live life in the present, while one utilizes the lessons learned in the past in a positive way. One Body in balance; physically, emotionally and mentally; (Body, Soul & Spirit)
12. **Creativity:** to utilize the energy of Spirit with the heart of Soul to create a positive life;
13. **Responsibility:** to understand that one's self is responsible for self. BE reliable to words, feelings and responses that belong to self;
14. **Compassion:** to dissolve judgment of self or others;
15. **Peace:** the ability to be present to calmness inside and out;
16. **Sincerity:** to live in purpose from the heart;

17. **Empathy:** to listen to God, self as well as others with purpose and intent;
18. **Serenity:** to understand the connection to God and self while allowing time daily to connect;
19. **Patience:** gentleness in a belief that this moment is meant to be;
20. **Humility:** to understand that success is available to all who choose to look within. The ability to recognize ego and choose to dissolve it;
21. **Self-worth:** the sense of BEing good enough in BEing authentic and respect of self;
22. **Relationship:** to truly live life is only established with a relationship with self.

Qualities listed above are present and available to all individuals. Loss of one or more qualities creates disharmony and imbalance. Incidents, illness, or disease are the symptoms projected by the Soul to facilitate opportunity to go within and repair qualities lost during life events, as well as to reconnect with God. (See Appendix B for more Soul Qualities.)

"Being silent means more than just holding your tongue. It means listening for the softest, most subtle sound of all-the sound of the Soul." Tijn Touber

All humans have the ability to find balance once belief in God and self is restored. Those who have difficulty to find resolve and reconnect only have to find silence within, to follow the heart to the path required.

Teachers will come when the student is ready. Believe that God sends what is needed everyday. It is important to BE present so the gift can be recognized and received. Balance is necessary in giving and in receiving from others as well. To refuse to receive has the ability to take away someone else's opportunity to give.

Everyday it is good to look at who has crossed one's path, whether by email, phone, text, in person, etc. What were they bringing one in knowledge or guidance? What did they need to receive from you?

While working on this book I used notes that had been tucked away over the past three years. One such item was an article about a book called *Tiger-Tiger, Is It True* by Byron Katie. On the same day I found this article, I also purchased Oprah's 10th Anniversary edition of *O Magazine*. This issue had special meaning that month as I had garnered tickets to Oprah's celebration in New York called "Live Your Best Life Weekend". In this edition was an article about Byron Katie. She believes that freedom is always just a question away and devised a program years ago called "The Work" that utilizes four questions developed around truth and thoughts one has.

The book is about Tiger-Tiger thinking his whole world is falling apart: He believes his parents don't love him, his friends have abandoned him, and life is unfair. A wise turtle asks him four questions, and everything changes. He realizes that all of his problems were not caused by things; they were caused by his thoughts *about* things. When wise turtle questions his thoughts, life becomes wonderful again. (See Resource List in the back of this book for information how to purchase.)

Mirroring

Mirroring is another means of indicating the quality that is necessary to retrieve at this time.

An example came to mind about a gentleman who used to come to the office where I formerly worked. His presence created a sense of irritation within me. After working through this reaction to identify what created the irritation, I realized he projected to me a lack of integrity. I had compromised my own integrity in little white lies over the past number of years.

This was a learned behavior from my father. Dad would hide my siblings and my self in the trunk to get several of us into the drive-in free; have a few identify ourselves as being younger to enter the Expo; even as a young teenager to hide his pint of liquor in my purse so Mom would not find out Dad was drinking. Growing up believing this was alright I followed slightly in his footsteps and lost some of the qualities necessary for my Soul to BE in purpose on earth. My Soul was identifying this through mirroring the gentleman's state I previously wrote about above.

Today, I respect while treasure the integrity God guided me back to. Not only is it possible to face this gentleman with integrity, also anything he says or does no longer creates a negative charge or reaction when I am present.

Whenever one is offended or brought to tears by an individual, it is helpful to look inside to locate the misplaced quality which initiated the reaction. The reaction is a symptom identifying a disconnection between God and one's Soul.

To strengthen the Energy Field that protects the Body, to repair the Soul, and to clear the path to wellness and oneness, an emotional piece from the past needs to be identified and forgiven. Restoration can be as simple as writing a letter to the individual from the past or present, ensuring all emotional feelings are expressed and forgiveness occurs in the letter. Next, sign the letter and flush it down the toilet, or burn it safely. If the occurrence still arises, the written word was not expressed entirely and has to be revisited with another letter.

Help is available from various natural health modalities if one is present to life and requests assistance.

Another example of mirroring: A few students indicated how emotional they became each time the phone rang while a relative they were upset with was identified on the display. The question to ask is, "Why does this emotional response occur?" It could be that the student is holding on to anger, fear, resentment or guilt connected to an event in the past. Until it is released, the person will always be affected by the other person or someone who looks, talks, or acts like them.

A person can quit a job due to a response to somebody in the workplace, yet the next job may also entail an employee with similar traits. A friend or acquaintance may also remind him or her of that negative person. God and the Universe align each opportunity with one's Soul to forgive past destructive emotional feelings, to remove the electrical charge, and to create balance and harmony in one's life. The cycle will keep evolving until the individual goes within; finds the connection and releases the harmful energy via forgiveness.

When the Energy Field around an individual has been weakened due to an emotional feeling being held in the physical Body, other individual fields identify with it as well. Animals, babies, children or adults can all be affected negatively via emotional feelings triggered by past experiences.

Has anyone ever walked close to one and suddenly, a feeling of irritation or sadness is present? The feelings are more than likely the other individuals and were felt via their Energy Field.

A former student was in the process of fighting for custody of her child. The student's mother and the student were emotionally upset, to the point of illness. The former spouse wanted custody for a negative purpose (control) and had hired a lawyer, as well as set a court date. The recommendation by my self was for each to write him letters, release all of the feelings present and forgive, because it was not about him and then destroy the letters. These were necessary to shift the Soul back into the driver's seat through retrieval of qualities lost during this relationship and as a child.

Within a couple of days of writing then destroying the letters, after months of negative conveyance back and forth, the ex-husband identified he no longer felt it necessary to have custody giving the student full custody. The mother and daughter's Energy Field had shifted, thus creating a path for the ex-husband's Field to shift as well.

Through the law of attraction, an individual attracts what is felt emotionally at the Soul level.

Illness and disease are symptoms created by the Soul when feelings are trapped within the physical Body, qualities are lost, and mental and physical toxins have accumulated that require release, to generate balance and harmony.

"Only from the heart can you touch the sky." Rumi

Emotional Feelings

The Soul draws on emotional feelings as directors of life. Feelings are important aids for the Body to take action to circumstances. Anger has its usefulness in life, as long as it is directed properly while without harm. It helps move an individual forward when procrastination may have stopped the progression of life purpose. Anger preserves the integrity of self and deserves respect as well as attention. Venting anger does not solve it, listening to self while feeling the emotion as one lets it go, does.

Organs in the Body hold different emotional feelings for a period of time, while the mental and emotional process is healed and the lesson learned. Those individuals unable to deal with the issue in a timely manner, due to loss of a quality of life from pre-birth to present, tend to hold on to the past or put it away using the Will (Spirit). Emotional feelings are controlled instead of released.

When an emotional feeling is not taken care of in a timely manner it can build-up in the initial organ and overflow into another organ creating chaos in the Body, while escalating physical symptoms from illness to disease. Individuals with strong diaphragms are able to release these feelings at a faster pace.

The process to locate these mental, emotional and physical symptoms plus their origin is simple. It takes only a small amount of time once the practitioner or individual has learned certain tools.

Diaphragm Breathing

The diaphragm plays a part in release of emotional feelings. During inhalation, the diaphragm contracts, thus enlarging the thoracic cavity and drawing air into the lungs. When the diaphragm relaxes, air is exhaled by elastic recoil of the lung and the tissues lining the thoracic cavity, in conjunction with the abdominal muscles. This process is also part of how trapped emotional feelings can leave the Body. Remember, emotional feelings have a reason: they move one forward in life. It is when emotional feelings stay that the Body starts to take on symptoms.

The diaphragm, in addition, helps expel vomit, feces, and urine. It also aids in child birth by increasing inter-abdominal pressure. A strong diaphragm prevents acid reflux by applying pressure on the esophagus.

Women used to be the ones with shallow breath compared to men, this is now shifting. Seventy-five percent of men and women in today's society, as well as ninety percent of children, have weakened diaphragms due to inertia and low breathing practices. Women also put others first, negatively affecting their Soul level and reducing life at the breath level. Strengthening the diaphragm is necessary at all levels; physical, emotional, and mental. Men have also become more inert in their daily lives.

With children, inertia of the physical Body because of television, video games, computers and cell phones, rather than physical exercise, has shifted the make-up of the human Body by weakening the diaphragm. In North America, more illness is apparent at the childhood level such as asthma, allergies, emotional issues, and cancers, than at any other time. Furthermore, the negativity projected by some television shows, computer programs and video games can disconnect the Soul from the Body as well as from the Universe.

How to further strengthen the diaphragm

- Reduce television and computer time to an hour each day.
- Protect personal energy with Electric Magnetic Field (EMF) eliminators, by placing them on electronic games, cell phones, computers, cordless phones, etc.
- Exercise thirty minutes daily five days per week.
- Put self first; emotionally, physically and spiritually.

Susan Manion MacDonald

Breathing technique

- Ensure breathing is at the level of the diaphragm: Place two hands on diaphragm with middle fingers lightly touching; breathe in and out; ensure the finger tips naturally separate with the breath.
- Practice twice daily: Ten minutes for adults, five minutes for children.
- There is a possibility of sore muscle as one exercises the diaphragm muscle.

To breathe correctly is not just for the physical aspect of life, it is for the Soul and Spiritual level as well. Breathing can transform matter.

Emotional Feelings Take up Residence

A sequence occurs with our organs, which the emotional feelings can inhibit. When the heart embraces guilt, that guilt will facilitate pain. Pain is a message to the Body from the Soul to work with the past while it removes guilt, regains qualities lost and moves into purpose. Even when one stubs a toe, it is a reminder to watch our thoughts and recognize where strength of a quality needs to be built. An accident will also identify a blocked pathway in the Body that needs to be resolved.

Look at all aspects of the whole person when one chooses to release and shift feelings. When the heart is opened to joy and happiness, the Soul will respond.

Emotional feelings are the language of the Soul (heart connection). How does one keep feelings under control? By releasing control and the feeling attached. Do not put it away, instead: feel it, move through it; say what needs to be said, whether in a letter or verbally. Remove the negative energy that will affect the Energy Field and thus the physical Body. Retrieve the quality of life that was formerly lost as it is necessary to keep on path. Allow the Soul permission to stay within while supporting a healthy Body.

**"Your soul cherishes every aspect of your life.
There is a Plan, and your soul knows what it is."
Deepak Chopra**

Endocrine Glands and Feelings

Each individual has a system of hormonal glands required for peace and harmony in the Body. Each gland supports organs plus Body parts in a rhythmic flow.

The endocrine glands also process emotional feelings. As mentioned earlier, the <u>adrenals</u> are blocked when resentment is present. One adrenal gland is seated on each kidney and when emotional feelings block the energy to the gland; this energy block also affects kidney function. Fatigue, low back pain and extreme emotions are signs that this gland has weak energy. Adrenal tire, the circle of fat at the belly button level, is also an indicator of long term adrenal issues.

The <u>thymus</u> is situated behind the breast bone and when an individual feels disappointment, this organ reduces its ability to function properly. Immune response is affected and the possibility of pressure on this area will arise, similar to the feeling of an elephant sitting on one's chest. Electrolytes will slow the heart, and loss of energy to the physical aspects of the Body will be felt. Pain or discomfort in the right arm is also a symptom of blocked energy at this juncture. Carpal tunnel can be a side-effect of this emotional feeling. The thymus is connected to one's heart rhythm: the music of which one is. Look at what sounds one is making at home, office, with family, friends, and more . . . BE aware of the music in one. Create joyful sounds from within to balance and heal.

The <u>thyroid</u> is at the base of the neck. This area is also connected to speaking one's truth, with the mouth, esophagus and ears being affected. Metabolism along with fatigue is also related to a thyroid imbalance. Hair loss is another symptom as well as a symptom of kidney weakness.

The parathyroid, although situated physically at the base of the neck, is energetically available for testing under the jaw. Its main purpose is to aid the Body in absorbing calcium. Energy blockage in this area is the main reason for arthritis, osteoporosis, kidney stones, bone spurs, rheumatoid fingers, cataracts, etc. Calcium which is unable to absorb in teeth or bones will collect in and around joints, including the spine. The feeling that challenges these glands is feeling a disloyalty from others or feeling disloyal to one's own self. Speaking one's truth also plays a part; one sometimes dislikes conflict, therefore chokes back saying what is of value.

Insecurity is an emotional feeling that affects the pineal gland. Disruption of sleep patterns is the symptom that occurs when this gland is not flowing properly. When one is having difficulty envisioning the future an energy blockage may occur in this area.

Disruption of sleep is a disruption of dreams, and dreams form a plan for the future. Insecurity is a detachment between the heart and Soul; therefore, balance will be found once it is re-established.

Hormones are controlled via the pituitary gland, which is energetically found at the base of the head. Energy blockage creates dullness, headaches, shoulder and neck issues as well as reduced functions of all the other endocrine glands. The feeling that affects this gland is loss of control. A reason for being unable to carry out duties properly can be understood, when an individual feels a loss of the ability to perform.

Individuals have two hypothalamus glands. One is located on each temple. The feeling related to both is the need to be nurtured. Left or right depends on whether the feeling registered is related to a female (left) or a male (right).

The Soul will signal the hypothalamus to nurture an illness or disease, similar to the Body's response when pregnant. If not pregnant, blocked energy in either hypothalamus occurs when the individual has not processed an emotional feeling within a certain time period of one's life. The inner reaction is similar to a child's reaction of lying on the floor kicking and screaming, when the child is unable to get something it wants. What does one want?

Caution is necessary when using Energy Balance Harmony to clear blocked energy in the hypothalamus area if it is possible the individual is pregnant. "Do not clear blocked energy in this case."

This process of emotional attachments and symptoms has been identified earlier as "The Fourth Principle". I named this after the realization that disease can be traced back to a major traumatic incident that happened four years prior. This incident becomes attached to an emotional feeling not cleared from the past as a child, which has similar properties. Toxins, which are present, complete the triangle.

A student with Colitis came to me for guidance and after a Live Blood Analysis it was determined that parasites were the physical toxin involved. The emotional toxin was more difficult to locate. The right hypothalamus was blocked; indicating male involvement and the spleen was also involved; indicating abandonment. The student's father was attached, yet his father was a great father, had not passed away or deprived him of any contact during his life. I had to locate The Fourth Principal, which was also more of an issue in this case. The student could not recall a trauma prior to the beginning of Colitis or the date defined via ERT, so we had a conversation about his father and mother. The student's father had only a small family and his mother a large one. Once children were brought up, it came to the student that he had become a Godparent four years prior to the diagnosis of Colitis. He is his father's only son and had made a decision to not have children. Since his reaction to choose not having children came into play as a trauma, it was necessary to discover what caused this decision. The student had been bullied as a child and when this was brought to the forefront, using conversation and ERT, tears started to flow, the feeling was up. Letters still need to be written to the bully or bullies even without knowing a name, the emotional feeling brought to the surface. Forgiveness; not of the incidents, however, of the humans responsible is necessary. Finally, flush or burn the letters to release the energy affecting the Energy Field.

I also used ERT to identify, and Energy Balance Harmony to clear a subconscious thought of not feeling safe to have children.

Subconsciously, the student wanted children; however, the bullying had created a trauma around that. He still may decide to not have children, although it is now his decision and not a decision created by a bully. If he does his homework, both physical and emotional, the Colitis will be history.

All emotional feelings are connected to a quality lost and to the Soul's desire to rebuild self. The Soul carries the individual's potential to motivate one to reach higher. The Soul is YOU. Ask the Soul for guidance, simply while with clarity; then wait for the response. Trust one's instincts. True guidance is not with fear. Sally Fields once said, "When fear makes the decision it's a mistake." Fear keeps us from being our authentic self. Ninety percent of individuals believe they have a Soul; it is time now to listen to what one's Soul is saying.

"Real power is usually unspectacular, a simple setting aside of fear that allows the free flow of love. It changes everything."
Martha Beck

Breaking Away from Fear

There are four types of fear that keep one from danger and other fears that are created from an overactive mind:

1. Instinctual: the rush of adrenaline when threats are near.
2. Emotional: a reminder of an event from the past.
3. Imaginary: a feeling of gloom, doom and ruin that may never happen.
4. Loss: of ego status, failure, humiliation, or death.

- Recognize what is causing the fear;
- Go into the fear and take a deep breathe;
- Listen to one's wise self and make a decision to reclaim one's power;

- Trust self; try again if one fails and use the failure as a stepping stone to success in the future. Take a chance and see the possibilities;
- Find one's centre.

BE grateful every day for what one has, and say a happy prayer of thanks for this new world one has awakened to this morning. Thank one for the ability to heal self and others.

Facilitate the process to heal, learn how to guide others to goals, without enabling them. Enabling occurs when an individual is looking for worth in the wrong place, and enables others as a false sense of self-worth. To enable another is to give them the knowledge while also to do the action for them. To enable another takes away their feeling of being good enough.

To BE is self-worth. A degree of learning, work ethic, time or money does not establish worth. One is worthy now, all are worthy.

The process of a protocol for disease is in point, to create a secure base for release of control and the need for approval. When an individual tries to control the enema in a healing protocol or another part of the process, anything and everything can go wrong. Laugh and let go! Learn about that which one is as well as one's purpose to BE on earth. Shift and transform to authentic self. That is the lesson of illness and disease. Accept the gift.

The Soul can get cluttered with all of the feelings and qualities that have been lost. Symptoms that identify this are: when one is driven, feeling stressed, pressure, always behind; the opposite is passion, perseverance and determination. A second symptom would be: distractions, too many targets, goals or visions; the opposite is focus. The third symptom is superficiality: being consumed with tasks instead of people with the opposite being empathy. Another symptom is materialism: one's need to validate self with things. The opposite too materialism is love of self.

Everything is connected and the information in this book should give you a fairly good understanding of how. A list is not necessary if one listens from within. Each moment is guided while each project has the ability to be accomplished on time with good quality, while one still feels energetic and purposeful.

One could ask, *"How can God or one's Soul do this?"*, when in fact it is one's self that creates the circumstance. God gave one free will and if one is connected Soulfully, God uses his connection to the Soul to try and grasp one's attention. Early childhood experiences, as well as processed food and toxins, deplete intuitive messages meant to guide. Symptoms then become the only way to identify to one that the Body is out of balance, and one needs to shift to BE, to put self first, forgive issues from the past, and BE grateful for the gifts learned. Yet one tends to utilize the mind (Spirit) and spend years in transition instead of in presence.

"The Soul would have no rainbow if the eyes have no tears." Native Proverb

Balance is attained when the Spirit, Soul and Body are in harmony. One form of identifying imbalance would be to recognize the emphasis on the Body. When recognition of weight, quality of clothes, etc. are identified before the quality of the person at the heart/Soul level, an imbalance would be indicated.

Once the past is brought forward and person or persons forgiven, the negative charge is released. The Energy Field that protects the Body will be strengthened. Individuals who participate in one's life will experience the transformation and respond in an affirmative way.

An example of this occurred when a student mentioned earlier in this book, was involved in a custody battle. The former spouse was determined to obtain full custody of the child at all costs, due to the need to control. The student and her parent let this affect their physical health due to past trauma as children. Once the student worked through forgiveness and regained the qualities lost, her Energy Field reflected a confident person. This shift of energy was detected via energy by the former spouse, who then dropped all claims to the child prior to trial.

Perpetrators subconsciously look for weakness in ones Energy Field as a way to garner control back that they perceive lost as a child. Confidence in another individual identifies the weakness in self. Instead of looking to shift that, they instead escape from it, which is what happened above.

In 2002, I was diagnosed with stage 4b terminal cancer. Part of the recovery was to go inside self and deal with past negative life experiences that had diminished my Soul while weakening my Energy Field. The weakness I was experiencing due to the disease stopped my ability to enable others. The cancer gave me the ability to say 'No' in most cases, for the first time.

The first clue that this was the right path to explore was not the fear of death, because I believe in God; instead it was the fear of dying and leaving a husband, daughter, sister, and friend who were use to having problems solved through me. "Oh my gosh! What would they do without me?" I was living life for them, not me. At the time, this did not register as being unusual. Thanks to natural means, tenacity I had gained from life experiences and an automatic shift to stop enabling, I was able to reverse the disease. A few years later, other health issues had me look deeper. As I regained strength and physical health I started to gradually enable the same people again. The individuals also gradually reverted back to old patterns.

Enabling others gives one a false sense of self-worth. Some would deny that I could have this issue when I headed organizations, multi-tasked and received awards for personal achievements. I concealed my low self-worth skillfully, even from my self.

Shifting from enabling was not easy. The people involved liked the fact that I resolved their problems instead of giving them the knowledge to let them resolve issues themselves. Communication was vital and when talking did not make this completely clear, they came back and attached like Velcro. I had not yet let go of my Velcro piece, on some level still wishing to enable them. I then resorted to letters. A few were offended, again mirroring their own issues. This knowledge made it easier for me to accept their response. A wonderful thing happened once the Velcro reaction ceased. They found what was always theirs, and began to grow in leaps and bounds.

Attachment creates enabling as well. Abandonment issues from childhood can lead us to believe others might also abandon us. Self-worth is compromised. Enabling can be gradual, ensuring that others have low worth also. The enabler holds the power of how to resolve issues, creating a vicious circle.

The best case scenario would be to ensure that there are no attachments to spouse, children, home, even to those we call self; Mom, Dad or Doctor, etc. Imagine putting everything one owns into one's house, including vehicle and job titles. Now envision a fire which destroys everything. What would be the top five things with meaning on the list of losses?

Now write down on a piece of paper those five items and ask the Universe to release any negative attachments. Do this until there are no attachments. It is wonderful to love and support one's family, yet when attached, there is no growth, including repairs to one's home when an attachment to that home is present. If one becomes attached to a book one authored, the second one will not be written.

Tears when reading a book or watching a movie can indicate the need to look inside and understand the heart connection. A piece of the Soul is in need of restoration and tears are an indicator. Listen within, and it will be identified. Ask God to assist in reconnecting the strands of light energy.

As children, the knowledge of life's path is already formed in one, yet circumstances can dissolve that memory. Children live life in the present. They have not developed an analytical process which interferes with intuition. Children are spontaneous beings.

James Hillman, author of *Soul Code,* uses a premise called the Acorn Theory. He believes that an individual image belongs to one's Soul. Be present to children and ask, *"Who is this child that happens to be mine?"* Keep an eye out for where the child's destiny might show itself, via an obsession or resistance. One needs to trust emotional rapport with children, to see a child's beauty. The Soul yearns for beauty.

Ideas are like children. A person can get one's children or their ideas into the world if possible, to support them and help them along. Nothing changes until ideas change.

One tends to approach people as they would a car, and ask *"What is wrong and how much does it cost to fix it?"* This concept is starting to shift, and it will take a heart/Soul connection to make it happen.

Mentoring is when one gets caught up in the fantasy of another person. One's imagination comes together. *What is one here for?*

Ask: *"How am I useful to others?"* *"What do people want from me?"*

When one considers the archetypal, historical, and cultural background of whatever one does, it gives a sense that the occupation can be a calling and not just a job.

Each human has a calling. Look at the accidents, curiosities, illness, oddities, and trouble in the past or present and relate it to being a symptom that is forcing one to go deeper.

Astrology and Palm Reading are connecting the Soul with the Universe and identifying some points. These points can move one forward or backward and depending on how one reflects the response, can utilize higher or lower self.

"Ethics were more important than aesthetics."
Carl Jung

The Soul is referred to in the Christian tradition as "the Christ within, the inner divinity" in each person. The realm of the Soul is called "the kingdom of God." In the Jewish tradition, the Soul is sometimes referred to as "the vital principle." In the Hindu tradition, it's called the "Atma" or "Self." In the Buddhist tradition, it is "the Buddha Mind," "the mind of enlightenment (bodhichitta)." In ancient Greece, the temple of the Oracle at Delphi proclaimed, "Man, know thyself, and thou wilt know the Universe and God." As one knows our Soul, the microcosm, one will understand the macrocosm.

There are three situations that can misdirect the Soul: the need for approval, control or security. Fear and Shame are the emotional feelings that direct these inappropriate needs. They are learned in childhood when a loss of control has occurred and are self-imposed as an adult. The situations become a story one tells ones self when the issue has not been cleared from the Soul.

There are different methods used by perpetrators to take control of another person. In some instances the wronged person negatively takes back control, rather than feeling the pain and clearing the Soul.

Methods of negatively taking or losing control:

- mental or physical abuse;
- molestation and/or rape;
- theft;
- fire or an accident;
- lack of nurturing;
- murder of a loved one;
- enabling;
- toxic overload;
- lying—even little white ones;
- clutter or hording;
- procrastination;
- illness or disease;
- fraud;
- weight gain;
- smoking, drugs, alcohol, shopaholic, sexual addiction;
- disobeying rules and laws.

Taking Control Positively:

- laughter/fun;
- leadership or mentorship;
- volunteering;
- being a team player;
- education or knowledge;
- being a friend;
- loving self;
- BE authentic;
- learning guitar, piano, dance, painting, photography, etc.;
- success such as writing a book;
- building a relationship with self.

Modalities for improving one's skills with the purpose to strengthen the positive are listed in the order of their benefit status. Those on the same line are equal in nature:

1. Belief in God with prayer;
2. Energy Response Testing & Interpretation;
3. The Fourth Principle;
4. Acupuncture, Naturopathy, Body Talk & German New Medicine;
5. Chakra Balance, EBH, EFT, AFT, Dowsing & Pendulum;
6. Shaman & Akashi Records;
7. Clairvoyant & Feng Shui.

"Our greatest happiness lies in practicing a talent that we are meant to use." Goethe

Stop pursuing happiness and one will find it right here!

One gathers information and stores it in the mind. The brain uses past experiences to interpret and react to this information, sometimes incorrectly. The filters of past life experiences limit choices for creating a joyful, abundant life. The wonderful message is that filters can be changed and habits reversed.

Habits

A habit is a shortcut that has occurred with loss of qualities in life and that now affects the Soul and Spirit.

Do not fight a habit! Instead look at it objectively. Ask, *"Why was it chosen? Was it chosen because it felt safe or familiar? Does the habit protect one from negative emotional feelings? Does it provide a quick fix for pleasure or security? When did one lose the quality needed to reverse this? By whom did this occur?"*

The benefit of a habit is usually at a hidden level, where the inner child wants safety, comfort or security. Approval is also connected to habits as is the need for control.

Be honest with why the habit was chosen and realize that it is a form of in-action so that change cannot take place as it can be frightening or threatening. For example; look for the quality lost while one chooses to forgive. Release the issue and emotional feelings so that the emotional weight can now disappear.

Why does one need to be a victim? Ask one's self, *"Is this an easy way out from accepting responsibility for something or someone? When and by whom was this learned?"*

Try to find a way to replace the old habit with a new, good one. Make the reason for doing so convincing and remember one can make choices.

Break the power of "NO!" to regain the power of choice.

Subtle action changes energy positively.

- Go inside and declare the change that one wishes to make.
- Believe in getting results.

- Do not resist the process of change.
- Write those letters of forgiveness and release emotional feelings.
- The Body effortlessly shifts at the physical level, once balance is achieved at the Soul level.
- Repeat until one has mastered the change desired.

Habits cut individuals off from their senses.

Senses

The five senses are the bridge to the world via the organs of the Body, while the sixth sense, intuition, is the connection to God by way of the Soul.

Music is a vibration and vibrations act as stimuli to ears. The rhythmic movement in the womb begins the connection. Note the difference in hearing and listening. Hearing is when the sound reaches one's ears, a physical ability. Listening, however, takes place when it reaches one's brain and becomes a skill.

One builds each part of one's world from the senses. Eyes are stimulated by light and beauty. Smells can bring back memories good as well as bad, again an opportunity to notice negative feelings and forgive while one releases the past. Smells have the ability to ground a person or to bring moments of serenity to an otherwise busy day.

Has one ever thought about why foods taste different? It's really quite amazing. The tongue and the roof of the mouth are covered with thousands of tiny taste buds. When one eats, an enzyme named amylase that resides in the saliva of the mouth is activated to help breakdown food. This action causes the receptor cells located in the taste buds to send messages through sensory nerves to the brain. The brain then informs one of what flavors are present.

Taste buds play the most important part in helping a person enjoy the various flavours of food. Taste buds have the ability to recognize five basic kinds of tastes: sweet, salty, sour, spicy and bitter.

Every other taste is experienced via the nose. Pinch the nose while eating and observe how little one tastes. Smells trigger vivid memories of events from one's past—even that cinnamon bun that Granny made. Negative feelings can arise as well as positive ones from smell if a traumatic incident occurred during a meal or when someone wears a certain perfume or aftershave. When symptoms show up, BE present to the time and place. Smell can also bring balance back to the Body with aromatherapy.

While the four senses (sight, hearing, smell, and taste) are located in specific parts of the Body, the sense of touch is found all over. This is because the sense of touch originates in the bottom layer of the skin called the dermis.

The dermis is filled with many tiny nerve endings which give information about items with which the Body comes in contact. They do this by carrying the information to the spinal cord, which then sends messages to the brain where the feeling is registered.

The nerve endings in skin can tell one if something is hot or cold.

They can also feel if something is causing pain. The Body has about twenty different types of nerve endings that all send messages to the brain; however, the most common receptors are heat, cold, pain, and pressure or touch receptors. Pain receptors are probably the most important for safety because they can protect one by warning the brain that the Body is hurt!

Pain is also a symptom the Soul is sending one to release guilt.

Intuitiveness

There are different levels of intuitiveness, while it's interesting to note that a child is very intuitive at birth. It is the guidance given from the moment of birth that formulates withdrawal from use, or exhilarates this potential.

Processed foods, alcohol, drugs and toxins, as well as emotional or physical experiences can suppress intuitive response.

Intuition is the result of receiving input or ideas from within the heart/Soul, while connected to God and the Universe. It is a guidance system like no other. To BE intuitive is to feel, sense, see, attract, and predict past, present plus future events in flow with one's self and God.

Learn and listen to the music of life, the vibration that one presents to the world. Does it bring harmony, love, or joy? One is the conductor of one's life. What does life ask of one? How does one respond? Who would one need to become?

Look around and ask what friends, family, community as well as strangers want from one. What does one have to give?

Oprah asks, *"What do you know for sure?"* I know that to live life there needs to be a relationship with God and self. To deny a relationship with one's self is to deny self-worth, while to deny a relationship with God is to deny one's existence.

Individuals come up to me and say what great courage I have. My past life experiences, my failures and successes, as well as the reaction to them, all affect who, as well as what I am today. Closeness to God plus the part He plays in my life everyday was a hard lesson to learn and not one I will ever forget. The new love for self came from that closeness. We all need to love self and God!

Intuitive decision making is far more than using common sense as it involves additional sensors to perceive and receive information from outside. Sometimes it is referred to as gut feeling, sixth sense, inner sense, instinct, inner voice, spiritual guide, etc.

There is no excuse or shame. When the Soul is attuned to God while in vibration and harmony with the Universe as well as earth, it cannot be moved to a negative response.

Messages come from a variety of avenues, even the craving of food or smells. Understand the reason behind the message, and if it doesn't resonate, let it go. Something or someone will arrive to bring light to it if one is present.

Test drive one's intuition, it is like strengthening a muscle. Spend quiet time with self, pay attention to shifts in the physical Body. Keep a journal of synchronicity.

"Come, Come Again" Rumi

Good or bad, it is the lesson one is here to learn. Go back to what ignites one to life. Reflect on one's values, standards and boundaries then choose to live within them from the heart/Soul connection.

Art is like music with its own vibration and can change the energy of a room, transforming the Soul as well as Spirit. To some, a specific instrument or song will ignite their Spirit while to others it may be art. Find the ignition that self-ignites one and spend time there listening to one's Soul.

Attention doesn't wander because something is dull-life looks dull when attention wanders. When attention flows to the past, energy is wasted as it is when worrying about what might happen in the future. Energy is what keeps one alive. When the mind connects with the heart and stays in the present, all vitality can come back. It is important to still the mind, remove fear, heal, and rest completely in each moment. Meditation brings one to a place with no time or space while it connects one to Soul. The present is all one has. It is where the gifts are.

Before I Began

A morning prayer in the style of Matthew

Lord thank you for life and the world
And for everyone with whom I share them.

Thank you for today.
Let me choose today's goals wisely
And live today perfectly.

Thank you for everything I touch
I embrace all of creation,
From the leaf in my hand
To the farthest ridge and mountaintop.
Let me use your riches respectfully,
Let me be a partner in your creative love.

Thank you for all the light that reaches me.
Let me transmit it further,
Especially where warmth and light
Are most needed.

Thank you for challenges.
Let me respond prudently and passionately,
Let me understand risks, prepare properly,
Then act with total commitment and courage.
When my action is completed,
Let me celebrate with my friends.

At the end of today,
May I remember to thank you
For all my successes and failures.
May I continue to grow through them
Until I reach the perfection of being
To which I am called.

A friend away in China on her inward journey sent me this letter. Stephanie lives life from her heart while listening to her Soul.

TCM & my Inward Journey-August 18, 2010
Written by: Stephanie Allen

In the past two weeks my journey has moved from an outward exploration of a new country to an inner journey through my inner landscape of motives and intentions. Being in an environment where few can speak one's language can leave one to listen closely to the inner voice. I have been in constant dialogue with my heart around what in which I want to invest my time and energy after I return from China. Who will I become due to this journey? Who do I want to become and how do I want to reinvent my life after this life here overseas? These questions have left me pondering the places where I have spent my time and energy. Now I am re-evaluating my life force and asking myself if I want to continue to spend my energy in the way I have in the past.

Since arriving in China, we have been making a conscious effort to put our energy in places that most benefit our learning, loving and health. Every morning we do our spiritual practice, followed by a healthy breakfast. We spend the day learning TCM and socializing with our classmates. After school we head to the gym for a quick workout and then go out for a meal in a place we haven't yet experienced (to stretch our culinary comfort zone). Each evening we discuss what we are learning and we ask each other questions about who we are and what we want to become in our lives. We write these things down and look at what has been the struggle or obstacle that has prevented us from making these intentions and dreams reality. It has expanded our awareness and opened our hearts to ourselves and to each other. What a remarkable way to co-create together and deepen intimacy with joy and courage!

Enrolling in the study of TCM has opened my creativity and child-like wonder to the world my heart knew but my mind had forgotten. This healing work is more than a science. It is a rich spiritually founded paradigm that requires an artist's approach. I love the philosophy of Yin/Yang and the 5 elements and that it is applied to all things in our lives, be it health, business, relationships or consciousness. Nothing is separated. Everything is woven into a beautiful, artful web that connects everyone and everything together. I believe that the next 3 months will not only change me but will also enhance and enrich all that is connected to me. As for now, I am enjoying being in the mystery of the sacred practice of Chinese Medicine.

Summary of Chapter 2

1. The Soul has an individual divine plan-we each have one;

2. Qualities guide the Soul, if lost during one's life they can be restored;

3. *Tiger Tiger is it True* by Byron Katie a story of thoughts creating life;

4. Mirroring-how one's perception of others relates to self;

5. Feelings can get trapped in the physical Body, creating illness and disease;

6. The diaphragm requires deep breathing to strengthen it so the Body will have the ability to release emotions naturally;

7. Separate emotions connect to each organ and gland. Whether they stay or leave is one's choice;

8. Fear has a message: listen, forgive and release;

9. Attachments disable self as well as others;

10. Approval, control and security-three needs that can misdirect the Soul;

11. Habits, senses and intuitiveness-it is within each one to change.

CHAPTER 3

Spirit of Adventure

Spirit is firmly active in jarring the Body physically, when a person falls off life's true path. Spirit wants life in balance, personally as well as professionally. Too much or too little of either and the Body will show symptoms of physical distress. Is one present or does one listen? Not likely! It is necessary on a daily basis, in a relaxed mode, to breathe for a minimum of ten minutes while one just listens. Forget lists, students, housework, children, etc. and focus on one's inner being and what it is trying to build-a relationship with self. When indifference shows up with time or energy constraint, look into one's eyes in the mirror while saying, "I love you." Be present to self, by being as well as doing what lifts one's Spirit. Spirit will process gifts, create quality time, and show how to increase one's energy as one accomplishes professional or personal goals.

Doors have opened for me to a deeper Spiritual path, with purpose and meaning as well as a connection to all of creation. Spirit is what lifts one, yet it takes awhile to recognize and listen, while understanding the connection of Spirit, Soul and Body. It took another lesson that almost brought death for me to wake up to the possibility.

In the last chapter it was mentioned about my Soul wanting to leave, in the same incident where my Spirit announced loudly that I had been ignoring it. While in Newfoundland presenting lectures on BALANCE, it became apparent that I was totally out of balance. On the second day, during a lecture, a pain gradually started in my right side, liver area and by the morning of the third day, my liver had doubled in size creating violent pain. James wanted to fly over to take me home, my friend and colleague who had set up this lecture series suggested the hospital. Instead, I asked God for help and was guided to a Homeopathic doctor, Gloria Penny who had been a former nurse. She had dealt with liver pain as a nurse while working in a portion of the hospital that did liver biopsies. Within twenty-four hours of following her natural protocol, the pain and swelling had subsided, although I was still weak.

James and our daughter Charlene met me at the airport in Nova Scotia so one of them could drive my vehicle home as I still had no physical strength. After two days at home, I realized I was in serious trouble. When I had been diagnosed with terminal cancer seven years prior to this, my will (Spirit) was strong and healing was possible. This time, with only a virus, it felt like I would not make it through the day. James called on two friends, Kim and Dianna who are Intuitive Healers. They worked on my Soul and Energy Field for hours. A third practitioner, Stephanie, came that evening and guided me through a Spiritual integration that took three hours, the longest she had ever had to do. What I learned through this process, which included Energy Response Testing, was that my Spirit plus Soul were leaving. I had put all my energy into the opening of a natural health centre and had forgotten about self, family, friends as well as community.

In 2005, when I started this business in the basement of my home, I had gradually, without even realizing it, started the process of distancing myself from my husband, family, friends, housework, and self. My Spirit plus Soul had given me simple symptoms that I had ignored up until this point.

In this moment, I had to follow a protocol to get back on path, given to me by Spirit and Soul, identified via questions as well as Energy Response Testing. This protocol consisted of no more than thirty-three hours at work per week; three hours daily of connecting with my husband, and one hour each day for me to BE creative through music, art, dance, etc. I was also required to drink two vegetable juices, one fruit juice, and eat healthy meals; awaken at six in the morning, breathe fresh air for ten minutes, then go back to bed and lay down for twenty minutes thinking only of self. No telephone, books, or getting back up until this was complete and then stay in bed until eight in the morning. I had to be in bed by nine in the evening as well, with the same rule of no books, phone, etc.

It was necessary to do this protocol for eleven days. The hardest part was laying down while listening to self. At first it took quite awhile to really pay attention, as lists formed and tasks tried to prioritize themselves in my head. Once I finally got there, it was the most wonderful journey.

During those eleven days, I was scheduled to go on a trip to Alberta to attend a seminar with Adam "DreamHealer". It was necessary to find a flight that left late and arrived early so I could stay within the time frame of this new sleep pattern. Being alone in Edmonton was wonderful for both my Spirit plus Soul. I had fun spending one day at the Edmonton Mall and even got an organic spray-paint tattoo on my ankle.

I visited a number of book stores and introduced myself as an author; attended a Turkish Festival going on in old Edmonton; visited the market; ate kettle corn and Bing cherries. The best times were with inner self, identifying what I liked and who I was. My lessons were powerful information that led to the writing of this book, and a different understanding of life, as well as a stronger connection to God.

Early in 2003 was when the first consciousness of Spirit came to me loud and clear. My husband James asked me this question, "If you die from cancer and leave this world, how I will recognize you when I get to heaven?" My reply was, "If I were brain dead in the hospital on life support, would that Body lying there be who I really am?"

One is a Spirit within one's physical Body, with a higher conscious and lower subconscious. It is one's higher self that is meant to journey on life's path, yet negative lessons learned while growing into adulthood can lower or remove the qualities necessary for the future. These can affect one's Soul and place the Spirit in the driver's seat. Spirit is connected to "Will."

Fighting, yelling, name calling, loss of integrity, hitting, molestation, and rape, all have the ability to steal a piece of one's Soul and weaken one's Spirit.

When intuitively blocked, the Soul then may respond using symptoms as a guide, out of fear, anger, resentment, worry or guilt. These emotional feelings are what can be held in organs of the Body and correspond to illness or disease. Guilt usually resides in the heart; fear in the kidneys; anger in the liver; resentment in the adrenals and worry in the stomach. Positive emotional feelings will also guide the Soul to a wonderful life where the heart wants to be in love, joy, peace and harmony, surrounded by beauty. The choice is within each one.

An emotional feeling from the present has the ability to draw upon a stored emotional feeling from the past. In combination with a toxic Body, it has the ability to block energy, prevent absorption of nutrients, thus creating illness or disease.

Emotions stand for energy in motion, they make one human. It is the inability to release emotional feelings that create illness and disease.

The heart and Soul are connected. Is one listening to them? They drive the show while Spirit is the energy force. The heart/Soul is the higher self and caretaker of emotional feelings, while the Spirit uses energy as well as the mind. The energy of Spirit can be driven by the heart/Soul if chosen. Most often individuals leave Spirit in the driver's seat, hence the mind instead of the heart. When the Soul drives life, it is no longer a struggle and is truly a place one wants to be. Use Spirit as intended as the wind beneath one's wings and life runs more smoothly.

The human Spirit knows it can do anything. It is very powerful and knows when one is lying to self.

"When I present a question to someone, 'I want what your Soul says, not what your mind is telling me'." Kim Ripley

Feelings Attract

A feeling is a response to a thought—an interpretation based on Spirit. It is necessary for feelings to be felt in order to bridge Spirit and Soul. This will connect one to the Universe and attract positive or negative reactions in one's life. There are three feelings: pleasant, unpleasant and neutral. Feelings as well as vibrations are the same thing. A Human is an energy vibrating being who lives within the magnetism of the earth. As the axis of the earth shifts gradually heading into the 2012 time frame, a human's vibration will reduce. One has the power to raise this vibration.

The only power a present condition has over one is what one gives it. Negative vibrations or feelings, mean one is out of sync with "God". There are no accidents; it is what one attracts with feelings that create one's life. To attract better, one must feel appreciation for self, others and the beauty around one. Connect with Spirit on a higher level of vibration. When one connects to a higher vibration, illness and disease, even cancer, can be cured.

I have met many people in the past nine years since being diagnosed who have died of cancer. This does not have to happen. One lady recently passed away, a wonderful woman, wife, mother and career person who did not believe or value self. She put everyone else in her life first and was not actually living life to the full. This lady did not know how much she was appreciated and most importantly she did not know how to appreciate herself.

A person can tend to look for the goodness in others and forget to look for the goodness in one's own self. One can hide it well, and usually has friends who care and family who love one dearly. When one does not love self, the vibration of which one is reduces the vibration of Spirit. Then if emotional as well as physical toxins are present, disease manifests itself and death will occur.

Practitioners! Students must not believe we will cure them. They need to understand what we give is knowledge and guidance. The healing is within them. Disease is created in a low vibration (Spirit) and then the disease reduces vibrations as well. Doctors who do not understand the concept that it takes the whole Body to heal, may offer medication, chemo and radiation that also reduce vibrations.

Raise the vibration and the illness or disease will go away.

Depression is a negative feeling brought on by emotional and physical toxins. It is believed to be anger, which has turned inside out. Once in play, if what one watches on TV is negative, or negative individuals are around a person, then it is hard to reverse this without changing the chemical make-up of the Body with medication. This can be done naturally by changing ones surroundings, looking inside for that good feeling one experienced in the past and hanging on to it. Remove the toxins that are affecting negative liver functions. Write letters to someone from the past, releasing all emotional feelings and forgive them, not for what they did or did not do, since it is not really about them. Sign the letter, then burn or flush it down the toilet and emotional toxins will be released. Physically, toxins can be released by infrared saunas, ionic footbaths or coffee enemas. Juicing and certain herbs facilitate the process as well.

A positive feeling such as gratitude, excitement, or wonder raises one's vibration and shifts the course of one's future by attracting positive reactions! This is called, "The Law of Attraction." *Excuse Me Your Life is Waiting* by Lynn Grabhorn is a practical book that has the ability to help individuals understand this concept.

A question to ask when one is ill would be, *"What does this give one permission to do or not do?"* When a quality of life has been prevented from enhancing the Soul, the Spirit nudges the mind to remember plus resolve the past so that this quality can be returned to the Soul. It is indeed necessary as part of one's life mission to BE authentic in who one is and all qualities are required for this to occur.

The same can be asked of any incident that occurs in life. For example, on the way home from a wonderful week in Las Vegas, where James and I attended the retro wedding of our niece Laura, the camera that held all the pictures was left at the inspection point at the airport. James and I had also visited the Grand Canyon while there as well as two of my sisters, whom I do not see often, were also in Las Vegas for the wedding. Many special photo moments had occurred. The airport there is quite intense, with thousands leaving and coming hourly, even at five in the morning which was when we were there. Following the path backwards, we were told it might be impossible to locate the camera. Nevertheless officials gave me a lost and found number. At first I cried. James consoled me, thinking it was the photos I was upset about losing. My actual loss was that after this beautiful week something could create this negative response in my mind (Spirit).

Once on the plane, I became calm and listened to Spirit plus Soul while an idea soon came to me. I started to write feverishly, got up and went to the bathroom to tear up the letter I had just written and flushed it. I came back to my seat smiling. James noticed the difference and wanted to know what took place.

While in Las Vegas, my older sister, Terry, whom I love dearly, yet only see once every four years or more, seemed to take charge of our little group, including where we ate. We let her, yet I felt a tension that I was not present to at that time. Basically I ignored my Spirit plus Soul. I should have debated where we ate, because I did not like the food advertised. I was still not speaking my own truth, and therefore lost part of my authentic self, leading to the loss of the camera. To debate and lose to the majority is still being authentic, something I did not enhance at this moment in time.

The letter was written to self. I addressed what needed to be said, forgave self, signed and disposed of the completed letter. I then realized the camera would be back within a couple of days. After calling lost and found at the next stop, we soon arrived home to a phone call which assured us the camera had been found and was on its way via express mail.

I was a person that had a tendency to hold negative emotional feelings, therefore, illness or negative incidents showed up occasionally. Once present to the emotional feelings and the lesson was learned, the symptoms went away quickly. I knew that to release emotional feelings, one needs a strong diaphragm and understood how to do that, yet it was not until I spoke to a dear friend and practitioner, Madachanda (Gugi) that I understood the physical Body will also hold on to negative emotional feeling when the Body is not in alignment. Gugi positioned me on my back on the floor, with knees bent so, the bottoms of my feet touched. To show alignment means that the thighs and knees would then be touching the floor. Not so, in this case they were raised quite a bit. To regain this ability, I am to practice this exercise as well as; lie in bed at night on my stomach in this position when possible. Osteopaths and Chiropractors will also help to reestablish balance if one is unable to accomplish this alone.

Individuals who hold negative emotional feelings also absorb more physical toxins than ones who do not. Emotional feelings are aligned with the Soul.

Growing up, I was taught to work hard. The tendency was to forego fun. Dad did take us to the Ottawa Exhibition or a picnic while fishing, yet the majority of what he taught us was to work. Fun was usually attached to a practical need with Dad, like catching the fish since we needed to eat, or attending the Exhibition because he had received free tickets from working there part-time. This taught me the lesson that to have fun always meant to organize it and to have another purpose in mind. It has taken me awhile to switch this behavior. When I worked at the Cumberland YMCA, Clare was my supervisor and we had fun doing our job each day. Since she gave me permission to enjoy work by her own actions and example, I was able to let go and have fun. Fun led to prosperity for the YMCA during the years we were there. To give, let go and just BE with fun in all aspects of life is still partly on my learning curve.

Conscious fruits of the Spirit are fellowship, kindness, gentleness, love, wonder, gratitude, and appreciation. Meditate on the fruits of the Spirit in the inner secrets of the consciousness, while the cells in the Body become aware of the awakening of the life in their activity through the Body. In the mind, the cells of the mind become aware of the life in the Spirit.

"Doubt, fear, avarice, greed, selfishness, and self-will; are considered the fruits of evil." Edgar Cayce

"A Return to Love"
Lecture notes of Marianne Williamson

*Our deepest fear is not that we are inadequate. Our deepest fear
is that we are powerful beyond measure.
It is our light, not our darkness that most frightens us.
We ask ourselves,
"Who am I to be brilliant, gorgeous, talented, fabulous?"
Actually, who are you not to be?
You are a child of God.
Your playing small does not serve the world.
There is nothing enlightening about shrinking.
So that other people won't feel insecure around you.
We are all meant to shine, as children do.
We were born to make manifest the glory of God
that is within us.
It's not just in some of us; it's in everyone.
And as we let our light shine . . .
We unconsciously give other people
permission to do the same.
As we are liberated from our own fear
Our presence automatically liberates others.*

Dreams

"I will sleep deeply and soundly, awaken refreshed and relaxed and remember my dream", is a wonderful statement with which to fall asleep. Dreams are a Soul/Spirit connection and can be an amazing way to guide one through life. When one is ill, dreams become less prominent as if Spirit

is not strong enough to carry out this task. Once wellness has been attained, they come back.

One can take a dream to a higher level by actually entering the dream. Visualizing an object such as a hand is a start. James can enter his dreams, yet in an awakened state is not able to visualize it. He cannot see an apple and close his eyes and see it in his mind's eye. Whereas I have the ability to see the past clearly in all aspects, as well as visualize a scene when going into a meditative state with a wonderful waterfall, butterflies and lush surroundings.

Dreams can be sacred moments in time that illuminate the future. They all hold tidbits of information that can make the path to enlightenment and life much smoother. God has given one great abilities, now is the time to accept the connection each one has. Intuition can help piece together the meaning of dreams. There are also great dream books that can point one in the right direction.

"Gracious Spirit, you have given everything to me. In your goodness, I have been made whole. Thank you for your love and your grace." (Creative Communications for the Parish)

Faith without generating vibration and harmony can lead to absence of life. The heart always sacrifices lower self while if not doing that, higher self is digested and wasted. When lower self is driving, the Soul is in the trunk. Higher self (Soul) is that which supports the Spirit and Will, as well as chooses from love. Passion will digest the indifference of lower self. Through love, grief becomes passion. If one has an illness that involves the lungs, love self and what one does, or shift to what one loves then grief will become passion and dissolve the illness. Illness gives time to learn about self.

Death is a step into the next layer of life. When one embraces death, one can embrace life. Stephen Covey wrote a wonderful book called, *Seven Habits of Highly Effective People*. In the book, Stephen suggests that a person picture himself at his/her funeral, listen to what is said by a friend, loved one, community member. Look to death to give life. This is also the beginning of being friends with death. The way one begins anything in life is how one feels. If one states a negative instead of a positive, then reverse that right away. The brain only sees negative if shown. Yet, the safest place to be is vulnerable. One has to BE vulnerable to the truth.

"We are not human beings on a spiritual journey.
We are spiritual beings on a human journey."
Stephen R. Covey

Authentic self stands up for self, does not apologize for light or power. Work calls one out! What calls one in? How is self ignited? By what one values. What I value is the beauty of nature and the tradition of family.

Enlightenment is when personal energy is handled with love while one walks through fear to reach clarity as one connects to the power of God and the Universe.

"Live with intention, walk to the edge. Dare. Listen hard.
Practice wellness. Laugh. Continue to learn. Play with abandon.
Appreciate your friends. Do what you love. Live as if this
is all there is."
Mary Anne Radmacher

The Spirit responds to the mind in conjunction with the Soul. To heal can be done by one's self when it is realized the power to do so is within us all.

Take for example the desire to eat junk food. The mind (Spirit) is making this choice. After eating junk food, the Body feels uncomfortable, sluggish and fatigued until twenty minutes later, once the sugar rush has worn off. The Body wants to feel good. It wants energy. It wants to feel alive plus energized and able to serve as one lives life authentically. Trust one's heart connection to Body; it knows what to eat, while one's mind may not. The mind may scream for chocolate cake, however the Body might be asking for an apple instead. Using a piece of cake as an example in Energy Response Testing, a person can ask, *"Is this good for the Body?"* and the mind will respond, *"Yes."* When higher self is asked and the question reworded to say, *"Is this good for the health of the Body?"* the answer is, *"No."*

A disconnect between the Spirit (mind) and Soul (heart) will create space for one to hold an addiction. Addictions are related to emotional feelings and specific organs in the Body not having enough energy flow. Take the kidney for example; it is where "Will" is stored. If the kidney is weak from fear or shame in one's life, then Willpower is hard to call forward. The balance of Willpower is needed when trying to stop smoking, overeating and other addictive behaviors. The liver, which holds anger, is where it is possible in a weakened energy state to become an alcoholic. Releasing anger can release the addiction.

The Spirit is what gets one up in the morning and gives one the vibrations to move in life. It is one's Shen. In Acupuncture the Shen is referred to as the heart. It is necessary in life for the heart to be joyful to enhance Spirit to its maximum; however, in co-operation with the Soul (heart) connection, the vibration raises even higher. Guilt and regret will diminish both the Spirit plus Soul. Joy as well as beauty will enhance it.

The soul and the spirit are connected, but separable (<u>Hebrews 4:12</u>). The soul is the essence of humanity's being; it is who we are. The spirit is the aspect of humanity that connects with God.

I grew up in a strong Catholic household, where my paternal grandmother was the matriarch over certain rituals like attending mass once a week. Dad wasn't as proficient, as he would leave the house with us, drop us off at Church while he went to the Corporal's Mess Hall to drink and then pick us up later. Mom, who was Anglican, would stay home except for Church holidays which Dad would also attend.

Most of my scholarly upbringing was in Catholic Schools, by nuns. There were many rules plus a thick black leather strap used on the palm of the hand if the students did not follow them. Due to the rigid rules, I did not go through the system without having a few strapping's on my hands. One example was as a young child when I ended up with my brother, Michael's lunch instead of mine. The rule at breaks and lunch during school concerned girls not associating with boys. To switch lunches, it was necessary to see my brother. At a young age the thought of breaking a rule did not enter my mind, after all, he was my brother. I went around the back of the school to the area boys occupied and was caught. When I went to Catholic school there was only black and white; I broke a rule so was strapped on the hand a number of times as well as spent time in the hall. The story my mind facilitated from this moment in time stayed for many years which became part of the reason I stayed in an abusive marriage for eight years.

When I turned sixteen, I left home to marry my first husband, and married outside of the Church. I attended funerals plus the occasional Christmas or Easter Mass over the years; however it was not until I was diagnosed with terminal cancer in 2002 that I returned to the Church. The deciding factors were a sense of community as well as energy that is felt in a Church. To be close to God does not necessitate the need for Church, as one has the ability to connect self to God at any moment in time.

Centuries ago, energy was used in deciding where to build a new Church. A staff and rod facilitated this choice; similar to dowsing rods or a pendulum today. The most energized spot was located in this way while the altar was designated to the centre of this Energy Field. The door opened to the east and the altar faced the door. If one has never experienced the energy in Church, find one that still goes by this positive method and when one goes close to the altar for Eucharist or sits in front, one will feel the energy. The feeling reminds me of when I was at the Grand Canyon and the strength of the energy I felt vibrating from the cliffs.

Churches were built with granite rock, which is high in energy. The vibrations emitting from the rock plus the positioning of the altar and door towards the east, attracts a magnetic force from the earth. When one's vibration is reduced and illness present, this higher vibration can heal.

Music is a great example of Spirit in motion as well as another benefit of attending Church. Churches are enhanced by the choir which also emulates a vibration that affects many in a positive way. Not all music does this and if one can test energy through Energy Response Testing, it can be identified quickly. An active intuition will also provide this response.

Sometimes an artist's complete CD or album will have positive vibrations while other times only a song or two will create the positive energy the Spirit requires.

My favorite moment with Church music was in York, England at a historical Cathedral called "York Ministry". My sister Cathy and I had gone to England on a mission to follow in the footsteps of our mother and father's meeting, falling in love, as well as marrying in England during the war. This Cathedral was a part of that process. Approximately one hundred altar boys were practicing singing in a choir in Latin as in the former years of the Church. It was an amazing sound to be heard in this huge Cathedral with vaulted ceilings plus dark wood with stained glass windows. My Spirit soared and each moment of that day was garnered in the present with that sound vibrating within.

James and I spent a number of years attending music concerts, enjoying a variety of artists. Recently we have returned to this practice, attracted by the musical vibration as well as connection to Spirit. James now plays the guitar and sings. I have taken up piano for fun, and the connection it gives us both to Spirit. Dancing to Rock 'n Roll plus Hula hooping also raise my Spirit. What raises your Spirit?

"Where the spirit does not work within the hand there is no art."
Leonardo da Vinci

A vibration from a singing bowl will enhance healing of the Body and strengthen the Energy Field. One's Energy Field surrounds the Body while it protects in the same pretext that the white around an egg yolk helps hold its shape without damage. A singing bowl is crafted out of brass with wonderful carvings inside and out. A wooden stick comes with it which is used to tap the outside of the bowl. The bowl is placed flat on the palm of the hand and once tapped the stick is pressed against the outer portion of the bowl lip. The tune depends on the bowl as well as the user. The sound is amazing. Once it is in motion, move the bowl close to an area of the Body that needs to heal. This method can restore the vibration of the affected area and heal while strengthening the Energy Field that protects the Body. This process also raises the Spirit of the individual to a higher level. Depending on the weakness of the Energy Field, it may take thirty days to see or feel results.

Brain Cortices

Spirit involves the mind and works with the brain's logical plus creative side. Certain conflicts in life can stop the logical or creative flow. Brain Cortices exercises will resolve that in most cases. James learned this process when he was in training as a Body Talk Practitioner. The Cortices process can be performed on one's self or on others. This process relieves confusion and brings clarity. It re-adjusts reversed polarity (energy) as well as balances physical frequency (vibration). The Brain Cortices exercise is helpful to practice before exams or any learning process, or when writing a book, starting a new project, etc. This process is also recommended for someone with Alzheimer's disease or Parkinson's disease.

The process of balancing Brain Cortices is simple. Place one hand on the base of the skull while tapping the top of the head; ensure both sides of the center line are reached. Breathe in while tapping the head; then breathe out while tapping the breast bone. Repeat!

Place one's other hand above the first hand while touching the first hand and remove the first hand; repeat above. Repeat this whole process until one has reached and completed the area at the start of the forehead. Then take both hands and place them on each side of the head, covering the temple areas. Remove one hand and repeat the above process. Place the other hand on the other side of the head and repeat again.

One of the main principles in Naturopathy education is the multi-causal principle. This is the connection between mind plus Body and how the core concept of viewing the past history of the student plays a role in illness as well as disease. The connection is greater once the Soul is added to the equation. Another discrepancy is the notion that it is Spirit, mind plus Body when quoting one's attributes. Soul, Spirit, Body and Energy Field are the attributes of humans, or in essence this is called the Energy Body. Soul relates to emotional feelings, Spirit to the mind. Therefore, one could actually depict it as Emotions, Mind, Body and Energy.

Five Elements

How past history plays a part is unique. It takes in the five elements of earth and self. The elements are Fire, Earth, Metal (which in some books is related to Air), Water and Wood. They identify with different meridian and organ systems in the Body, as well as the seasons, climates, growth stages, fluids, emotions, shapes, plus colors. This knowledge is helpful in predicting what area of the physical Body can be weakened when an emotional feeling or physical toxin is trapped within. It is normal for one to identify with the element presented in a parent or parents. For example, my father characterized wood and fire while my mother characterized earth. I identify in physical shape and attributes with the elements of wood as well as earth.

Organs and Elements:

- Fire: Heart, Small Intestine
- Earth: Spleen and Stomach
- Metal: Lung and Large Intestine
- Water: Kidney and Bladder
- Wood: Liver and Gall Bladder

Fire sparks life

When one awakens in the morning, one can identify if Spirit is up for the day or whether it needs a boost. The Spirit provides the energy to produce the effective presence for life that day. Spend the first moments of each day recognizing how one feels. Be present, notice in life what raises Spirit and use this upon rising when one's Spirit needs a lift. Start each day in a positive light with the energy that is one's privilege to own.

Medications cover symptoms and reduce the spark of life, yet are necessary until one learns how to be responsible with natural support to clear the cause, thus no longer requiring the cover of symptoms. Physicians are on the threshold of learning this while individuals such as Oprah, Dr. Phil, and Dr. Oz are facilitating some change. It is up to us to allow the inner knowledge to transform each of us into our authentic self, to create a joyful, peaceful life with one's self in harmony with Earth.

In nature, the fire element is related to summer, a season of heat, daylight and flowing streams and rivers. This is similar to the inner workings of the Body with blood flowing via veins and arteries as the cardiovascular system works in balance giving one a clear mind. The heart holds within us joy, intuition, insights, imagination, optimism, enthusiasm as well as communication.

Earth is about nurturing and creativity

Earth is at the Soul level, yet as with all elements it takes Spirit to move one. If one puts Spirit in what is created and lets that energy transform, it takes on wings. This is even so with one's own children. To let them have wings and soar is to allow Spirit in one's life and release control. The job of a parent is to provide knowledge plus guidance.

The lymph system responds positively to the creative Spirit flowing while detoxifying the Body. Non-Hodgkin lymphoma is connected emotionally to the flow of life thus has increased by one hundred and ten percent in the past thirty years. It is a call to transform back to nature and nurture one's creative side. Fungus is also a sign of imbalance in this element.

Worry, abandonment as well as loneliness are the emotional feelings in the stomach and spleen that revolve around the Earth Element. Digestion of ideas plus ideals is necessary to transform nutrients into energy in each cell of the Body. Enzymes are natural sources that facilitate digestion and move food through the system proficiently. Emotional plus environmental toxins stop production and utilization of enzymes throwing the Body out of harmony. The Earth is similar. In the same way that one looks inside to resolve one's own disharmony, one can look outside and move one step at a time to help resolve Earth's disharmony. Let Spirit move one's self.

Metal is dry yet easy to transform

It takes strength to accomplish that. Metal has to do with one's physical strength. If a person cannot open a jar that is tightly covered, it could mean low Po. When Spirit wavers, so does physical Po. Try opening that jar when Spirit has been lifted with one's favorite music or when the grandchildren have given one oodles of love.

The organs involved with metal are the lungs and the large intestine. In the same way that metal can tarnish as well as rust, so can grief bring sadness and a "tarnishing" of the lungs when they cannot breathe normally! Grief is a version of control, when one senses a lack of control in one's life. Grief prevents oxygen from transforming life and transporting fluids in the Body. Loss of Spirit has set this in motion though one can reverse this effect by letting go of control while moving to one's harmony. BE authentic; find what creates Spirit in one.

The large intestine is all about forgiveness of self and others. When one moves the past using forgiveness, the harmony in the Body shifts while the flow of debris that is meant to leave the Body does so at the appropriate level. If the process occurs too fast, diarrhea may result. The nutrients lack the ability to adhere to the cells and one's energy is depleted. If the process is too slow, fecal matter stays in the intestine too long creating a build-up of gas, bloating, as well as toxic waste. Water, as a conductor of electricity, helps this reaction assimilate properly. Mucus, phlegm plus yeast are all symptoms that the Metal element is in disharmony with the spleen (Earth element). Autumn is the season related to this element—a season for harvest.

Water is a master element

Willpower is a predominant feature of this element and Spirit is about Will. Without the Spiritual energy to move, one can get stuck. Smoking, overeating, while even pedophilia, are signs of a weakened form of Will, which occurs when a past negative emotional feeling is present and a quality is lost. The season is winter—cold and dark with a deep power.

Loss of head hair, as well as bone or cartilage issues, are all symptoms of disharmony in this element. Too much or too little saliva is also an indicator as are hearing issues. The Kidneys are the main proponent of this element and when in disharmony can lower or raise blood pressure and react with the spleen as well as the pancreas to create diabetes. They hold one's qi (energy). Arthritis can also be kidney related as magnesium absorption is another process attributed to the kidney. When a magnesium low occurs, the symptoms of arthritis are present: joint pain, muscle spasms, heart palpitations, plus restless legs.

Fear and shame are the feelings related to this. A cycle with Spirit can form, where fear depletes Spirit, yet it takes Spirit to transform fear to clarity and then to personal power. Living life authentically can overcome this cycle. Wearing what one loves, listening to what empowers, seeking company of others with higher Spirit, serving others, loving what one does, choosing where it is done and for whom are all builders of clarity plus help to transform fear. BE present to receive the gifts in life.

The Bladder is also a part of this element. Fluids are carried at the appropriate level when this element is in harmony. Swollen ankles, ascites, and incontinence are all related to being "pissed off" with life, either with one's own life or with another whose life affects one's own.

Wood is new growth

Wood is aligned with the liver and gall bladder; as well it is related to spring. The Soul and the affection part of emotional feelings lend credence to this element. As with other organs, it takes Spirit to energize plus generate positive functions. Tears are the fluid that is connected; too little or too much indicates disharmony.

Muscles and tendons respond to disharmony in this element. Wood in life is a builder. As trees are a filter for sunlight, the liver is a filter for the Body. It builds momentum in the Body while it filters toxins out. Feces need Spirit to generate energy in the Body to extract toxins. This is why it is essential to find those things in life that generate Spirit in one self. For me it can be as simple as hearing or seeing a Blue Jay, or watching a butterfly flutter by.

Anger, irritation, rage as well as unhappiness all affect the liver and when unable to filter debris, will transform it to the skin as a rash. Where are muscles not supporting ones Body? Again, check in with Spirit. The eyes are directly linked with this element, therefore affecting most eye disease and sight issues. Anger distorts one's vision of what is right or wrong so that one does not want to see the direction one has to take to shift to a higher level at times. Looking into one's eyes is the connection to the Soul. The link of Spirit plus Soul is not an accident. Nothing in life is an accident, it is a thought transformed to an emotional feeling.

Vibrations

I am sitting here at my kitchen table typing this portion of the book and notice the items on the table I have recently purchased, again not an accident. There is a Belly dancing DVD with a free hip scarf complete with coins attached. There is also a Louise Hay CD on self-esteem affirmations. James and I were at an Edgar Cayce convention this past weekend and I was drawn to both of these items-one for the fun I can have plus share with James, while the other to help with raising my self-esteem: worth and confidence to prevent illness. One needs to love self, believe they are good enough as well as worth it (self-esteem), so emotional feelings do not take up residence in the Body. The CD is a great addition to our center's lending library and a great tape personally to raise Spirit while keeping to a higher vibration in this path I am on.

Kevin Todeschi spoke at the convention (2010) and defined bringing Spirit to the earth in three ways: Spiritual ideals, attunement plus application. The ideal I chose was joyfulness, while the question I then asked was what it would look like. How could I attune to it as well as take action to make joyfulness occur in my life? Laughter, acceptance, approval and a positive attitude were my attunement. Ways to apply it were playfulness, openness, a celebration of life moments, positive affirmations, watching as well as listening to comedy. The main part of all this is to feel while in attunement and action so as to raise one's vibration.

Vibrations are energy force acting for or against the physical Body directed by thought (mind-Spirit) and activities. Emotional and physical toxins lower vibrations in the Energy Body, resulting in illness and disease. That is why it is important to prevent illness or while ill to raise the vibrations of the Energy Body in all dimensions. The Soul needs one to BE its authentic self to generate one hundred percent vibrations. Spirit needs to be lifted, and that is why it is important to focus on positive things while enjoying TV, radio, CD's as well as individuals' one chooses to be around. What raises one's Spirit is different for each person. Check in with one's own Soul. The Body needs the vibrations raised with food, and that is why the eighty—twenty rule works: eighty percent raw food plus twenty percent cooked. Live food or slightly cooked is still living and has its own vibrations. Slightly steamed retains vibration while activating enzymes in the vegetables to ease digestion.

Water also has its own vibration as Dr. Masaru Emoto's work has shown. His name is a registered trademark in forty countries. *The Message from Water and The Hidden Messages in Water* were translated and published on a global scale while Dr. Emoto has been walking around the world as a water messenger ever since. Energy of words as Dr. Emoto's work shows can transform water as other positive energies can also. The company called "Enagic" delivers this message, using Kangen machines that transform water to alkaline, therefore changing the vibration to a higher level.

Words can raise or lower vibrations in the Body. That is why to BE authentic plus stand-up for one's self is important. Otherwise a person could get involved with someone who would mentally or physically abuse him/her or take advantage of children or the elderly. Words can change the meaning of a sentence, such as the word *"but"* relinquishes what was said in the words before it. *"Should"* is a prerequisite to not doing something, whereas "could" is a positive action word. *"Just"* devalues the person plus process. For example if one walks into their home while announces "It's just me", one has devalued self.

Vibrations are the building blocks of all creation, a fingerprint that can be left behind. Let's say one has had cancer and has been housebound for any length of time. Once the illness has been transformed to wellness, the home also needs a transformation since it is still in the vibration of illness. Pets as well as children sense this negative vibration more than adults, especially if the adult is not intuitively connected.

Music, laughter, or the use of a singing bowl is a way to transform the home over a thirty day period. Notice the difference, and see plants grow while pets respond to this positive vibration. Jewelry can even hold disease or negative vibrations from a past relationship. Transform it with love, joy, laughter, etc. It is important to factor in harmony with the Energy Body. Even cell phones need to be in harmony with one: an energy eliminator is necessary to protect the Energy Field from the negative response of the cell phone battery. A simple prayer will also work while holding an object. Speaking "The Lord's Prayer" can result in a higher attunement.

Did one ever realize that individual cities and towns have different vibrations? In the past when I traveled, if my vibration was low I could pick up an agitation when coming into a different town or city. Connecting with God while reciting a prayer will harmonize one and the feeling will dissolve in moments. Being present plus authentic will ensure that one stays in harmony while travelling. Check in with self before a trip. Ensure water is consumed during travel as water is a conductor of one's electricity.

Shadows from the past need to be resolved so that Spirit can be fully present in one's life. They reduce one's vibration. The information in the last chapter and a following chapter will help locate as well as resolve these issues. Resource information in the back of the book lists other modalities that can provide aid and guidance.

Values, Standards and Boundaries

A person is meant to have personal values, standards and boundaries as one goes through life. These support Spirit while it gives one a measuring tool to identify imbalance. To BE valued, value another.

Values: Identify one to three key values that one stands for or that ignite one to act. An example for me is love, hope and beauty.

1. **Love:** self, God, family, friends, serving others, community, country, and more. Being loved, a lover, plus loving is what comes from that value.
   - Love of creating gives me self-ignition;
   - Connection to The Way of the Heart™ and courses offered in that and other modalities give me knowledge to transform life's vibrations, thus creating a deeper love of self;
   - Love of family as well as traditions both ignite and ground me.

2. **Hope**: Before there can be hope, self love is needed. Self love is the spark that can ignite hope. As a practitioner, self love is a value that is mirrored to the student as hope is nurtured. If the practitioner is lacking self love, then interest, not hope is experienced. One's Energy Field is a value and mirrors that which one is.
   - Hope with love and knowledge transforms one from living in the past to being in the "NOW"!
   - The Fourth Principle as well as other modalities can give one tools to move the Soul back into the driver's seat of life, while keeping Spirit ignited.

3. **Beauty:** is where I get the most self-ignition from; the sky, clouds, butterflies, birds, water, music, storms, words, children playing.
   - The beauty of transforming others via knowledge and guidance; of transforming self on a daily basis self-ignites me;
   - Self-help courses plus books create the tools, community and field for one to go deep, release and rise in a safe container. This is similar to an effect of transformation from caterpillar to butterfly;
   - Sitting on a rock beside the ocean, smelling, hearing and seeing the wonders around me transform who I am at this moment in time.

Standards are what one stands for in life, yet are not only self orientated. Does one permit another person to smoke in one's home or car, to tell racial jokes, to mentally or physically abuse another and so much more . . .

- The above are standards I let occur in my life for a number of years until taking stock of who I really am, thus was able to release the past and learn to love as well as respect myself.
- A way of knowing one's authentic self is to be committed to one's standards. A relative emailed me a racial joke that depicted blacks in a negative tone and I emailed back that it was wrong. If one does not respond when it happens, then one is not being authentic to one's standard and it will affect Spirit plus Soul, eventually causing illness. If a standard is compromised, then don't let it slide thinking it does not hurt anyone. It is hurting <u>you</u> internally.
- Oprah has a standard that most of us have heard of: not texting or talking on the cell phone while driving. That is a standard or boundary I have taken for my own. In other words I will not travel in a vehicle with someone who does this, for my protection.

Boundaries are a self protective shield one subconsciously develops over time, utilizing values and standards. The difference between values and standards is that crossing one's boundaries can create physical safety issues, as in the above example.

- Not getting into a vehicle where one has been drinking more than one drink in a couple of hours without eating is a boundary I follow. Two shots of alcohol in one glass are considered two drinks.
- Standards and boundaries can be close in nature, such as not leaving small children alone in the bath. One is protecting self from loss of precious parts of life while protecting the children.
- When one lets another person cross a boundary that has been set, the effect can sometimes be seen on the physical Body. In some cases psoriasis or eczema will occur. The skin is the

Body's boundary as well as protective shield, and can react when subconscious boundaries have been crossed.

While editing this book, a friend emailed and reminded me of how important being authentic is while knowing one's boundaries. Someone she new just lost a grandchild in a drowning in the bathtub. The mother left the child for a moment as she answered the door. In Society one is falsely taught that to answer a phone, text or door are of value and to ignore it one might be discriminated against. When one stands for self, the understanding is to BE present to life and worth (value) come from that. One loses qualities growing up or forgets they are in control of life, not the person on the other side of the door. This child had a purpose; the story has the ability to save other lives from this tragic reminder of how important boundaries are.

"When you know who you are and what you stand for, you stand in wisdom." Oprah Winfrey

Spirit is what one presents to the world in flow with the Soul. View everyone as an extension of self. Look at people around one and without judgment; identify the differences in Spirit of each one. Can one see or hear the difference? Then look and listen to one's own self to learn who one is. A great message I received recently from Oprah at Radio City Music Hall in New York, was that she had discovered she is not just her hair. An incident had occurred in her early TV history that taught her this lesson. One is Soul plus Spirit; the physical Body is not who one is in essence. The Body is the container for one's Soul. I rather like that aspect as it takes the pressure off of the physical.

Spirit of the Game

Spirit is the energy of movement, the wind beneath one's wings. When aligned with God plus attuned to Soul as well as authentic self, the Spirit will soar.

Life is a game one plays that starts in the Universe before conception and the first molecule that becomes us takes place! The Spirit arrives first as the energy to transform this molecule into a child.

Games are played daily from all walks of life, while the Spirit of a game is affected by the connection one makes to the outcome. This connection is not about winning, it is about the journey, the fun, the obstacles overcome, and the feeling one puts into it. We all have a dream of winning, yet it does not have to be the first, second or third spot. Winning is the feeling one gets when one has achieved. It is the Spirit of the game.

Spirit is a mindful thought which in turn are vibrations. Once connected to the Universe with positive vibrations, anything is possible. Great athletes connect in this way such as feeling the ball hit the bat before it happens, then experiencing how they would feel when this occurs. This is attracting the action to happen.

A thought or vision will only produce positive attractions when connected to an emotional feeling (Soul). Spirit speeds one's wellness if one is there to receive the healing as it arrives.

Cancer or any other illness and disease can also be considered a game, one where winning is valued. Again, vibrations play a major role in wellness. Once a person identifies if he or she has cancer, their Spirit can break down if it reverts to situations in the past where they have felt like a victim. When one reacts to disease one's mind gives it the power to grow.

Find something of value about self each day and build on that positive emotional feeling to transform Spirit and raise one's vibration to heal. Feel it deeply and hold onto that emotional feeling as long as possible. See self as healed, not only wishing to be, actually healed. How does that feel? What would one do or not in life? Make a wish list as well as question why each item is on the list until one feels for each item. Use a vision board to enhance this list, feel each picture or word as it is attached. Attract instead of trying to control the present and future. BE in wellness, not illness.

"Illnesses such as cancer are methods that the Soul (higher self) uses for an individual to release control, based on a lesson needed in life to transform and shift one to authentic self."
Susan Manion MacDonald

Chakras

Light and life need to also be in harmony in the human being. Chakra means the wheels of light in Sanskrit and connects Body with Spirit. There are seven main chakra's identified that are positioned at certain vital points over as well as surrounding the Body. The chakras are likened to color therapy for the Soul, Spirit, Body and Energy Field. Musical vibration can raise or lower their energetic ability. Chakra colors plus notes coinciding with them are listed below.

Root Chakra: The color is red, the musical note C and it is located around the base of the spine. The purpose is to ground one to earth plus this chakra is connected to all the other chakras. A deficiency would create a feeling of ungrounded, feeling spacey, blocked passion and a feeling of insecurity;

Sacral Chakra: The color is orange, the musical note D and it is located at the belly button (the seat of the Soul) to harmonize the life of the Body as well as works in conjunction with the heart chakra. Imbalance may show up as loss of integrity or diminished ability to overcome;

Solar Plexus Chakra: The color is yellow, the musical note E and it is located above the belly button in the gut to enhance the intuitive self while it strengthens the communications chakra plus vibrates calmness. The need for approval is a sign of imbalance here;

Heart Chakra: The color is green, the musical note F and it is located at the heart to enrich communication with the Soul plus connects to purpose via the third eye chakra and life in harmonization with sacral chakra. An individual would have trouble with acceptance if this was not balanced;

Communications Chakra: The color is sky blue, the musical note G and it is located at the thyroid and it connects the Spirit plus Soul (mind and heart); a guidance system utilizing the solar plexus chakra. Lack of expression as well as the power of choice is limited when this chakra is imbalanced;

Third Eye Chakra: The color is indigo blue, the musical note A and it is located between the brows to enhance one's vision of greater possibilities (to see the way) and connects with the communications chakra. Symptoms of imbalance include visual problems, migraines, dizziness, or vertigo, issues with memory, imagination and visualizing are also signs;

Crown Chakra: The color is purple, the musical note B and its purpose is to allow light plus energy into the Soul, Spirit, Body and Energy Field so, that all the chakras are enhanced. Being present to one's life is the symptom to look for;

An example of working together: if the thyroid is not functioning properly it would benefit the thyroid to enhance the solar plexus by tightening muscles.

A protocol for thyroid would be to remove toxins; communicate to others verbally or via letters, thoughts or emotional feelings buried from the past or present; release energy blockage by acupuncture or Energy Balance Harmony and strengthen the solar plexus using a hula hoop or Belly Dancing. However silly this might sound, it has the possibilities to regain full use of the thyroid for individuals who have been on thyroid medication for years. A drop of iodine placed on the inside wrist is an easy method to detect iodine deficiency, which can lead to thyroid problems. The iodine should stay on the wrist over a five hour period. If it disappears into the Body, a deficiency is suggested.

To clear chakras is about drawing upon white light from God, the Universe and angels; seeing as well as feeling it emanating through each chakra color surrounding the physical Body; seeing the colors getting brighter while this occurs as the color expanding around one.

Balancing the chakras is a process of enlarging one's chakras to be equal in size. Simply holding the intent to clear and balance will also work. Check resources at the back of the book for contact information if help is required.

Spirituality

Spirituality is not one faith. It is a multi-faith connection to one's self, to the Universe and to all creation. Spirituality can reside in community, a culture or in one's self via meditation.

Spirituality is the feeling one gets when connected to Source; where one is derived from, the divine Spirit of life; God. When the feelings are positive and raise vibrations that heal self as well as the planet, then one has found Spirituality. It is not what wars are made of, nor is it atonement of the past. Spirituality is attunement of the present, forgiveness of self and others, the connection to higher self plus appreciation of all that is.

"In the name of the Father, Son and Holy Spirit"

The Spirit is the wind beneath one's wings, the feelings that accomplish purpose of the Soul. To do this, one has to reach a higher vibration with appreciation of life and death, accompanied by an understanding that the power is theirs to have and to hold whatever one values. Align self, BE authentic, this is one's journey.

Summary of Chapter 3

1. A relationship with self is a priority in life;

2. One is a Spirit within a physical Body;

3. An emotional feeling is a response to a thought-"The Law of Attraction";

4. Look for the goodness in self;

5. Dreams are the Soul plus Spirit connection and guidance system;

6. When one embraces death one embraces life;

7. A disconnect between Spirit (mind) plus Soul (heart) will create a space for one to hold an addiction;

8. Spirit is connected to Energy attuning Life force;

9. Brain Cortices-the balancing of logical and creative sides of Spirit;

10. Five Elements; Fire, Earth, Metal, Water plus Wood guide one to discover individual strengths and weaknesses;

11. Values, Standards plus Boundaries support who one is and measure balance;

12. The Spirit of the game-life is a game about the journey;

13. Chakras the light of life-a color therapy that connects Body and Spirit;

14. Spirituality is a multi faith connection to self, to the Universe and to creation.

CHAPTER 4

The Energy Field that Surrounds One

Rub one's feet on a carpet and touch something metal. Did one receive a small shock? Balanced electrolytes (calcium, magnesium, potassium as well as sodium) and the proper amount of water to conduct electricity are necessary for this to occur.

Humans are energy! Energy emanates around as well as through the Body while acting as a protective coating, similar to the white part of an egg protecting the egg yolk. Emotional feelings that are trapped create static in the Energy Field surrounding the Body, and physical toxins are then able to decrease the energy of the physical Body, creating illness and disease.

Similarly, the earth is protected by the ozone layer and any weakness will cause a disruption in the flow of balance on the earth.

A human's Energy Field can be seen and measured in many ways. A number of modalities in the natural health field utilize this information in guiding students to achieve balance. I am one of those practitioners. I use Energy Response Testing a form of Applied Kinesiology and Muscle Response Testing, as the main source of connecting to a student's higher self, their subconscious. George Goodheart and then John Diamond brought this way of connecting to the forefront. James utilizes this same method in connection with an international program called Body Talk. A practitioner who is grounded while connected to God (Source) knows the answer without checking; the test is for the student.

Dr. George Goodheart Jr. DC has been called the "Father" of Applied Kinesiology. In the 1960's he discovered that muscle testing could be used to gather information from the Body.

One of the foremost senior holistic healers is Dr. John Diamond. His remarkable Body of work includes his discovery of the link between the acupuncture meridians and the emotions. This embraces a wide range of disciplines, which are the results of over fifty years of research and clinical practice. Dr. Diamond began his career in psychiatry then expanded into holistic medicine, concentrating on the totality of the sufferer. In his fifty years of practice, he has increasingly recognized that there is within us a great healing force, Life Energy, the healing power within. With his increasing involvement in this concept, his research has led him to concentrate on the enhancement of the sufferer's Life Energy so as to actuate his own innate Healing Power.

For the past nine years, starting first with resolving imbalance in my physical Body, then Soul plus Spirit while working with my Energy Field I learned to be in harmony with myself, God, and all that surrounds me. Through working with others, studying under different teachers and modalities, I discovered The Fourth Principle while doing research and development.

The Fourth Principle is a new modality using the Energy Field and Body to relax while it obtains information from the Soul plus Spirit.

The Fourth Principle represents the knowledge that four years prior to being diagnosed with a disease, a person has experienced a traumatic incident. This brings forth deeper emotional feelings that one had experienced as a child or an adult, which were put away without being dealt with entirely. The process of putting away emotional feelings stops one from feeling at the Soul level and also hinders one from being who he or she is fully meant to BE. In conjunction with physical toxins in the Body since conception, these three factors combine to create the path of knowledge necessary to transform one's life to a higher level of purpose on earth. The Soul (emotions) plus the Spirit (mind) work with the Energy Field and Body to bring this forward. In other words; one's self creates illness and disease.

"Illness and disease is a gift of knowledge to learn about one's self, to go inside and awaken the Soul plus Spirit while retrieving qualities lost from incidents from the past."
Susan Manion MacDonald

An individual's natural Energy Field range is approximately the length of the individual's arm, surrounding the Body, including over the head. A number of practitioners and individuals have a far wider range of field due to mediation, energy work as well as healthy living. A sudden negative emotional incident can reduce this immediately, while a positive one can raise this energy.

The Energy Field can be measured using Energy Response Testing, a special infrared camera called Kirlian, Dowsing Rods, a pendulum, bio-energy machines or the human hand.

James can feel someone's Energy Field and with their permission can move their Body using the Energy Field only. Students at our center love this while James enjoys the response. Sometimes an individual's Energy Field is less in front than the back or vice versa. A recent incident brought back how powerful this process is to awaken another to the possibilities.

A new student came with their spouse as well as their adult daughter to gain knowledge and understanding on how it might be possible to heal naturally from terminal cancer diagnosed in the liver. The diagnosis had only been two days before and emotional feelings were intense. James had the daughter close her eyes while he placed his hand outside her Energy Field and slowly moved it toward her. He had her notify him when she could feel his hand approaching her Body. At arms length their daughter could; she did not have her arms out while this was taking place. James then proceeded to do the same behind her back and received the same response. Their daughter could feel his hand approximately arms length from her Body.

He then wanted to identify to the parents the effect the mind has on the Energy Field that protects us. He had her parents think bad thoughts of their daughter while he repeated the above measuring and her Energy Field was reduced to less than half, by a thought; not a spoken word. James then had the parents thoughtfully praise her and the measurement she felt was expanded far beyond her arms. James then, with her permission while her parents watched, took his hand and grabbed her Energy Field, as if he was grabbing clothing and pulled her backwards; their daughter started to fall.

When the family left with the knowledge of emotional feelings, the effect of the mind (Spirit), Energy Field, Soul and information on the Body healing naturally, they felt empowered. It shifted the energy of the room, creating laughter as well as joy. Whether, the student encompasses life while being self or not, a better quality of life or death will occur due to this experience alone. Fear left the room and life was present.

Emotional feelings create a weakness in the Energy Field and thus a weakness in the physical Body. Disease reduces the Energy Field, as do negative words, thoughts or actions including those found in TV programs, radio, CDs, DVDs as well as computer games.

Lack of exercise can also create static in one's Energy Field. There is a specific amount of energy necessary in the Body and Energy Field for the Body to be in harmony. Exercise is the filtering system for negative as well as positive energy in the Energy Field. To keep the Body in harmony physically plus energetically, thirty minutes of exercise at least three days a week is required. Five days of exercise provides an optimum amount. Lymph needs to move, and simple rebounding or a gentle walk will be effective.

Rain comes when there is harmony within the Rainmaker. He prays until that happens, similar to the story of Ho'onopono who first cleared himself and then healed all of the mentally ill patients in the clinic where he was in charge. One's Energy Field is a powerful source if one becomes harmonious with the Universe while releasing control.

The reason natural health practitioners recommend juicing, organics and eating raw or slightly cooked food when working with illness or disease is the energy or life they hold. Once eaten, they are retained by the physical Body starting at the cellular level. This of course is only possible if the individual is also taking essential fatty acids (flax, omegas, hemp, or fish oils) to support the cell so it can hold the nutrients. If one is eating fish four times weekly, along with lots of nuts and seeds plus olive oil, then they are getting enough essential fatty acids without the need of supplements. A digestive system that is operating optimally is also essential for nutrients to be received.

To increase energy in vegetables as well as herbs in the form of vitamins and minerals, it is recommended to plant those that grow above ground before a full moon. Plant those that grow below ground after a full moon. Pick vegetables that are above ground around eleven in the morning, and those that are below the ground in the evening. This will keep the sugar up in the plant and prevent fast spoilage. Picking at the time of the full moon ensures that additional nutrients are present in the fruits or vegetables due to the magnetism of the earth at that time. Circular beds grow better than rectangular. Positive symptoms which will show that the garden has taken on extra energy are the presence of birds, bees and butterflies.

Emotional feelings plus physical toxins reduce the energy of the Body, as well as the Energy Field. Remember, eighty percent of illness and disease is due to emotional feelings. In the majority of cases, illness is a means of lost control. When one has low self-worth specifically, that person has learned to control his or her life in another form. Letting go of the control of others is vital in the path to wellness. It is necessary to find one's authentic self by strengthening all parts of which one is: Soul, Spirit, Body and Energy Field. To BE authentic is to love self more than to love control. A positive relationship with one's self is essential.

A wellness protocol has the ability to shift control of others to one's self, thus creating a pathway for balance. When an unwell individual who is capable of giving him or her self a coffee enema if required, however chooses instead to have the partner, child, sibling, etc. do it for them then balance will not be achieved. Energy is not flowing nor connecting in a healthy way, when this is occurring. Control of others is still an issue. Individuals attached to control have difficulty facing the pain of the past as well as being vulnerable. They need knowledge to connect to feelings of life.

Feelings get submerged when one does not want to deal with them and are forgotten consciously, however not subconsciously. One's life shifts and detours off path without even knowing it, until the negative emotional feelings have been released. Releasing also means having to BE vulnerable while feeling again.

Overeating is the negative energy which surfaces from not feeling. When an emotional moment presents itself, a person can tend to go to the cupboard or fridge rather than to feel the emotion. The emotional feeling then gets trapped further in the Body as it fragments the Energy Field, until the Soul (one's true self), with the help of Spirit, presents symptoms of illness or disease. The positions in the Body of the symptoms are related to the emotional feeling and attached organ or gland. In the next chapter this may become clearer as symptoms are explained further. The bottom line is a person needs to become a feeling being again!

One can experience another's feelings if in tune via their Energy Field. Has one ever gone to a party and felt strange when someone was closer than arm's length, possibly feeling an emotion that was not related to an event one experienced? That is possible, as sometimes one can feel another's emotion via their Energy Field.

I had a wonderful experience in 2009 when I visited Edmonton, Alberta and attended a seminar by "DreamHealer" Adam McLeod. At one point he had the audience connect with each other via their Energy Fields and he used the connection of the approximately seven hundred individuals to raise their physical vibration. To work with the group in this way saved time while it enhanced the group as each concentrated on healing and balancing one's self.

For those who do not know about Adam, he is a young man now in University who is working energetically with famous research scientists on the molecular structure of cells. Adam started with natural healing as a teen when he used his Energy Field to guide energy from the earth and God through him to heal his mother of MS. Since then Adam has become famous by working from a distance with Ronnie Hawkins to cure his pancreatic cancer. Adam has also written several books.

One may have heard about Chris Angel, a "unique magician", and some would call him an "energy worker". He has an amazing performance whether on TV or in person. Chris uses energy to transform items as well as his self. By watching Chris or Adam, one can start to better understand the concept of energy surrounding each person plus the connection each has with self and others. Again, it is one's choice to connect or not. For positive results, it is important to ask another for permission to access their Energy Field. Not only would it be disrespectful; the results may be distorted without first obtaining their permission.

The Body has meridian channels that transport magnetic energy and heat slightly below the surface of the skin via pathways that connect the Body to the Earth plus Universe as well as to and from each organ. Infrared photography confirms energy at each point. Acupuncture uses these meridian points to unclog blocked energy in the Body. Energy healing is the oldest, safest and most accessible healing in the world. The Body is designed to heal itself.

Acupuncture is a treatment based on Traditional Chinese Medicine (TCM), a system of healing that dates back thousands of years. At the core of TCM is the notion that a type of life force, or energy, known as qi (pronounced "chee") flows through energy pathways in the Body called "meridians". Each meridian connects to one specific organ or group of organs that govern particular Bodily functions. Qi maintains the dynamic balance of yin and yang, the complementary opposites that are reflected in all beings as well as throughout nature. Yin is about structure, fluid and conservation, while yang is about energy transformation. Together, in harmony they create balance.

When too little or too much qi exists in a meridian or when the qi stagnates or is blocked, illness results. By applying needles to certain points along the meridian lines, acupuncture restores equilibrium and health by correcting the flow of qi. Acupuncture points, or the specific locations where needles are inserted, are places where the energy pathway is close to the surface of the skin.

While writing this chapter I was currently studying acupuncture through The College of Acupuncture and Therapeutics Inc. in Kitchener, Ontario, Canada. It took a few weeks in class to get the connection so as not to feel congested with the knowledge of many points plus the flow of channels. Once acclimatized and familiar with the procedure, I have found it has become a wonderful new pathway to enhance what I have already learned. The teachers, Louise and David, each have different styles yet complement each other while creating a classroom that is fun to be in.

Releasing blocked energy that supports pain in the Body has been the biggest "Aha!" moment as I worked with my case studies. In connection with The Fourth Principle and emotional feeling of guilt, the knowledge of how to release that blocked energy both emotionally as well as through acupuncture, has completed the dotted line for me. Acupuncture also works with the elements of the Body as mentioned in Chapter 3. The elements are fire, earth, metal, water and wood. Air is replaced by metal in some knowledge based acupuncture, therefore indicative of lung and large intestine. I see it more as a sixth element attached to the brain.

Recently I watched a number of short videos on YouTube by Donna Eden who has been working with energy for a number of years. I recommend listening and learning the techniques she has adapted. Nothing in the Universe is limited, all is meant to transpire.

Through the energy of my book, *BALANCE nature's way to heal your body*, I am contacted by different individuals who have energetically changed my life. Joanne Works is one of these special individuals. Joanne owns and operates Avalon Natural Health in St. John's, Newfoundland and has invited me there many times to lecture. We inspire each other to increase knowledge and attain to a higher self.

Recently, I met Ruth Hoyt from Saint John, New Brunswick. Ruth is a cancer survivor and vibrant lady who opened her home to friends plus family so my husband and I could teach there. She introduced me to energy healer Donna Eden's work and the knowledge which complements Acupuncture. I visualize Ruth and her friend Nancy Baker transforming the medical industry one person at a time, while attuning them to the harmony of natural healing.

Another source of energy building took place a number of years ago with Juli Oxford. Juli connected with me offering her meditation room as an office, so I could work with students in Halifax. The Way of the Heart™ also connects us to a network of vibrant individuals who are now leading life from the heart in a softer, joyous, more peaceful way to achieve dynamic success. Juli operates Pathways to Wellness, P.A.U.S.E. Wellness Centre and is completing a retreat in Musquodoboit, Nova Scotia.

Gugi (Maduchanda) LeRoc learned massage while blind. She surrendered to the Universe and received her sight back. We connected a number of years ago while we worked out of each other's centers to provide knowledge and energy of natural healing to others. When Gugi massages, she sees from a different place what needs to be worked on or with whom, and transforms that information in a way that others listen to her. It is rare to find someone in Moncton, New Brunswick, who does not know this vibrant woman. She nurtures me in many ways, including with Indian cooking.

It is the energy these women and others emit that connects us as well as provides greatness for expanding one's limitations. Look at each moment to who enters one's Energy Field and connects to transport information or receive. That is the journey plus the way energy flows from one to another. To attain a higher flow, one must transform as a caterpillar to a butterfly. Looking inside to one's authentic self while being surrounded with positive energy will expand Spirit and create a wind beneath one's wings.

James grounds and supports me in life, allowing me to learn who I am without fear of losing who he is. When one chooses a partner in life, there is a need to stand first for self or one may fall for anyone or anything. To lean on another person weakens both, however support is different. Partners need to support each other in attaining higher self. Is one leaning, supporting or carrying another?

In December of 2005, I purchased a Boston Pug for James for Christmas. He named her Lila. Talk about energy at its highest; that was this puppy! Lila demanded and one responded, whether it was for food, affection or a walk. She got us off the couch and moving, she energized us. It was not a drudgery to get up to her, the Spirit she contained was high. We noticed she had a deformity in her hind leg and hip so we took her to a natural veterinary center in Dartmouth, N.S. By using acupuncture and electrodes, they were able to stimulate the growth of the hip and Lila was then able to walk again. No hip replacement was needed. This can also be done with humans. It is transforming energy at its highest.

Lila became mentally ill close to her one year anniversary, and began falling over, foaming at the mouth, while running into walls. Back then, James and I had not learned about energy to the level that we have today, as well as her addition to our life was part of our journey to learn. The natural veterinarian could not help by herself so James took Lila to the veterinary hospital in Prince Edward Island. The hospital agreed to work with the natural veterinarian. Lila's Spirit enabled this amazing sharing of information. She came home better, however it only lasted a short period and she died. We all cried for the loss of this wonderful Spirit.

It is not the time one spends on earth; it is what one succeeds in accomplishing while here. Lila accomplished a lot in her short life and we thank her for the memories. Why did it happen? The breeder interbred dogs which created cellular damage. By using the transformation of energy James and I have learned in the past five years, I believe this could have been resolved. One person or animal at a time can shift energy plus transform change. Let energy flow and one can be that person!!

Tools to Measure Energy

There is a variety of energy measuring tools available to suit individual professions, taste and fun.

Dowsing

Before technology came about that would allow one to "see" into the ground, people depended on dowsing (also known as divining or water witching) to find water wells, metals, gemstones, and even missing people, as well as unmarked graves. Although dowsing has never been scientifically proven to work in a controlled setting, the practice remains popular in many parts of the world. It's been suggested that humans may sense electric and magnetic energy that is invisible to the eye (as many animals can) and subconsciously manipulate the dowsing rods or pendulum to reflect that information. Whether one is a stout defender of dowsing or thinks its hogwash, it is both educational from a historical perspective and fun to experiment.

Dowsing, on the other hand, is one of the easiest ways to access a repository of unlimited knowledge. Carl Jung referred to it as the "collective unconscious" or the "super conscious mind". There are many books available about the art of dowsing. One book in particular can be accessed online free by master dowser Walt Woods from www. lettertorobin.org. Dowsing, as in Energy Response Testing, is about gaining access to unlimited knowledge via one's Higher Self. Dowsing can be used to obtain ANSWERS and information about *anything*, providing the question is correctly framed.

When one dowses, a dialogue transpires with one's Higher Self and other Spirit guides who are trying to assist in obtaining the information a person seeks. A question is asked, most often framed with a 'yes' or 'no' answer. When learning more advanced dowsing skills, one can ask for answers that go beyond this framework, however most dowsing questions are answered using the 'yes' or 'no' format. Very simple indicator tools are used in dowsing to help accurately recognize the information one is trying to obtain.

The three most common dowsing tools are:

1. Pendulum;
2. "L" rod;
3. "Y" rod.

There are other types of dowsing tools beyond these three however, these three are the ones most often used.

During my journey to wellness, I made a discovery in my own neighborhood. Within a triangle around my home were three electric transformers and a number of homes which housed victims or survivors of cancer. After contacting the utility company to find out if there ever was a leak of any transformer in this area and not getting an appropriate answer, I contacted an elderly gentleman who dowsed. At that time I had only a vague idea of what dowsing was. Within fifteen minutes he was in my kitchen. Jack is a wonderful man who loves dowsing and people in general. He gave me knowledge on electrical magnetic fields as well as information on the Curry/Hartman Grid. This Grid is a natural and manmade electrical field that when crossed, results in a powerful altering of human or animal Energy Fields. Cows will not milk if in a stall where these lines cross, babies tend to be fussy and will not sleep peacefully, and disease will grow. Infertility can also occur, and anger or agitation, become a part of one's temperament.

Jack proceeded to dowse my home with metal L-shaped rods and located both of the above Grids, indicating the crossing points. I could move the furniture and still have issues if standing in those affected areas. I chose to have him rectify this by planting magnetized crystals in a triangular position outside my home. Once this was done, he again dowsed and it was no longer possible to pick up electrical magnetic fields in the home or outside the home. Years later, this was done at our center as some students felt agitated while there. Once it was rectified, a calm wonderful feeling came over the center and is still there today.

James and I both learned to dowse for fun plus professional reasons. Items that were lost have been found, as well as Energy Fields around individuals have been measured. We have even discovered mold in the basement in specific corners or spots. Prior to our experience with cancer, we had been skeptical and wary, with lives of hard work and thoughts of bad or good luck. I knew of God and had attended school surrounded by theologians for years, yet did not understand why religious beliefs separated individuals. Today, I believe we are all connected to one God, no matter what name he or she is given. The rules of society are meant to protect an insecure world that was created out of disconnect.

I have realized since working with energy that the word "cancer" does not create fear in me anymore. I create my world!

To love self and live life authentically encourages a strong Energy Field, Soul, Spirit and Body. The only control one has is over one's self. When one gets the connection, the realm of possibilities in life on Earth, become endless.

As with all energy work, there is a need to ask the question properly to receive the answer that is relevant. In Energy Response Testing, if it is an important question, then a request for "higher self" to respond is in order. "Could I . . . May I . . . ask this question?" is important as well to ensure that respect is given to the response.

In earlier history, the staff and rod were used as dowsing rods to locate energetic positioning of the altar of a Church. Dowsing can also take place using a Pendulum.

Pendulum

A pendulum swings back and forth, as does the needle on a string used at a baby shower to identify whether the baby is a boy or girl. One's Spirit plus Soul get together when using this form of energy measurement. I use washers on a string when identifying this in a workshop, because it is so basic and easy to explain.

The washer demonstration identifies how much the mind (Spirit) plays a part in illness and disease. When the audience holds a string with the washer and uses their mind to move the washer in a circle, then back and forth without using movement of their arm or fingers, they understand. It is simple.

Pendulums are beautiful, made of basics such as wood, stone, crystal or metal. They are in different sphere shapes that work with one's energy to identify negative or positive items that can affect the Body. Take a list of vitamins or minerals and go down the list with the intention of identifying what one needs today to keep in a healthy balance. Test it, have blood tests done to verify the choices. Take the vitamin or mineral and see if there are fewer physical symptoms. Trust energy and connection.

Use a list to identify qualities that have been lost as a child. *(See Appendix B at back of this book.)*

Pendulums become personal and adhere to one person's energy so it is recommended to use a prayer to clear another's pendulum before using or simply to purchase one's own.

Most questions asked when using a pendulum have "Yes" or "No" answers. Before one starts, it is necessary to determine the direction one's pendulum will take for their "Yes" and for "No".

Pendulum Instructions

- Hold the pendulum in one's hand. With the other hand touch the point/bobber to steady its motion. Keep one's eyes on the point.
- Address the pendulum and say, "Show me a 'Yes'." It will soon swing in one direction, which could be side to side; back and forth; or circles.
- Now say, "Show me a 'No'." It will swing in another direction. Be certain the pendulum is not being guided by the movement of one's hand or fingers.
- Once the pattern has been determined for "Yes" and "No", one is ready to begin.

There are times that the answer is unknown or the Spirit requires more information. At that time the pendulum will generally swing diagonally or not at all, and the faster the movement the stronger the energies.

Sometimes a pendulum will appear to bob or dance up and down. This is usually an affirmative response. The point of a pendulum is sometimes called a bobber. There are generally no rituals involved with pendulum use, though some people hold their pendulum in the palm of their hand before they begin, to 'charge' it.

When a question is asked, one may want to record the answers in a journal.

When ready to begin, ask a specific question. Start with something simple. Once one gets the 'swing' of it, move on to personal questions. Remember to only ask a question ONCE.

If the motion of one's pendulum increases or the circle gets larger, the energy is increasing and one can expect change linked to the question being asked. Pursue further questions to get additional information.

One major benefit of the pendulum is the ease of carrying it compared to dowsing rods.

Last summer I attended the Gem Show in Parrsboro, Nova Scotia, with James. I was specifically looking for a pendulum, and was letting energy guide me to the right one. Finally I came to a table where seven pendulums were hanging, and one crystal pendulum started vibrating. When I moved away it stopped and when I got closer it started again. It was amazing, and of course I bought that pendulum. When one pays attention to the present, the gift unfolds.

Energy Response Testing (ERT)

ERT is similar to a process that was identified by a chiropractor named George Goodheart in the nineteen sixties (Applied Kinesiology) and the extension of testing emotion was added in the seventies by a psychiatrist named Dr. John Diamond (Muscle Response Testing) while the Fourth Principle was added by myself in two thousand and nine.

Energy Response Testing is an indicator that is valuable to many procedures and treatments. It is a viable, efficient as well as effective tool for determining the Body's needs. MRT is currently being used by many healing disciplines: Naturopaths, Naturotherapists, Medical Doctors, Acupuncturists, Chiropractors, Osteopaths, Holistic Dentists, Veterinarians plus other natural health practitioners, from which I envision ERT to evolve as a higher form of testing.

Controlling will stop the whole process of Response Testing. Energy Response Testing is an art and only suggested for use when an answer is unable to be found in any other way. When the Body is in tune and contains the right amount of energy, it will pick up the connection to the Soul via gut instinct therefore not needing the test.

A few reasons a person cannot test self or others via this method:

- Dehydration;
- Rushing, therefore not grounded nor connected to the energy of the Universe;
- Trust issues;
- A magnesium low (cancer, heart disease and diabetic individuals usually are low in magnesium);
- The practitioner or student is trying to control the other person or the outcome;
- The presence of a watch, pager or cell phone on the Body can significantly interfere and reduce ability to test, due to the energy they transmit.

I love teaching a course on Energy Response Testing as it gives the student personal independence. Children can be taught in five minutes, because they have true belief and trust.

Our seven year old granddaughter Gia, was having a constipation issue last year. She called upon her Papa and me to help her as it hurt to poop. By using Energy Response Testing, we were able to determine a fear that was blocking energy. The fear developed when she watched a movie shown at school which taught the students how to leave the home when it is on fire. We used Energy Balance Harmony to resolve the issue, while discussing with her the positive aspects of the movie, and it has never occurred again. The wonderful part of all of this is that Gia understands that emotional feelings affect different organs. This was demonstrated this year when one of her friends had a tummy ache and Gia showed her how to release the blocked energy of worry. Her friend was fine within five minutes.

Since this incident, her Papa (James) has become a volunteer fireman and I believe the energy of that experience with Gia helped this to transpire.

I use Energy Response Testing with students to check the Endocrine System for energy blockages, emotional feelings trapped in organs, and to supplement quantity or necessity of natural health products. I also use ERT to identify The Fourth Principle when the student's conscious self cannot access their sub-conscious. The question has to have a yes or no answer and be asked specifically.

An example would be asking if a piece of chocolate they were holding was good for the Body. Their answer may be "Yes" if the person really wants the chocolate. Yet if the question was, "Is this good for the health of the Body?" the answer could be "No." If not able to test; check self and then ensure the student has water, and that they have removed cell phones or watches from their person. Finally, have them hold a bottle of magnesium while testing, which usually resolves the problem.

Whatever is in the Energy Field of the Body can be tested or can affect the test; therefore, just holding a bottle of magnesium will energetically transfer that energy to the field so one can be tested. One can have fun with all of these forms of testing energy.

Kirlian Camera

Kirlian photography is a process that uses high frequencies and electron streams to take a picture of invisible radiating Energy Fields that surround all living things. It is a unique tool for research, experimentation and fun to understand the energy flow of life.

When one wants dramatic before and after photos, to illustrate the effectiveness of protocols, or wants useful information about the Body's energetic and physical state, Kirlian photographs can meet one's needs in ways no other tools can. With practice as well as training, the subtle cues of bio-energy photography become apparent.

Kirlian photography has been extensively studied in reputable labs. It has shown not only consistent correlation with emotional and physical states in any life energy source, as well as the state of the energy meridians flowing through them.

On my vision board is a picture of a Kirlian camera, a future goal. This type of photography is a dynamic way to introduce others to the knowledge of the energy surrounding us. Some suggest the energy is an Aura, and I too have accepted and researched to the satisfaction that it simply is.

Casaroma Wellness Centre in Dartmouth, Nova Scotia uses a unique probe of the full hand with its reflexology points to identify Aura in each individual and actually transform this onto print. It's not a Kirlian camera, though it has a similar ability. When I had the above test done by Casaroma, the aura was wonderful and indicated positive energy.

During the process, a lady at the expo came up beside me, entering my Energy Field. She commented that this was not something she could do as she recently had a child pass away. Immediately, I took on her sorrow and the color shifted on the reading, with gray matter appearing. It took a few hours for me to resolve the emotional feeling, and then re-testing indicated I was fine.

It proved to be a lesson in staying grounded while present to self so as not to take on someone else's negative energy. Empathy is fine as long as positive emotional feelings are transferred via the Energy Field by the practitioner, using Universal energy which creates an uplifting experience for both.

New life and light emanates from every cell, while an aura appears as the energy of all cells functioning in synchronicity with the vibration (frequency) of whom one is.

There are certain gifted individuals who have the ability to see one's aura, thus also seeing where gray matter indicates an energy block or shift of emotional feelings. They can also see when a person has a beautiful glow of white or colors. There are books available which can teach a person how to read auras. It is not something one can control or will to happen, seeing an aura takes a connection to self and the Universe while being present to life.

Royal Raymond Rife

Vibrations are everywhere in one's life and affect each moment. Royal Rife, an American inventor, identified this when he invented a super microscope (31,000 x). He claimed that this invention proved that the blood, not the germ, is responsible for disease (pleomophism). Once the virus was identified, he produced a Beam Ray Rife Machine in 1939 that used the frequency of the virus to destroy it without harm to the Body. Royal Rife believed cancer is a virus.

According to the *San Diego Evening Tribune* in 1938[4] *"We do not wish at this time," Rife commented," to claim that we cured cancer, or any other disease, for that matter. But we can say that these waves or the 'ray' has the power of devitalizing disease organisms, of 'killing' them, when tuned to an exact particular wave length, or frequency, for each different organism. This applies to the organisms both in their free state and, with certain exceptions, when they are living tissues."*

Dr. Rife's work was ruined by the American Medical Association, his machines as well as paperwork destroyed. He died a broken man a number of years later, knowing he had been denied the ability to save lives. The rise plus fall of a scientific genius deserves to be widely viewed and spoken of as a tribute to scientific discovery and the misuse of power.

Live Blood Analysis

This procedure is a wonderful measuring tool to find where the Body is out of balance. It is important to ensure that the microscopic technician also does Dry Blood Analysis because this method verifies the Live Blood and picks up further imbalances. The ideal situation would be if the technician did a DVD or photos so a comparison could be made in the future to determine if the protocol chosen has been effective. Chemical changes can be detected up to four years prior to a normal blood test. This method of testing blood has the potential of indicating over fifty possible imbalances in the Body such as vitamin or mineral deficiency, anemia, sluggish immune system, free radicals, parasites, yeast, digestive issues and so much more.

James is a Microscopic Technician and we find this tool important in identifying imbalances as well as severity of the imbalance, thus giving us as well as the student a tool to measure progress while alleviating the fear of the unknown.

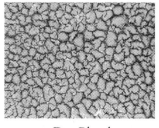 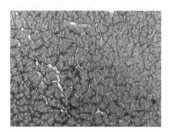

<table>
<tr><td>Dry Blood</td><td>Dry Blood</td></tr>
<tr><td>Normal</td><td>Indication of Chronic Fatigue</td></tr>
</table>

Hair Analysis

Hair is the second most metabolically active tissue in the Body. The hair tissue is affected by the blood, perspiration, environment, genetics, hormones and enzymes. The hair represents what is occurring inside the cells as well as the sub-molecular figures of the Body. A regular blood test shows what is happening outside the cell and the waste material being discarded. The hair gives a reading of what is being stored in the Body. For example, if mercury is high in the hair, a higher concentration of it would also be found in organs like the kidney or the liver.

A hair analysis identifies deficiencies of vitamins, minerals and other nutrients as well as accumulation of heavy metal toxicity over a long period of time.

Iridology

The eyes are often referred to as the windows of the Soul. Iridology, or iris diagnosis as it is often called, is a method used in natural medicine to analyze the health status by studying colors, marks and signs in the iris, pupil, plus sclera of the eye. What is revealed in the eyes mirrors the state of health of the entire Body. The iris of the eye is actually a map where each place represents a different Body organ or system. An Iridology examination is an absolutely safe, non-invasive, painless and reliable method of obtaining information about the health status of an individual is one of the few real methods to view all of the Body organs and systems as a whole as well as how they interact with each other.

Iridology begins as early as 1400 B.C. when a study of the eyes was found in the tomb of King Tutankhamen of Egypt, and goes on to many others including the work of the gentle Greek physician, Hippocrates in 460 B.C. It then takes one throughout Europe, Australia, Russia, the United States, and many countries of the world illustrating how many great men plus women risked their lives and stood trial in order to continue their valuable research in iridology. A great deal of information is given about the life as well as work of the Father of Iridology in the United States, Dr. Bernard Jensen.

Traditional Chinese Medicine notes the whole eye when looking for patterns within the Body. The upper lid coloring is indicative to the spleen, lower edge the stomach, corners the heart, white the lungs, iris the liver and pupil the kidney. This alone does not produce the whole picture, however in conjunction with the tongue, pulse, plus history of the student, produces a larger picture of what is happening within the Body.

Tongue Analysis

For the Japanese and Chinese, tongue diagnosis is essential when it comes to reading a person's health. They believe it reflects the state of one's digestive system, including the stomach plus spleen, heart, lungs, kidney, liver and gall bladder.

It is also believed to relate to the throat Chakra, which indicates communication both internal; (inner dialogue causing issues with digestion) and external; (one's thoughts and words).

There are a lot more tongue cancers now in North America. This is possibly an indicator of disturbances in Electric Magnetic Fields due to the use of cell phones without EMF protectors, in conjunction with issues in the throat Chakra (communication).

A normal tongue is described as pink in color with a thin white coating. The tongue should not be overly wet or dry, without cracks or movement as well as it should not be too long or short, stiff or flaccid.

Tongue Colour

- Pale tongue can indicate deficiency or anemia.
- Red tongue can indicate excess, fever and infection.
- Red sore tongue can indicate vitamin B12 deficiency.
- Red tip can indicate stress on the heart.

Tongue Coating

- Scant or the coating is absent indicates a lack of vitality.
- White coating indicates mal-absorption of nutrients.

- Yellow coating indicates fever or elimination issues.
- Thin indicates blood deficiency.
- Quivering indicates adrenal fatigue.
- Swollen indicates vitamin deficiency and/or thyroid issue.
- Scalloped edges indicate spleen problems or prostrate in men.

Pulse Analysis

For final verification in Traditional Chinese Medicine, the pulse is the main indicator of what direction to take. The right wrist has three positions, indicating lung, spleen and kidney energy. The left wrist indicates the heart, liver and the other kidney. Strength or weakness, rapidness or slowness, are only a few of the indicators noticed in this analysis. It takes about ten years to perfect the ability to read all the levels plus to determine the cause more quickly.

I recently learned pulse and tongue analysis while taking Acupuncture. Tongue is much simpler, however without pulse can send one in too many directions. Although I have not yet perfected pulse reading enough to determine instantly a mushy or wide pulse, I find the more individuals I work with strengthens and speeds the process. With Energy Response Testing plus Live Blood technology as my main tools of analysis, this additional TCM information is an added tool I am glad to have adapted. In Acupuncture it is vital.

AMAS

This test measures anti-maligan antibodies in serum (the portion of the blood containing immune bodies) which reflects the immune system's response to cancer. It is ninety-five percent reliable and can detect cancer nineteen months prior to conventional tests.

"Negative" means no cancer (when the last malignant cancer cells are destroyed in the Body)

It is meaningless to use this test on high dose chemotherapy or radiation therapy and on end stage cancer patients as they cannot produce enough anti-maligan antibodies to make the test positive. Once emotional and physical toxins are removed, cells strengthened plus nutrients added a test would be appropriate.

PSA

This form of testing for prostrate cancer is not accurate in determining cancer present. Eighty-five percent of test results indicating a high PSA have proven to be false.

The prostrate can be irritated or weakened for a number of reasons. To much caffeine, not enough water for the Body size, toxins which affect the parathyroid therefore producing excess calcium which can cause inflammation as well as infection are a few reasons for a false reading. Low amounts of essential fatty acids, flax or fish oils, can also weaken the cells. Saw Palmento helps with enlarged prostrate, repair of inflammation plus distress of the prostrate. It is also reported to help in male pattern baldness, therefore working with the kidneys. Doubt and nurturing are the emotional feelings that are involved.

Bio-Meridian Testing

This is a non-invasive way to accurately assess the energy in the meridian channels that flow through the Body and determine the function of organs plus tissues.

The technology found in the Bio-Meridian machine combines the life work of two doctors. First, Dr. Reckeweg spent his life documenting the six phases of six hundred different conditions and their progression. The second doctor, Dr. Reinhold Voll, documented the acupressure points that when measured, accurately show the functions of the tissues and organs associated with that point. In under an hour, an individual may be tested using a small current on Voll's sixty acupressure points that measure the resistance of the tissues and combine them with Reckweg's phases of progression of conditions. This gives the individual an easy to read graph showing where one stands in overall health. It then allows the provider to use the software to match up the best nutritional choices available from whole food supplements or herbs.

Our eldest daughter uses this device in her nutritional practice and recently we have added a small hand held unit to our own practice. It works with Auricular meridian testing, while it can also be used on the meridian points in the Body. The ear is another part of the Body that has the ability to indicate imbalance while the earring was originally started as a meridian enhancer and test point. Addiction services often have great results with individuals when using Auricular acupuncture. If one added The Fourth Principle and Energy Balance Harmony *(See Appendix C.)* it would enhance positive results.

N.A.E.T.

Nambudripad's Allergy Elimination Technique is a system for dealing with allergies. It is a natural, drug free, painless and non-invasive method which can be used safely on individuals of any age (infants to the elderly) regardless of the individual's health. Allergies can be eliminated through N.A.E.T., along with the symptoms arising from the allergens. Clear fluid in glass vials representing the vibration of each allergen is held by the individual as the N.A.E.T. specialist utilizes Muscle Response Testing to assess the Body's reaction.

Allergens are treated then cleared one at a time with this technique. Best results are obtained if allergens are cleared in a specific sequence. Normally only one item is treated on a given day. The substance must then be completely avoided for twenty-five hours following the treatment unless the practitioner has access to a cold laser, at which time the avoidance is not necessary. In most cases, only one session is needed to eliminate an allergy. Individuals who are highly sensitive may sometimes require additional combination clearings.

What I have discovered through my research, is that food allergies are ninety-nine percent caused by yeast infection, affecting the colon. When the condition escalates, rhizoids (string like lesions) can attach to the colon, and in some cases create holes. Small food particles then have the ability to flow through into the blood stream where the immune response attacks the particle which creates an instant food allergy. If this condition is not resolved, an autoimmune response can occur such as Lupus or Wegner's Disease.

A student once came to me barely able to eat any food without an allergic reaction. After a Live Blood Analysis was done as well as Energy Response Testing, it was apparent that yeast was a factor. Most individuals that have gotten to this stage also have such a reduced immune system that parasites are able to proliferate. After sticking to a thirty day cleanse with a Kroeger Candida Kit followed by a parasite cleanse as well as a series of ionic footbaths to remove toxins, the individual was able to eat food again that formally created illness. Today, this person has a distinctively healthy appearance.

Two simple physical signs of parasites are drooling while sleeping and grinding one's teeth. See below for further indicators. A person's partner also needs to follow steps to remove signs of yeast plus parasites or these will transfer back to the individual during intercourse. A strong immune system will reduce the symptoms; however, the partner is advised to follow this protocol as well to ensure the continued health of the other.

Parasites are meant to take the Body to dust. During an illness or disease the Body can start this process due to low immune response created by an accumulation of emotional and physical toxins. Dr. Hulda Clark believed that parasites create cancer and once resolved, cancer can be beaten. Parasites eat what one eats while robbing the Body of precious nutrients. They multiply on the full moon as well as become active in the Body at this time. Parasites have the ability to enter and destroy organs plus glands. Tapeworms have the ability when rolled up in the

Body to appear on scans or x-rays as an apparent tumor or foreign object.

I had a tapeworm that was noticed through symptoms of hunger. I was always hungry, eating more than James, and was losing weight. Catchexia will also resemble the same symptoms. Over a period of time I had both.

Tapeworms can grow up to twenty-five feet long and block off many areas of life flow in the Body. After using a product to kill the tapeworm naturally, it did not expel via feces. A friend who is a massage therapist was able to feel this unusually large worm in my stomach/intestinal area. I opted to have colonics; a flushing of the bowel, at which time the tapeworm visually left. In India some women are known to swallow a baby tapeworm and let it grow until they lose weight as well as then coax it out via the mouth with milk. This is definitely not something I wish to ever have again, nor recommend to others as a weight loss program.

pH Testing

There is a whole chapter designated to alkaline and acidity in my first book *BALANCE, nature's way to heal your body.* Disease will not grow in an alkaline Body: period. Litmus paper or certain machines designed specifically for pH testing will indicate the level of alkalinity in the Body. The test needs to be of both urine and saliva as each component indicates the ability of certain organs or functions. The urine could be okay with a 7.4 reading while the saliva could be off in the 6.0 range. Saliva has a requirement of 7.0 to be of proper alkalinity.

A person who is not drinking enough water may have a varied urine test that is not diagnostically correct.

The tumors which were present in my groin plus neck area melted like butter when I was able to transform pH from 5.5 urine and 6.0 saliva to normal ranges of 7.4 urine and 7.0 saliva.

Dr. Tullio Simoncini from Italy is an Oncology doctor who works with cancer. He is able to transform cancer cells by raising the alkalinity of the Body using simple baking soda (sodium bicarbonate). He believes cancer is a fungus and has written a book called *Cancer is a Fungus*.

A simple Alkaline Therapy that binds maple syrup with baking soda can be found in *Appendix D*. The cancer or diseased cell accepts this protocol which has the ability to transform the cell to alkaline. This creates a pathway to wellness. Baking soda should be aluminum free to bind properly and to prevent extra heavy metal toxins from being added to the Body.

Too much lactate acid in the Body can create kidney disease, gout, etc. It can be reversed by drinking a glassful of water with a tablespoon (15ml.) of baking soda dissolved in it daily for approximately thirty days, depending on the person as well as condition. Emotional plus physical toxins still need to be removed so that the Body is in balance and does not create this again. A reduction of red meat and processed sugars is necessary as well; especially products that contain corn syrup. "Elevated sugar levels are the cause of eighty-five percent of the crystal formations that create gout." *(Dr. Mercola)*

Blood & Urine Tests

These are the usual modes utilized by traditional medicine. Tests are important while a comparison of past tests should be a priority. The results usually show a high/low reference for each indicator and the positive result would be to have a number in middle range. Most often the doctor will not notice the indicator unless it is below or above the average reference which is indicated with an L or H. It is important to check the variance.

There is a natural way of determining cancer with the Navarro Urine test that measures human chorionic gonadotropin (HCG) a hormone produced during pregnancy and is specific for cancer however; it can be used to measure the health of a person as well. Developed in the late 1930's by the renowned oncologist, the late Dr. Manuel D. Navarro [his son, also an M.D., currently does the test], the test detects the presence of HCG in urine. It indicates the presence of cancer cells even before signs or symptoms develop. Dr. Navarro found HCG to be elevated in all types of cancers. www.navarromedicalclinic.com

Magnesium low can be indicated in blood tests; however, a magnesium urine lode test is more proficient. A urine lode test requires twenty-four hours of urinating in a container retrieved from the lab at the hospital. Lines on the earlobe are a natural way of recognizing a low magnesium lode in the Body, as well as cramping toes, fingers, restless legs, Charlie Horses, and palpitation of the heart. Other than diet, a magnesium low can occur due to the presence of fear; fear of or fear for someone or something. This affects the kidney and its ability to process magnesium in the Body.

Blood tests measure many things, however, they cannot tell the whole story. Blood strives to maintain normalcy even at the expense of tissue. An example is when calcium shows up in the test as close to normal while the person may have osteoporosis. The calcium has to be absorbing in the bones to be of value. Osteoporosis is a symptom that indicates calcium is not absorbing in the bones.

We are all different, although we need the same food factors such as protein, fats, minerals, vitamins, and fiber. Although this is true, we do not all need the same quantity or food from the same source.

Diagnosis by Smell—Odor

Within the category of listening diagnosis, Oriental practitioners included the diagnostic technique that uses the sense of smell. A disorder with either member of an organ pair will often generate a particular telltale odor. The solid, physically yin organs (spleen, lungs, kidney, liver, heart) are considered to be the source of these specific smells. However, the hollow, yang partner organ (stomach, large intestine, bladder, gall bladder, and small intestine) will be affected whenever imbalances develop within its complementary partner.

People who have good health plus eliminate daily do not usually have a problem with Body odor. Deodorant and all the other fragrant alternatives mask the Body odor problem, thereby further complicating the real present and future dangers! Body odor, whether it is emanating from underarms, feet, or breath is a clear as well as immediate sign that internally a person needs to get his or her health in order.

The physical Body is able to heal as one's natural vibrations are restored. Releasing emotional and physical toxins raises vibration. Eating organic food with its enzymes intact raises vibrations. Drinking healthy water at the appropriate amount daily raises vibrations as it conducts electricity. Radionics, N.A.E.T., Energy Balance Harmony (EBH), Essential Oils, Acupuncture, supplements, etc. raise vibrations of the Body.

Chemotherapy and radiation reduce the Body's vibration, destroy healthy as well as bad cells, increase the toxin level in the Body as well as add emotional and physical stress. Medications mask symptoms while creating new ones as they affect the liver and its five hundred functions. Surgery can remove parts needed by the Body such as the gall bladder. Hardened stones are emotionally caused by hardened thoughts, and physically caused by too little essential fatty acids plus too much saturated fat. A simple ten day lemon with olive oil flush at bedtime resolves the issue in ninety-nine percent of cases, yet the government spends millions yearly in Canada as well as the USA to remove gall bladders. This removal weakens the support of the liver and causes other issues in time if the liver is not detoxified.

It is not necessary to believe the process to have it work; belief has to be in self and one's connection to God.

Interference comes when the strong need for a protocol to work becomes greater than one's presence in the healing. A few individuals are invested in not getting well; for example, those who finally are being seen due to illness. In a nursing home one will find this, as some seniors have gone through life not being seen, even by their spouses and suddenly are.

The positive written word as well as speaking with one's true voice raises the Body's vibrations. A journey to wellness requires both the written and spoken word.

The next chapter has additional information about symptoms which lead to the cause and how to recognize what is occurring. During my journey to wellness, plus education in the natural health realm, it was my privilege to learn many different modalities and meet a number of natural health practitioners. The following are additional natural health modalities I have experienced which work in different aspects to raise the Energy Field to its appropriate vibration for healing to occur. Emotional feelings that are not released can keep one in a cycle of illness and disease.

Natural Health Modalities

Attraction Field Technique (AFT)

David R. Hawkins MD, Ph.D., author of *Power Vs Force: The Hidden Determinants of Human Behavior,* adapted this protocol after twenty-five years of historic research into human consciousness. AFT techniques interrupt the energy flow through the meridians used by acupuncturists. There are no needles and no discomfort. This method is comprised of tapping a specific amount of times on different meridian points, depending on the symptoms or cause of the illness or disease.

Dr. Hawkins releases his book with the protocol on line for free at www.the-tree-of-life.com/gogscrc.htm

Emotional Freedom Technique (EFT)

This is similar in many ways to AFT however more emphasis is placed on the individual taking responsibility. Gary Craig is the founder of this modality and self help tool. EFT works with the Body plus mind (Spirit) to shift as well as change that which holds one back. It is a great tool for fears such as airplanes, spiders, etc, and for larger concerns such as pain.

EFT works directly with the meridian system, stimulating points by tapping or massage while repeating the appropriate affirmation for the symptom. This e-book is also available on line at www.123eft.com

A simple process to aid the liver/gallbladder is to tap the edge of each hand, starting at the tip of the little finger to the start of the wrist area. A gentle massage will also help.

Radionics

The Body vibrates in tune to the earth and its atmosphere. Radionics analyzes plus measures energy (vibrations) of the Body, soil, seeds, vitamins, etc. The Body energy is measured through hair or saliva to work with its DNA. There are one hundred and twenty-eight emotional vibrations, and emotional feelings are usually eighty percent of the cause behind illness or disease. Taking the Body back in time to when the condition started to occur, by remembering the symptoms, will help locate the emotional feeling. Using Energy Response Testing as well as The Fourth Principle will help those who cannot locate it.

The Radionics machine can broadcast the vibration of nutrients to raise energy in vegetables. For example, vitamin B12 broadcast via vibrations into a vegetable will reduce the need to have protein. *(Charles Hubbard)*

A master of radionics and dowsing who does lectures all over the world is Charles Hubbard. He and his wife Judith operate a bio-energetic farm in Shinimicas, Nova Scotia. Their home is nestled against the Shinimicas River, buzzing with bees and birds and abundant in wonderful organic vegetables. His farm has the ability to sustain his extended family. We are friends and I enjoy taking my grandchildren to his farm to pet the animals and walk the Labyrinth on his property. See resources for information on his book.

Essential Oils

Essential oils, known as nature's living energy, are the natural, aromatic volatile liquids found in shrubs, flowers, trees, roots, bushes, and seeds. The distinctive components in essential oils defend plants against insects, environmental conditions, as well as disease. They are also vital for a plant to grow, live, evolve, and adapt to its surroundings. Essential oils are extracted from aromatic plant sources via steam distillation, plus are highly concentrated and far more potent than dry herbs.

While essential oils often have a pleasant aroma, their chemical makeup is complex and their benefits vast—which make them much more than something that simply smells good.

Historically, essential oils have played a prominent role in everyday life. With more than two hundred references to aromatics, incense, and ointments throughout the Bible, essential oils are said to be used for anointing as well as healing the sick. Today, essential oils are for the purpose of aromatherapy; massage therapy, emotional health, personal care, nutritional supplements, household solutions, and much more.

Young Living Essential Oils, the leading provider of essential oils, offers more than three hundred essential oil singles and blends. All Young Living essential oils meet the YLTG standard. This means that every essential oil Young Living distils or sources has the optimal naturally-occurring blend of constituents to maximize the desired effect.

Everything on this planet has a frequency. One can measure frequency in rocks, plants, animals, people-everything. A frequency is where there is a positive and a negative charge.

Normal Body frequency should be between sixty-two and seventy-eight megahertz. The Body is generally sixty-two and the brain soars to seventy-eight when in use. Cold symptoms show up at fifty-eight megahertz, flu at fifty-seven, Candida at fifty-five,

Epstein Barr at fifty-two and cancer at forty-two; as the frequency of the human Body diminishes; disease enters.

Essential oils range from fifty megahertz to three hundred and twenty megahertz. Disease cannot live in a host where the frequency is higher than its own self.

Young Living is the best and most recognized, yet a person can also make their own product. Recipes are everywhere. By using the information mentioned above, along with growing the plants in a circular bed and a nutrient ground, plus by planting as well as picking them according to the moon, the product will have a great start.

All oils used on the Body should be of such quality that one could eat them. The skin absorbs everything in contact with it and the substance is delivered into the blood stream and transported through the Body. If one cannot eat the product, then it is not chemical free. Potent aromatherapy oils should be mixed with a balancing oil so as not to burn the skin.

Also understand that smell only takes seconds to go to the brain. Smells trigger thoughts and actions within the Body plus mind, therefore can heal or create illness or disease depending on the emotional charge attached. We are more than our Body.

It is advised to purchase products, whether oils or other items, in glass containers. Glass, wood plus stainless steel all have energy and keep the vibration of the product, whereas plastic does not keep the product at its higher vibration.

Raindrop Therapy is based on Lakota native healing and designed by D. Gary Young to present essential oils in a protocol to the Body. Nine essential oils are dropped onto various points of the Body and then feather massaged. It is a relaxing while energizing method associated with wellness. In our area of Amherst, Nova Scotia, Kim Smith uses this technique with clients during a massage when requested.

Bach Remedies is another specialized essential oil company which utilizes oil combinations for emotional feelings. An example: willow is good for resentment and self-pity. They are famous for their rescue remedy used to calm a child, adult or animal.

Hydrotherapy

Fever is one of the Body's defenses against disease. Fever causes the Body's temperature to rise above normal in an attempt to destroy invading organisms while it sweats impurities out of the system. Hydrotherapy is the use of water in the treatment of disease. Through water, ice and steam, hot as well as cold temperatures are in contrast to each other.

Hot water stimulates the immune system and causes white cells to migrate out of the blood vessels and into tissues where they clean up the toxins.

Cold water discourages inflammation by means of constricting blood vessels. It is beneficial for incontinence, tones muscle weakness, stimulates adrenals and other endocrine glands, reduces congestion, alleviates inflammation, as well as improves liver detoxification and digestion. *(Dr. Richard Schultz)*

Dr. Richard Schultz also advocates having two hot/cold showers daily when ill, concentrating on the affected area for approximately sixty days, then once a day. A cold sheet treatment every seven to ten days for the first four months of illness, then two a month for the remaining year are among his protocols as well.

I have not done the cold sheet treatment, yet I do enjoy an occasional hot then cold shower. While in Germany at a spa in Baden Baden a number of years ago, I experienced wonder at their process. A hot spring from a rock wall in one alcove, then a cold spring in another, followed by a mineral pool to swim in was rejuvenating. The area I was visiting was rich with healthy people, and the markets were overflowing with produce, all without pesticides. Individuals with fibromyalgia, which is basically toxins trapped in tissue and muscle will benefit from hydrotherapy.

Ho'oponopono

This process helps a person make things right with all individuals with whom one has had a relationship; beginning from ancestors through current. It may involve correcting the wrongs that have occurred in one's life, such as incorrect goals once aimed for, harm that one has caused to others, excesses that have been allowed in one's life, or disobedience of society's rules or one's own personal standards.

It is connected to the Hawaiian code of forgiveness. When one forgives another, he or she is also forgiving one's self.

The process of Ho'oponopono can help one to align with and clean up their genealogy, as well as to clean up relationships with other people who are currently in one's life.

The Process:

Bring to mind someone whom one does not feel aligned with or supported by. Then construct a small stage below one (in one's mind's eye)

Imagine an infinite supply of love and healing flowing from a source above the top of one's head, which fills up then overflows out of the heart to heal the person on the stage. The person on the stage must first identify they will accept the healing. While the image is still present, discuss this with the person on the stage, forgive them, as well as ask for forgiveness from them.

Let go of the person and see them float away. Cut the aka cord (etheric connection) that joins both (if appropriate) or if a primary relationship, assimilate the person inside.

Do this with every person in one's life with whom one is incomplete, or not aligned. The final test is to ask, "Can I see this person or think of them without feeling any negative emotions?" If one does feel negative emotional feelings when one asks the question, then do the process again.

Reconnection

Dr. Eric Pearle, the founder of Reconnection, talks about the gift of being childlike. To be in awe, to view everything with genuine wonder is a gift which gives reverence to the purity of the child, an inherent connection to God. Being childlike releases the desire to diagnose, explain, try, fake, force, push or exert effort. It even releases one's need to take credit.

Reconnective Healing is a form of healing that is here on the planet for the very first time. It reconnects one to the fullness of the Universe as it reconnects to the fullness of one's being and of whom one is. Reconnective healing is considered to be able to reconnect one to the Universe as well as to one's very essence not just through a new set of healing frequencies; through possibly an entirely new bandwidth. The reality of its existence has demonstrated itself clearly in practice as well as in science laboratories.

The Reconnection is the umbrella process of reconnecting to the Universe, which allows Reconnective Healing to take place. These healings and evolutionary frequencies are of a new bandwidth brought in via a spectrum of light and information. It is through The Reconnection that one is able to interact with these new levels of light plus information, while it is through these new levels of light and information that one is able to reconnect. This is something new. This is different. This is real: it can be entrained in everyone.

Healing energy comes to the earth when one allows one's mind to reach a place where one is not exactly awake and yet not exactly asleep.

Listen with ones hands, using hands to do energy work keeps one in the now. REM (rapid eye movement), breathing, tears, laughter, finger movement, head rotation or other Body movement, stomach gurgling are all indications that the Body is registering some moment in healing.

Color Therapy

Color therapy is often known as chromo therapy and is classified as a vibration healing modality. All the primary colors reflected in the rainbow carry their own unique healing properties. The history of color healing has its roots in ancient Egypt.

Color is simply a form of visible light, of electromagnetic energy. The sun alone is a wonderful healer! A therapist trained in color therapy applies light and color in the form of tools, visualization, or verbal suggestion to balance energy in the areas of one's Body that lack vibrancy, whether physical, emotional, spiritual, or mental.

Tools Used in Color Therapy

- Gemstones
- Colored fabrics
- Candles/Lamps
- Color bath treatments
- Crystal Wands and glass prisms
- Colored eye lenses

Color is introduced to one early in life. Pastel pinks as well as blues are used in nursery decor to welcome newborn babies into a gentle and restful atmosphere.

Scientists who have studied color and light extensively recognize that colors bring about emotional reactions to individuals. One's reactions as well as attitudes to colors differ from person to person, which makes an interesting study in itself.

One's attraction to certain colors may very well signal areas where one is imbalanced. Understanding why certain colors affect one favorably, while others bring about negative feelings, helps one along their healing journeys.

The colors worn can reflect one's emotional state and will create positive or negative energy. When teaching Energy Response Testing, I have the students go through their closets and relate to what they wear. This is fun and informative as it enables the individual to recognize limitations they may have set at one point in their life that can influence their potential. Certain colors cause a person to blend into their world rather than stand out, and there may be moments when this is a good thing. All clothes may do this, as the authentic person hides within.

I mention my first husband disliked the color green, to the point it was a color he would not allow me to wear. This would indicate that the color was prominent in something negative in his life that he had not resolved.

The Way of the Heart™

"Field," said Albert Einstein "is the only reality." He defined matter itself as simply denser and denser fields. And as one now knows from quantum field science, everything in the Universe is not only connected through the Energy Field, it is involved in a constant dialogue, regardless of distance or time. Everything, literally everything *speaks*. Scientists call this phenomenon "quantum non-locality"; the mystics have simply called it "unity".

There is an actual language through which the fields converse and interact with one another. The miracle is that one has access to this language: knowledge. The gateway is through the heart.

I first connected to The Way of the Heart™ several years ago. I believe that without the process of clearing past negativity, supporting my Energy Field by doing the work within, dealing with the fear of success and failure that had been attached to my Energy Field from childhood,

I would have been deterred from starting my own business as well as having a Best Selling Book.

It is not about what one writes; on the contrary it also involves the positive energy surrounding it that carries it to the world. I now enjoy the community of like-minded beings plus the endless possibilities I have for the future. Connie Fisher and Stephanie Allen, both authentic human beings, hold the field in the Atlantic Provinces for The Way of the Heart™. Their friendship and leadership is with peace.

Herbs

Herbs supply the Body with natural energy. Caution is important in their use, however, as they can react negatively with certain medications or with each other. It is best to have the help or guidance of an experienced natural health practitioner.

Hanna Kroeger was a famous North American Herbalist. Her inspiration came from her upbringing, where she learned that natural healing came from within the Body. According to her teachings, the Body becomes ill due to experiences that leave trauma and congestion in the energy pathways, organs, glands, muscles or wherever the physical Body feels pain as well as discomfort.

Neglect on top of this causes long-term illness. Hanna taught that all dis-ease began in one's emotional framework and manifested inwardly to one's physical Body. Hanna believed that dis-ease from the past could be triggered today in response to a new stress totally unrelated to the past condition, yet similar from an emotional interpretation. Most importantly, Hanna believed that reversing all of these conditions would create a flow of energy that would resolve the issue and cleanse the Body, eliminating most of these repressed emotions and physical setbacks. (Exerts from an article that was written by a student of Hanna Kroeger; Reverend Louise White, Sydney, Nova Scotia)

Kroeger Candida as well as Parasite cleanses are the best in the market plus they work the first time. Reverend White is a natural health practitioner in Cape Breton, Nova Scotia who took courses from Hanna, and now utilizes her work. Information for Reverend White and accessing courses as well as books are listed in the Resource section of this book.

I work with a wonderful variety of dried herbs used for tea that have a healing energy and facilitate a response more efficient than supplements.

- Pau d'arco for the immune and yeast;
- Papaya leaf helps with digestion, parasites, worms, IBS, Celiac Disease and has cancer-fighting abilities;
- Hibiscus is a potent vitamin C and cholesterol lowering tea;
- Celery seed cleanses the kidneys and aids fungus;
- Fennel helps aid anemia, diarrhea, indigestion, respiratory problems and bronchitis;
- Passion Flower reduces the adrenal tire: bulge around the belly button area);
- Rooibos is a wonderful antioxidant.

Akashi Records

Akashi Records are described as containing all knowledge of human experience and the history of the Universe. The cosmic energy of that which one is!

I had the opportunity to communicate through a phone call with a wonderful woman named Kateri. I agreed to be one of her case studies as she became certified in reading Akashi Records. Nothing in life is an accident. I was allowed to ask three questions. They were answered through the use of records of who I was in past lives.

The insight was profound for the moment in time. The questions I asked were:

1. Why do I keep letting others' energy affect my well-being? She listened and connected while she talked of a seed that grows in a crack in the sidewalk. If left there, the weed or tree will eventually destroy the whole sidewalk. We are all equal, no matter how big or small. Perception of strength is not measured by this world's standards. When we are affected by others, it is an opportunity to be aware of ourselves, a reflection of life. Ask for guidance and get the best use of knowledge from all who come in contact.

2. Why am I not allowing my inner child to play? The answer was a strong belief from a prior life as a nun who took a vow of service and poverty that was still in play with my Soul in this life. I was advised to write a vow of poverty plus service and offer it up in fire then replace the vow with one open plus expansive; as well, ask for wisdom from nature (seeds such as tomato) and share abundance as they do. One seed does abundance produce. Visit with one's five and ten year old self plus release the need to put others' needs before self. Visit with now knowledge and re-educate the inner child to what is truly possible as well as how many more can be helped when we are flourishing and happy.

3. I procrastinate, yet love what I do. This procrastination reduces my ability to receive; why do I do this? Some relation to question two was part of the response. Additionally, when I feel self up against an opportunity to take action, I need to allow that grace; a break is needed. This is the force of grace offering me time to play and nurture my inner child. I can play in full honor and knowledge without guilt. When a wall comes up, mentally turn around and see where the wall is directing me. Look left at new avenues. Know that there are many more ways of doing things than we can imagine, and this moment in time of procrastination is to stop-look-listen. An image came up to her as she related this of a sheet billowing around me and I can't see opportunities, she directed me to stand on the sheet to create movement to clear the veil. Spend time on vistas that surround me while I allow wind and peacefulness to calm my mind, lift and inspire. Be sure to express acknowledgment received and give thanks.

Kateri thanked me for seeking guidance from who cares about me deeply and acknowledged there is much support when I ask. Ask and one shall receive

Affirmations

One of my favorite authors is Louise Hay. She uses affirmations to release emotional feelings and increase vibrations towards wellness.

"We are each responsible for all of our experiences. Every thought we think is creating our future. When we really love ourselves, everything in our life works." Louise Hay

As a conference presenter and author, John Major Jenkins, points out in *Maya Cosmogenesis 2012*, "The Maya understood the principle of enantiodromis (a principle introduced by psychiatrist Carl Jung that the superabundance of any force inevitably produces its opposite) and believed it was driven by one's changing orientation to the field-effects of the Galaxy . . . The Maya believed that the twenty-six thousand-year Great Year of precession is a spiritual gestation period for humanity, and that the 2012 alignment will catalyze the birth of what has been growing on this planet for twenty-six thousand years. For the Maya, Father Sun's movement into union with Cosmic Mother's heart also signified the insemination, or seeding, of what will come to fruition in twenty-six thousand years. The 2012 era is about the birth of something new on this planet however, it is also a death, the rupture of the womb-world that held one comfortably warm for millennia, unaware of the larger world outside of one's limited sights.

So what does that mean? To me it means a new wondrous world where individuals who understand the connection of Soul, Spirit, Body plus Energy Field to the Universe have the ability to live in joy, peace and love. That luck has shifted to choice and blessings. Individuals have awakened to discover it is within them to heal, to rise to greatness as well as have a wonderful life, one which they imagine, feel and attract. Material things are not attachments that a person longs for or misses when lost, so fear is no longer a part of one's self. It is possible to celebrate life each moment and to be present to authentic self.

Nurturing Energy

The Law of Attraction

The Law of Attraction is all about vibration. All existing things have vibrations. This energy is either positive or negative and is easily transmitted to other existing things. Dr. Masaro Emoto has proven that water can actually respond to information.

Albert Einstein said all energy reaches a vibratory rate faster than even the speed of light. Matter is energy and energy is matter.

Vibrations move when they have two poles: positive and negative. When response testing self or someone else, it is the rule to check the negative and positive field before testing to ensure the right response is achieved. Emotional feelings, toxins, trauma, etc. can shift the polarity of a person, reducing their vibration and Energy Field. This can be shifted back by crossing arms and placing hands on both shoulders, hold for twelve seconds and then reverse crossed arms (aligning acupuncture meridians). In some cases, simply place the right hand on the head and then the left hand for twelve seconds each: a Mind Gem.

Humans can create different vibrations mentally, emotionally and physically. In response, other people, things, or events which have similar vibrations will resonate with those signals and attract.

One can quickly see why and how one attracts into one's Energy Field whatever one is giving energy to on a consistent level. Everyone is the co-creator of his or her own life. Be careful what one asks for since a person attracts what one thinks and feels. The written or spoken word has energy.

"To attract good health, prosperity, or abundance to name a few, first and foremost ask clearly what you want, with no if, and or buts. Remember written or spoken, words have vibrations and attract." Mary Jo Rugggieri, PHD, RPP (excerpt from International Energy, spring/summer 2007).

Before we learned to Energy Response Test or connect with our intuitive self at the level we do today, James and I would ask a simple question. When we wanted to know if what we thought to put out to the Universe is right, we simply asked for a visual red light or green light as in a traffic light, which would stop us or move us ahead. James was contemplating performing comedy in Halifax and asked for a visual to help him manifest the right response. He had never done comedy before. On the way to work in Oxford, many cabs heading in the opposite direction kept passing him with Halifax on their signs; this was a phenomenon that had never occurred before. They indicated his question was answered and that performing comedy in Halifax was indeed the step he needed to take.

Labyrinth

A labyrinth is an ancient symbol that relates to wholeness. It combines the imagery of the circle and the spiral into a meandering, however, purposeful path. The Labyrinth represents a journey to one's own center and back again out into the world with a broader understanding of which one is. Labyrinths have long been used as meditation as well as prayer tools.

Labyrinths and mazes have often been confused. A labyrinth is not a maze. A maze is like a puzzle to be solved. It has twists, turns, plus paths that end. It is a left brain task that requires logical, sequential, as well as analytical activity to find the correct path into the maze and out.

A labyrinth has only one path. The path leads one on a circuit path to the center and out again. It is a right brain task involving intuition, creativity, while using imagery. The choice is whether or not to walk a spiritual path.

A Labyrinth works with the Energy Body of Soul, Spirit, Body and Energy Field to positively affect one's health. The shape is a medical tool.

It is recommended that angry individuals should release anger before they walk in it so as not to transform the energy of others. One's energy, whether negative or positive, affects one's life path if not standing for authentic self.

Pyramid

Ancient Egyptians had used the pyramids as graves and temples, as well as a way to ground along with convert cosmic energies.

Healing energies can accumulate in objects placed inside pyramids. Ions reproduce and repair Body cells. They're transmitted into the Body through the air supply and are circulated by the blood. Too many positive ions (the result of air pollution) can cause depression, as well as ultimately sickness. Negative ions have a beneficial effect on the Body.

One can test this idea for oneself by remembering or experiencing how one felt in a large city, or if one was on the receiving end of automotive exhaust. This is the effect of positive ions. Contrast this to the feeling in the air after a heavy rainfall or how one feels when one sits near a waterfall. These situations are examples of the effects of an abundance of negative ions.

Pyramids generate negative ions. In addition, they are believed to have a generally balancing effect on the Energy Field of the Body. This effect is enhanced by the particular materials used, such as pure twenty-four karat gold or copper.

- Charging Crystals. This is a popular use for pyramids. It is generally believed that quartz crystals are most effective for this use, as they may hold the charge for several weeks. These crystals can then be used for healing purposes or for programming a specific positive thought.
- Large pyramids (the kind one sits inside) are often used for meditation, distant healing, massage, acupuncture, as well as Reiki.
- After sleeping inside a pyramid, many people find that they need less sleep while they feel more relaxed and at peace when they wake up.
- People put their drinking water in pyramids to imbue it with the negative ions which are a particular aspect of pyramid energy. It is recommended to put a glass inside a pyramid for about half-an-hour, and large quantities overnight.

Do not use wood to build the pyramid as it will twist as the energy moves through it. Gold is the best to use. Copper is second, and more economical.

A copper pyramid can be placed over a greenhouse to enhance growth and supply heat. The best case is to ensure the copper is inserted into the ground so the copper will draw energy from the earth as well as the Universe. (See resources for information on making a pyramid)

"An imbalance of the Body can simply be caused by eating foods grown in another country. One's Body is in sync to the vibrations of where one lives. One can transform the energy of the food via prayer or other energy work. One is energy and requires constant energy for life!" Susan Manion MacDonald

Granite Circle

Granite is high in silica and quartz, a good yin/yang mix which opens the soil and creates energy. The outer planet has a specific pull which is seventy-five percent silica in the earth (Yang), while the inner planet; soft calcium holds onto energy (Yin).

I first became interested in granite circles when in Sedona, Arizona for a course. While there, I felt a shift in my Energy Field. I had not yet learned the lessons which explained this. Years later James and I visited the Grand Canyon with its wondrous vibrations emanating off the rocks and understood the connection.

Taking a course with Charles Hubbard completed the circle, and he supplied us with a recipe to design a granite circle for our backyard. The size of the circle depends on the size of the property. In our yard, we built an eight foot wide circle. The energy supplied via the circle can cover two hundred yards to one hundred acres depending on the size. The circle can have as many as eight spokes. In our case, three were required.

We used round pink granite stones, checking each for energy by dowsing. When placing the stones, we also checked for positioning to ensure the right stone was placed energetically. A space is left in the centre of the circle to stand in or for a hub stone. Our circle has a two foot center. When we stand in the center, facing east with outstretched arms the energy felt is amazing.

Medicine Wheel

This is similar to the granite circle, yet has four directions with prayer, and they energetically attract things to self. A garden circle where flowers are grown: yellow in the east, warm blue in the south for summer sky, red in the west and white in the north. It is also called a sacred hoop by Native Indians and represents the cycle of life as it develops an energy that keeps on flowing while building momentum. Energy can continue to flow around a circle forever. Sometimes one places a sick person in the middle of the circle while others stand around the circle equal in distance. One has a Spirit, an energy that is transferable. One also gets energy from nature, including rocks. Earth was not created by accident.

The light Body one has needs to be nourished in all ways. One needs oxygen. All organs survive on energy coming from the sun; food represents trapped sunlight. Every message from the Soul is encoded in energy while working with the Spirit, the brain turns love, truth, and beauty into physical activity. To nourish this energy is basic for life. Routine activity is necessary; BEing, taking pleasure in each day, having a personal vision as well as a higher purpose. One is likened to electricity; re-charge and let energy flow with purpose plus light.

It is easy to lie on a table and have energy "rebalanced" however things will not change unless it is linked to a path/purpose in a person's life. Healing occurs when one can relate to the feeling that arises when working with the whole body and connects to the Universe.

December 21, 2012

The sun is to align in the center of the Milky Way. This will complete a shifting in the earth's atmosphere affecting the magnetic field. One's Spirit will be more present to those who allow it to BE. One needs to BE fully awake in this life as Eckert Tolle has said in *The Power of Now*.

What is happening and will complete the cycle in 2012 was defined in a five thousand year old calendar by the Mayans. One has a choice of extinction or enlightenment.

We are one on earth-connected to God
Individually and as a whole

Illness is actually trapped emotional feelings needing to be resolved such as growth waiting to open a flower. Instead, the growth goes inward as one nurtures the past. The Body gets the message that a growth (in some cases a baby) is on the way and homeostasis stops its process of balancing the Body. One is nurturing disease or illness.

Past Life Regression is using the energy of the Spirit to guide one in resolving issues projected from this life or past life. *Mindwalking* by Nancy L. Eubel A.R.E. and *The Journey* by Brandon Bays are both books that give insight into this process. Rose Devine is a practitioner at our center who works with The Journey. *(See resource list in back of book.)*

One accumulates life force in the present moment. BE present to life!

Summary of Chapter 4

1. Humans are energy! Energy emanates around and through the Body;

2. The Fourth Principle represents the knowledge four years prior to being diagnosed with an illness or disease, a traumatic incident occurred bringing forth past buried emotional feelings while linking with physical toxins;

3. Emotional and physical toxins reduce the energy of the Body as well as the Energy Field. Remember, eighty percent of illness or disease is trapped emotional feelings;

4. Energy healing is the oldest, safest and most accessible healing in the world. The Body is designed to heal itself;

5. Look in each moment to those who enter one's Energy Field and connect with one to transport or receive information. That is the journey and the way energy flows from one to another. To attain a higher flow, one must transform as a caterpillar to a butterfly;

6. It is not the time one spends on earth, it is what one succeeds in accomplishing that matters;

7. Plant food that grows above ground before the full moon. Plant food that grows below ground after the full moon;

8. Before technology evolved that would allow one to "see" into the ground, people depended on dowsing (also known as divining or water witching) to find water wells, metals, gemstones, even missing people and unmarked graves;

9. Energy Response Testing is an art and used when an answer cannot be found any other way;

10. Essential oils, known as nature's living energy, are the natural, aromatic volatile liquids found in shrubs, flowers, trees, roots, bushes, and seeds;

11. Vibrations are everywhere in one's life and affect each moment. American inventor Royal Rife identified this when he invented a super microscope (31,000 x) where it was realized the blood, not the germ, is responsible for disease;

12. "Field," said Albert Einstein "is the only reality." He defined matter itself as simply denser and denser fields. One learns from quantum field science, everything in the universe is not only connected through the field, it is involved in a constant dialogue, regardless of distance or time. Everything, literally everything, speaks. Scientists call this phenomenon "quantum non-locality"; the mystics have simply called it "unity";

13. One's Body is in sync with the vibrations of where one lives. One can transform the energy of the food through prayer or other energy work. One is energy, and requires constant energy for life.

CHAPTER 5

Symptoms

"The Language of the Soul"

To be clear: symptoms are the Soul's language to identify an area of concern that is keeping one from living life fully. To live is not necessarily to live life. To BE is to live life. All symptoms are included, from the very small ones like stubbing a toe to the major ones like terminal cancer. Symptoms start out small and escalate as one continues to ignore inner self as well as the need to BE present in one's life.

Life is not simply breathing, eating, playing, working, loving, etc. The reason why the Soul came to earth in the physical form is around life purpose: BEing. BEing is who one is and what makes one joyful at a Soul level. At birth, unless trauma has occurred during conception or delivery, the qualities required to attain life purpose are present and clear. During childhood, qualities can be lost along with pieces of one's Soul, through traumatic experiences or what one perceives as traumatic. Some individuals can release the emotional feelings created by trauma effectively and others cannot. It is these feelings that have been put away that forge the base of illness or disease. As a human being, one is meant to feel and BE, not just exist and do.

The Energy Field that surrounds the Body extends in normal circumstances to the distance of one's outstretched arms around and above one. This Energy Field protects the Body as an egg white protects the yolk of an egg. Emotional feelings can become trapped in organs of the Body, thus creating static in the Energy Field. This static weakens a portion of the Field and interrupts its ability to protect the Body. The Spirit stays in the Body due to this Energy Field and when it is weakened, takes action along with the Soul to ensure emotional feelings are released while qualities lost are reclaimed. This is done via symptoms.

Nothing in life is an accident! Did one stub a toe today? Hit one's head? Cut one's finger? What was one not present to? Be present to life. Release the emotional feelings buried from the past, so one can live here, now, in the present. Humans are meant to BE in the present eighty-five percent of the time; in the past five percent; and in the future ten percent.

Symptoms appear in one's life to reveal the need for being present.

"The significant problems we have cannot be solved at the same level of thinking with which we created them." Albert Einstein

Indicators of Imbalance

Endocrine System imbalance includes internal glands that secrete essential hormones (pineal, hypothalamus, pituitary, thyroid, parathyroid, thymus, adrenals, pancreas, ovary and testis.) Toxins can block energy pathways for these glands to perform optimally.

Insufficient Essential Fatty Acids (EFA's) will affect cell membranes and hormone function, as well as play a major role in depleting the immune system. There is no substitute for EFA's.

Toxicity includes heavy metals (aluminum, cadium, copper, lead, mercury, caffeine, chlorine, fluoride, nicotine) which block pathways for elimination, hormone secretion and nutritional absorption. Cells hold memory as well as toxins.

Lack of nutrients such as protein, Vitamins A, B1, B2, Niacin, B6, B12, Biotin, choline, folic acid, P.A.B.A., Pantothenic Acid, C, D, E and minerals; calcium, chromium, iodine, iron, magnesium, manganese, potassium, selenium, plus zinc all reduce the Body's ability to protect and heal.

Organs that need support include the stomach, spleen, liver, gall bladder, colon, lungs, kidneys, bladder and heart. Emotional feelings play an eighty percent role in weakening their pathways.

Water Dehydration: the cells of the Body are like sponges and it takes time to become hydrated when given the proper amount of water. Joints require fluid to be in motion. Seventy-five percent of the Body is water and the brain eighty-five percent.

Science has discovered that humans were 'designed' to live between one hundred twenty and one hundred fifty years. However, given the poor quality of nutrition plus drinking water, as well as the ever-increasing levels of stress in the modern world, that range has been shortened by at least one-third or more. The human Body also has to deal with an onslaught of toxins, which after centuries of 'progress' has lead to record levels of cancer and heart disease in an all too toxic Western world.

Research has found that certain changes take place in the Body when it gets too little or too much of a given nutrient. By studying "Soul language" via the Body's symptoms, one can determine deficiencies or excess of specific vitamins, minerals, proteins, or other factors. The use of consistent patterns can be significant in determining deficiencies and the underlying cause.

Symptoms are warning signs

If ignored, misunderstood, covered up by medications or removed via surgery, symptoms could easily develop into a more serious disease process.

Seldom do sufferers look for the root cause of illness, disease or pain within the Body. Rather, they search for ways to cover those symptoms.

Taking time to stop, look and listen carefully to the Body is a process that can be carried out on a regular basis. Each Body is unique, and time must be set aside to ensure that one's health is a priority. A person is worth more than a set of tires! It is not unusual to spend more time, energy as well as money on a vehicle than on the Body that will carry an individual through years of life. Make today count!!

"Nature is the healer of disease"
(Hippocrates, 460-377 BC)

All forms of healing modalities use the same basic principle: to work with energy within or around the physical Body. The choice made is similar to working with a specialist in conventional realms. The Body has quite a few ways to clarify imbalance.

Symptoms are the most prominent. Other ways include Live Blood Analysis, Hair Analysis, Iridology, Pulse and Tongue Analysis, Bio-meridian testing (many varieties of this), N.A.E.T., Energy Response Testing, Blood and Urine tests, and pH for urine as well as saliva.

A Naturopath's or Naturotherapist's practice revolves around health problems that do not depend upon a diagnosis. People consulting with one of these practitioners usually get to keep their free will, as they educate and work with the whole person. The best conventional or natural health practitioner is one who will teach, plant seeds and let each person be engaged in his or her own wellness is the right choice.

Natural health practitioners can sometimes be just symptom orientated, therefore it is necessary to ask questions which ensure the person guiding is also working with the initial cause of the symptoms. Dr. Richard Schultz a Guru of natural healing from the seventies believes as I do, that there is no such thing as "incurable". When Dr. Schultz was practicing, he was very strict with protocols and whether they were followed or not. He had a waiting list of clients, and felt that if one of them chose not to follow a protocol, then that person's appointment time could be given to another who would. He now owns and operates the American Botanical Pharmacy at www.800herbdoc.com and The School of Natural Healing at www.snh.cc

**"The Universe is so compassionate; it allows you to draw on
what you need in order to heal yourself."
(O Magazine, March 2008)**

The part one does not realize is the connection to God (Universe) as well as the ability one has to ask for help and receive. It can never be about the money, material things or even wellness, instead what having them would do in a positive way for self first, then others. One also has to be grateful for current blessings and express this gratitude to God. When was the last time one looked at what one really has or gave thanks? For a day, see what one can attract. Start small with a parking place, then a person, item or opportunity. If a person is authentic and totally connected to God, one has the ability to receive and give in balance. To do this requires doing, BEing and giving thanks.

**"Where can disease come from when the emotional state
maintains inner composure?"
Canon of Medicine (Nei Jing)**

List of Common Symptoms

Liver Dysfunction

Anxiety, panic attacks, depression	Constant gas and bloating
Yellow or gray stool, foul odour	Nausea or headaches
Liver spots on hands and face	Constipation
Oily nose or forehead	Dark under eyes
White or yellow nails	Ascites or edema
Degenerative eye disease	Heavy or no menstruation
High cholesterol	Cysts, hemorrhoids, polyps
Difficulty swallowing	

Toxins

High or low blood pressure	Kidney disease
Hair loss, skin issues	Cramps or abdominal issues
Tremors	Diabetes
Memory issues	Loss of appetite
Frequent urination	Bone & joint pain, numbness, neuropathy
Diarrhea or constipation	Migraines
Allergies	Auto immune disease
Bladder infections	Anxiety, panic attacks, depression

Vitamins/Mineral Deficiency

Poor night vision	Dry eyes or cataracts
Warts, edema, dizziness	Sleep disturbances
Inflamed or itchy skin	Anemia or loss of appetite
Graying hair	Mood disorders, depression
Ruptured blood vessels	Loose or sensitive teeth
Cuticle tears	Fatigue
Joint pain, leg cramps, restless	Memory issues
Brittle nails, hair	Heart palpitations
Sore or swollen tongue	

Endocrine System Blocked Energy

Flu or infections	Motion sickness
Neck, head and shoulder pain	Shingles
Cold hands or feet	Overweight
Slow healing or little finger pain	Emotional
Fatigue	Kidney stones, bone spurs, cataracts, dowager hump or arthritis

Parasites

Children have blisters in mouth and on lower lip	Grinding of teeth
Chronic fatigue	Immune dysfunction
Constipation or diarrhea	Gas and bloating
Anemia	Allergies or nervousness
Unexplained rash	Drooling while sleeping
Epilepsy	Crohns or Colitis

Low Water Consumption

Asthma or allergies	Acid reflux and digestion issues
Ulcers	Headaches
High blood pressure	Constipation
Mental disorders	Edema or congestive heart disease
Degenerative disease	Stress
Joint pain and weak back	Diabetes
Colitis pain	Kidney stress

Symptoms can sometimes intertwine. For example, too many toxins will block liver and spleen function thus, keep protein from absorbing correctly. This can cause ascites, which is the accumulation of serous fluid in the abdomen. The liver meridian channel passes through the breasts and can attribute to breast cancer. Regulating liver qi has the effect of relaxing an anxious mental state, thus increasing the immune function so the Body can resist cancer. *(See liver support in Appendix E.)*

When Seasonal Affective Disorder (often called S.A.D.) occurs, the Soul needs adjustment since the Body is not storing enough light (energy). Food represents trapped sunlight and nourishes the Body as oxygen is delivered. Removing both emotional and physical toxins, strengthening cells with Essential Fatty Acids as well as getting the proper nutrients can resolve this issue. Light supports vision, and without vision it supports old habits plus closed off beliefs. Positive affirmations are a great way to dispel old habits and beliefs.

Acid Reflux

Medication is prescribed for a condition called Acid Reflux or Gerd that covers the symptom. Acid Reflux medication has the ability to inhibit the absorption of iron and create another symptom: anemia. Inflammation or anger is the emotional feeling involved with Acid Reflux, with a little guilt, therefore liver and heart related.

Acid Reflux is related to the Body having toxins and therefore unable to produce enough Hydrochloric Acid (HCl). Without sufficient HCl, food is unable to digest properly, thus extending the time in the stomach. In turn, this creates fermentation and an acidic response, causing acid to travel up the esophagus. Scar tissue can be created if this happens on a regular basis.

Removal of toxins has the ability to increase the normal production of hydrochloric acid, thus removing the original symptom. Doctors are partially right when they state that low hydrochloric acid is due to the aging process. The part they have not recognized is the relationship to toxins as they accumulate with age, and their ability to stop the natural process of hydrochloric acid. While one is removing toxins via a detoxification process, organic apple cider vinegar can be taken at the start of a meal to take the place of the hydrochloric acid until such time as it is again plentiful. The vinegar needs to include the mother in the bottle; the "mother" is made of living nutrients and bacteria. One can actually see it settled in the bottom of the bottle like sediment.

Vertical lines on the fingernails identify a digestion issue usually created by too many toxins in the Body reducing the ability to digest food properly. These lines are due to the lack of nutrients being received through the cells because of this whole process. They will disappear as the toxins are removed and digestion is brought back to normal. Supplements are just that, and once balance is restored, they are no longer necessary.

Eating is a process that requires a relaxed state. It is beneficial to abstain from reading, studying, watching T.V. or moving while ingesting. Enzymes work more efficiently that way. Worry can also keep one from digesting effectively. Saying grace at a meal is meant to calm and relax one before a meal. Meditation will also work.

Each symptom the Body projects can be taken deeper until the cause is located. Sometimes this happens immediately, and occasionally there are quite a few symptoms that have accumulated over time. In trying to find the cause, remember that taking over the counter medication or prescriptions hide symptoms.

One example is the gallbladder. Every year millions of people have their gallbladder removed when they are experiencing symptoms. The cause is usually related to insufficient essential fatty acids needed to break down saturated fat in the Body. Toxins in the Body cause an imbalance in the parathyroid creating a lack of calcium absorption, which in turn can irritate a blocked bile duct while also forming stones. These stones and the hardened saturated fat block gallbladder function.

Symptoms Relative to Organs

Gall Bladder

The medical term for gall stones is cholelithiasis. Chole is from the Greek meaning "bile". Lithos is "stone" and iasis is "condition of". So it is the condition of having bile stones. The usual center of gallstones is a mixture of cholesterol, bilirubin and calcium. These stones can be black, red, white, green, or tan-colored. The most common found during a flush is a pea-green color, which contain the highest concentration of cholesterol and are generally soft. As the stones grow and become more numerous, they clog the tubing, creating back pressure on the liver, causing it to make less bile. The back-up of bile can cause jaundice, which gives a yellow coloring to the skin and the whites of the eyes.

More symptoms

- Indigestion after eating, especially fatty or greasy foods.
- Nausea or dizziness.
- Bloating, gas, burping or belching.
- Feeling of fullness or food not digesting.
- Diarrhea (or alternating from soft to watery) or Constipation.
- Headache over eyes, especially the right eye.
- Bitter fluid comes up after eating.
- High Blood Pressure or Adrenal stress.
- Potassium low and Sodium high.
- Weight gain—obesity.
- Pain in the right shoulder.

Attacks often occur at night after overeating. Discomfort or pain will often, however not always, follow a meal with fats or grease. Pain may be worse with deep inhalation

Attacks can last from 15 minutes to 15 hours!

Harsh, bitter feelings toward oneself or others will create a hardening of saturated fat in the gallbladder, creating stones. Stones can lodge in a bile duct interacting with nerves, and can cause discomfort or pain in the right shoulder blade and neck area, specifically if the emotional feeling is about feeling burdened. Irritation from gallstones can also affect the pancreas, causing shingles, hypoglycemia, and insulin issues. A stone will interfere with the pituitary gland, thus creating pain in the base of the head, and neck.

A weak gallbladder can also affect hearing. The kidneys play a role in hearing as well. What does one not want to hear? Sometimes, this includes listening to one's inner self. Shutting out the sounds of laughter, due to a misguided feeling of responsibility and work ethic may cause an individual to believe that fun is not allowed. Doubt is the main emotional feeling of the gallbladder, which can delay decision making.

Beets may help to both thin and move the bile as well as to metabolize fats. Beets are an excellent source of betaine, which helps support healthy liver and aids in gall bladder function as well as digestion. They should be eaten in moderation, in other words, no more than four times weekly. It is good to remember that eating beets can cause the urine as well as feces to be red, and not to be concerned or alarmed.

Removing the gallbladder does not always reduce symptoms. In order to break down and digest fats, the Body must produce bile, which is done in the liver. The gallbladder is merely a sac for holding some of the bile that the liver produces. Whether or not a person had his or her gallbladder removed, the liver is still producing bile in order to digest fats. Without the gallbladder, however, the bile is not as readily secreted in the Body, and the liver can become overwhelmed when faced with large amounts of any fats, especially saturated or hydrogenated fats. For some people even small amounts of fats can cause discomfort.

Symptoms after gall bladder removal

- Dumping of bile which is now not as easily regulated and can send someone running to the bathroom immediately after eating. (diarrhea)
- A decrease in the secretion of bile.
- Bile produced by the liver can become thick along with sluggish, painful symptoms and bile stones can form.
- Large amounts of fats can also collect in the colon and block the absorption of vital nutrients.
- Weight gain.

It is in the best interest of the Body to ensure that enough essential fatty acids are present to break down fat and prevent the build-up of gallstones. *(An Easy Gallbladder Flush can be found in Appendix F.)*

Statistics

"A moderately increased risk of colorectal cancer in patients was noted in those who have undergone gallbladder removal." stated Dr. Yutaka Yamaji, University of Tokyo, Japan.

Liver and its 500 Functions

Some of the most important functions include:

Producing quick energy:

One of the liver's most important functions is to break down food and convert it into energy when that is needed. Carbohydrates such as bread and potatoes included in one's diet are broken down to glucose then stored mainly in the liver as well as muscles as glycogen. When energy is required in an emergency, the liver rapidly converts its store of glycogen back into glucose ready for the Body to use.

People with liver damage may sometimes lose the ability to control glucose concentration in the blood. They need a regular supply of natural sugar until toxins have been removed and the Body has returned to normal.

The liver also helps the Body to get rid of waste products. Waste products not excreted by the kidneys are removed from the blood by the liver. Some of them pass into the duodenum and then into the bowel via the bile ducts.

Fighting infections:

The liver plays a vital role in fighting infections, particularly those arising in the bowel. It does this by mobilizing part of the Body's defense mechanism called the macrophage system. The liver contains over half of the Body's supply of macrophages, known as Kuppfer cells. These cells literally destroy any bacteria with which they come in contact. Parasites and/or yeast in the colon plus a weakened liver via toxins are the cause of Crohns and Colitis.

A few daily functions of the liver:

- Metabolizes proteins, fats, as well as carbohydrates, to provide energy and nutrients. <u>Symptoms of distress</u>: digestive disorders, constipation, heavy menses, skin rashes, and more . . .
- Stores vitamins, minerals and sugars. A distressed liver could result in diabetes or hypoglycemia.
- Filters the blood and helps remove harmful chemicals, drugs and bacteria.
- Creates bile, which breaks down fats. Bile is then stored in the gallbladder.
- Seat of cholesterol production and regulation. Distress and toxicity can create high cholesterol.
- Stores and assimilates fat-soluble vitamins A, E, D, plus K. The liver can store enough vitamin A to supply an adult's needs for up to four years and enough vitamin D and vitamin B12 to last for four months!
- Stores extra blood, which can be quickly released when needed. A distressed liver can cause excessive menstrual bleeding, lining deficiency of the womb causing miscarriage or tumors.
- Creates serum proteins, which maintain fluid balance.

The liver also

- Produces heat for the Body. Liver stress can mean one is too hot (Yang) or too cold (Yin)!
- Liver distress can mean frequent headaches related to tension and stress or from eyestrain. Eye disease is a sign of liver stress.
- Skin problems; including acne and psoriasis, brittle nails, weak tendons, ligaments and muscles could point to liver distress.
- Catchexia is a muscle wasting disease that results from cancer and is intensified by chemotherapy. Fifty percent of individuals with this disease die. Spirulina is a natural algae that can prevent this from occurring. Catchexia is due to a toxic liver.
- Helps maintain electrolyte and water balance.
- Creates immune substances, such as gamma globulin.
- Breaks down and eliminates excess hormones.

Too many hormones in the Body has been linked to:

- Increased risk of gallbladder disease; production of clots and inflammation in the blood vessels; high blood pressure; hypoglycemia; breast, uterine, liver and vaginal cancer; emotional swings; food cravings; PMS along with hot flashes; anxiety, panic attacks and depression. The liver will process excess hormones when balanced as well as prevent these from occurring.

Excessive testosterone has been linked to:

- Over-aggressiveness; extreme mood swings; abnormal levels of sexual energy; dysfunction of reproductive cycle.

Toxins enter the Body via many pathways and over time can create a sluggish and distressed liver. The liver should gently press into the ribcage when one breathes, thus acting like a sponge. Toxins can cause the liver to lose its softness and become hard, creating pressure as well as sometimes pain in the right side rib area, center at sternum and back.

Toenails are also a good indicator of liver stress. If the white of the lunar moon is more than a quarter of the nail, the liver is in stress. Brown spots on the skin, specifically the hands, arms and face also relate to a stressed liver, as chemicals stain the skin when the liver's filtering action is not working up to par. The wonderful part about knowing this is that toxin removal and liver support can reverse these symptoms. One can have a large belly: a liver ledge so to speak, which is also an indicator of liver issues. Sciatica can also be related to a weak liver that is affecting muscles.

The liver looks after one's eyes, muscles, nerves and tendons, fingernails as well as aspects of the throat. It also controls the menstrual cycle and plays a major role in the reproductive process. For women, keeping the liver peaceful means the difference of excess blood during menstruation, miscarriages, fertility and mood swings. For men, especially the sporty type, a peaceful liver will prevent torn muscles, injured back, tinnitus and headaches. The emotional feelings that can attach to the liver are anger, frustration and irritation. Anger creates heat, which can affect the Body in many other ways, including acne (little spurts of anger), Rosacea (spurts of rage) and road rage is a severe burst of anger being released in spasms. Holding back anger over the years, combined with toxins in the Body, will cause reactions such as these.

Eyes are the other connection to the liver. Anger brings up the subconscious desire to not BE aware of the present. Anger blocks the connection to beauty and suppresses individual values. Combined with fear, anger will facilitate cataract growth, with the parathyroid playing a part. By itself, suppressed anger manifests macular degeneration. Glaucoma is not due to the liver.

The liver and gallbladder are in charge of life vision and decision making. When an individual is having difficulty in those areas, it's good to look for the emotional feelings which are connected, write a letter or letters to release the past by expressing while experiencing the emotional feelings, then forgiving-not the event; the person.

A vibration of anger will create a path for Parkinson's disease. When a person is vibrating or seething with anger and unable to release the rage, this illness can occur.

It brings up another story of a student that had Parkinson's disease. At the time she came to me I was starting to work with emotional feelings and facilitated a conversation regarding anger. Her reaction was startling in the fact she physically started to vibrate as she spoke of a relative in a situation from the past that was still acting out in the present. As well, even though this physical vibration was occurring, she was not noting the connection. Once recognized, she began to understand the connection of emotional feelings and physical illness or disease, a start on her journey to wellness.

Anger is meant to bring action and only develops into a negative response when an individual is unable to learn the lesson, move forward and release it. Damage to the Soul is at different levels and requires deeper vocation. To hold onto anger causes excess in life such as alcohol, drugs, material things as well as hording or clutter. One has often pushed the anger deep and does not feel angry or recognize it, which then facilitates the symptoms.

There are quite a few symptoms related to the liver alone. I have worked with individuals with cirrhosis of the liver, fatty tumors, cancer, high cholesterol, etc. and found with emotional and physical toxin removal, liver support, along with the release of blocked energy it regenerates, that illness and disease are history.

Lying down for ten minutes a few times a day can help support and energize the liver. Infrared heat applied directly to the organ will help. Eating larger meals earlier in the day; reducing or eliminating red meat; ingesting enough potassium through apples, potatoes, bananas, etc. is helpful. A castor oil pack works to gently re-generate the liver as it also detoxifies. (See Appendix I) Milk thistle combo tincture contains five herbs that cleanses the liver at a deeper level as well as repairs and is taken after meals. This protocol follows the three week protocol for castor oil and is complete when the bottle (50ml) has been taken. Severe cases such as liver cancer or cirrhosis of the liver require a further bottle.

I promote a progression of harmless removal which I hope other practitioners do as well. Applying a program of castor oil packs or milk thistle combo without first removing excess toxins via coffee enemas, ionic footbaths or infrared saunas, may push to many toxins into the blood stream and cause anxiety, depression, flu like symptoms, etc.

What one needs to understand is that names are given to symptoms in the form of illness and disease when one does not understand the pathway of toxins.

A toxin that people are not paying attention to these days is the new efficient light bulb: compact fluorescent (CFL). These bulbs contain mercury and are considered highly toxic even in very small amounts.

Should these bulbs be dropped, the loose mercury poses significant health risks. Vacuuming is not recommended, touching is harmful, as is breathing. When their life span is over, they are supposed to be disposed of at a hazardous waste depot.

Mercury build-up causes Autism, Alzheimer's, dementia and memory loss to name a few. The amount on the head of a pin is too toxic for a small child.

Fluorescent lights create an imbalance in the Energy Field of one's Body. Energy Response Testing is hard to achieve when one is standing beneath one of these lights. Yet, fluorescent lighting is found in classrooms where one is meant to have the energy to learn. Be aware of one's life; take action to protect as well as support in a positive way. LED lighting is a healthy choice.

Vitamins and Minerals

Calcium aids in equalizing the activities of the glandular forces as related to the circulation supplied through ends of nerve and blood supply, or the sympathetic circulations that aids principally in the return of the circulation when carried by the heart beat through the arteries and the deeper circulation. Especially as related to those glands, particularly the thyroid or those as related in part to the digestive system, and parts of those glands that cause these disturbances between the liver and kidneys; the glands that destroy or that use sugars in the Body. (Article 1727-2; Association for Research & Enlightenment True Health publication, October 2007)

So what does that mean when looking at symptoms? Calcium has a major influence on the health of the Body, not just in strengthening bones and teeth. Imbalance can affect glands, including the thyroid. Taking calcium does not always mean the Body is absorbing calcium at a healthy rate. Certain illnesses and diseases indicate an imbalance such as thyroid issues, enlarged prostrate, arthritis, or osteoporosis, cataracts, kidney stones, bone spurs or dowager hump. Toxins can interfere with the normal process of the parathyroid gland creating this response.

Other signs of calcium deficiency might be biting nails or having no half moons on the thumb and first two fingers.

Calcium should always be taken with magnesium. They are brother and sister in the Body. Calcium creates tension while magnesium provides relaxation in the arteries. One gets sufficient calcium through daily diet even without dairy products. In a diagnosis of osteoporosis, it is not excess calcium that is essential. Rather, toxin removal and support of the parathyroid are critical so calcium is again able to absorb into the bones and teeth. One could be taking calcium until the cows come home and not resolve the issue until the parathyroid has been supported. *(More information on this topic is included in the following Chapter.)*

BALANCE, nature's way to heal your body has extensive information on the importance of vitamin C and heart disease. When the vitamin is taken in excess, the Body will identify this by producing diarrhea. David Rowland has a wonderful patented product RTRE that contains high doses of vitamin C as well as a balance of other vitamins and minerals. This product works great in a protocol for individuals with a build-up of plaque related to heart disease, emphysema, diabetes and MS with its ability to melt the plaque in all the arteries, opening up the ability for blood to flow at a normal pace again. Cuticle tearing, plaque on teeth, loose or sensitive teeth are also an indication of low vitamin C. Smoking rapidly depletes vitamin C in the Body.

Potassium is essential for a well balanced liver as it holds up to thirty-three percent of the Body's volume. Salt (sodium) is potassium's twin. Too much of one will cause the other to reduce. When cancer is present in the Body, it is best to avoid salt and increase potassium levels to support the liver; it is not uncommon that potassium levels in the liver are low in conjunction with cancer. The liver and spleen both are energetically blocked by emotional and physical toxins for cancer to grow.

Bananas have potassium however potatoes and apples have a greater quantity. A lack of potassium will negatively affect kidney function, yet those individuals on dialysis are advised to reduce intake of this mineral. This is a contradiction of natural balance.

The cause of low blood pressure is the kidney. As noted below, to switch the symptom of malaise, sea salt (sodium) with water can shift this feeling while one works on fear and toxins.

Himalayan sea salt has a wonderful array of minerals that can enhance the Body's function. If one owns a reverse osmosis system that takes the minerals out of the water, a few sprinkles of Himalayan sea salt will create a healthy balance in the water. Some larger hotel chains, such as the Intercontinental Hotel in Toronto are now introducing this salt into their hot tubs and pools. Swimming in this water is like swimming through silk. It revitalizes one's weary Body.

Kidneys

Traditional Chinese Medicine teaches that the kidneys are not just there for filtering out toxins. They are the seat of procreation, the vitality center of the Body, the clarity of one's thinking, and the ability to regenerate one's Body.

The kidney's system supports the Body's reproductive organs: ovaries, uterus, testicles, prostate and the reproductive material: sperm plus ovum, as well as reproductive activity: sexual impulse, ovulation, ejaculation, fertilization, gestation.

The kidneys are defined as essential to the Body's youthful vitality!

The kidneys are responsible for development and regulation of the brain. The spinal cord, bones, teeth, blood, and head hair are all engendered by the kidney. They also support joints. Kidneys activate vitamin D in the Body and play a part in acid or alkaline balance as well as electrolyte balance with the absorption of magnesium.

The kidneys regulate the balance and circulation of the liquid substances in the Body, including tears, saliva, mucus, urine, sweat, cerebrospinal fluid, synovial fluid, plasma, and semen. The kidneys work with the liver to produce tears, with the lung plus spleen for mucus, as well as the heart for sweat.

Fear and shame are the most frequent emotional feelings experienced in this century. The kidneys hold these emotional feelings and when in play will stop the process of magnesium absorption, cause muscle spasms, palpitations of the heart, cramping toes, restless legs, and Charlie horses. High and low blood pressure, are also proponents of this emotional feeling's effect on the kidneys. Kidneys affected by fear or shame reduce the function of regulating the pancreas. When this is accompanied by the loss of the sweetness of life, diabetes may occur.

Kidney disease and failure occur when this feeling is held within the Body for too long. The blood stops cleansing properly and the Body starts to destroy itself via uric acid, inflammation, anemia and infection. Far Infrared saunas are a natural means to cleanse the blood. The fear can be of concern for someone such as a sick family member. Don't fight fear when in it, when calm and safe call it up. It is one's choice to move the energy of fear or hold it. It is not weak to have fear, only to hold on to it. Knowledge will set fear free.

Glaucoma is a part of the feeling of shame projected via the kidney. Shame has different levels, such as who or what an individual has not attained to, or something that was done to them or by them to another that does not fit their values, standards or boundaries. It may also be a perception that others see the individual or the family as inferior in some way. Peripheral vision (side vision) goes first, literally shutting down the ability to see what is around one. This reaction is a form of the subconscious protecting one from hurt and harm.

Traditional Chinese Medicine teaches that a weak or damaged kidney/bladder system can produce:

- Growth and development issues, including problems of fertility, conception, as well as during pregnancy;
- Multiple sclerosis, muscular dystrophy, and cerebral palsy; all relating to the central nervous system;
- Disorders of fluid metabolism including lymph fluid;
- Soreness and pain of lumbar-sacral region;
- Loose teeth plus weakness of hearing;

- Diseases of spinal column, bones, teeth and joints;
- Thinning or loss of head hair or premature graying;
- Weakness as well as pain of ankles, knees, and hips;
- Restless legs, Charlie Horse, cramping toes and fingers, as well as palpitation of the heart;
- Impotence, infertility, habitual miscarriage, genetic impairments, menstrual cramps and spasms;
- Loss of vitality and susceptibility to cold, inadequate sleep along with premature aging;
- High or low blood pressure.

Kidney stones can be derived from different substances: calcium oxalate, uric acid, cystine, or xanthine. Infection or dehydration can cause these to occur, as well as toxins which create an issue with the parathyroid therefore blocking the absorption of calcium. Fear or shame via the kidney can block the absorption of magnesium, also creating a magnesium and calcium imbalance.

Any edema of the knees, legs or ankles would require a kidney cleanse-emotionally and physically.

Kidney & Bladder Cleanse:

Watermelon seed tea taken three times a week is recommended by Edgar Cayce. Pour one pint of boiling water over ground or cut seeds, and steep (fresh each time). This will stimulate underactive kidneys, as well as cleanse and remove stones.

A whole watermelon can also be juiced: rind, seeds and fruit, using a quarter of a melon with a quarter of a bunch of parsley. Drink a sixteen ounce glass a day for three days.

Celery Seed Tea (Apuim Graveolens) is recommended by Dr. Hulda Clark. It is potent for kidney stones, chronic kidney disease, arthritis or diabetes as it increases elimination of water and speeds up accumulated toxins from the joints. The diuretic action affects the pancreas along with production of insulin as well as helps decrease the oversupply of uric acid (gout).

Notes:

- Celery contains large amounts of potassium and organic sodium. It stimulates skin, bowel, along with the kidney; re-balances alkaline levels; is good for gripe, flatulence, visceral spasms and flow of breast milk. Celery with dandelion can increase liver plus kidney toxin removal. It is also an antifungal if taken three times daily.
- Do not use in large quantity for kidney disorders. Take only for a short duration such as three days. After a break of several weeks, take again if symptoms return.
- Not recommended for pregnant women.
- Treats appetite loss and exhaustion as well.
- A tablespoon (15ml) of baking soda in water once daily for approximately thirty days will reduce abundance of lactic acid and also facilitate healing of the kidneys.

Two Naturopathic doctors in Australia put together a wonderful protocol that includes a tea that has the ability to repair the kidney and help return its vital functions. The tea is recommended for individuals with kidney impairment, and diabetes; the recipe is available online with the purchase of their book. Please use a natural practitioner as support while taking this product. *(See Resources in back of book for contact information.)*

Recently while attending Acupuncture classes, I experienced symptoms confirmed via my pulse and tongue, which indicated a deficiency involving kidneys. One symptom was the inability to retain fluid, thus pointing to bladder issues. The skin appeared fragile; there were excess wrinkles, and what one considers old age basically, when enough fluid was not being retained by my skin layers.

The lungs played a part in this as they work with the spleen which looks after transformation and transportation of fluid in the Body. The feelings involved were fear (left kidney), grief (left lung) and abandonment indicated via Energy Response Testing; the left side indicates a female involvement and a quick test identified it was about myself. The emotional toxins trapped in these three organs <u>together</u> facilitate lymphoma if physical toxins are present.

Another symptom was pain in my left knee when I walked upstairs. The muscles there are linked to the kidney function as well. The pain I felt was guilt related, as pain anywhere in the Body is always guilt. All of this was current in my life since opening the larger center, due to my inner reaction to financial issues. Reversal of symptoms required my being authentic professionally as well as personally along with a little help from Acupuncture, Energy Response Testing as well as Energy Balance Harmony. Natural health practitioners are not immune to holding emotional feelings or facilitating blocks in the Body that create symptoms, as we are also human beings. The opposite of fear or shame is gentleness and understanding, something I had not been towards self for a long while.

Adrenal Glands

<u>Definition:</u>

The adrenal glands are seated on top of each kidney, and are part of the Endocrine System. They are the internally secreting or ductless glands, which release their secretions directly into the blood stream.

The adrenals, often referred to as the suprarenal, are the Creator's most intricate chemical factories. "It would take acres of chemical plants" to synthetically manufacture "the fifty odd hormones or hormone-like substances" produced by the adrenal glands. (Ratcliff, 1975, p. 69) Not only do these hormones control all the oxidation processes of the human Body through the anterior pituitary Body, they also regulate growth, mental balance, sexual development and maintenance, plus a host of other phenomena. The adrenals, the pituitary, and the thyroid are functionally united.

THE ADRENALS ARE ABSOLUTELY ESSENTIAL TO LIFE!

A story I like to repeat took place a couple of years ago. I was at a book signing in Saint John, N.B., approximately two hours from my home. James had purchased a Mustang the previous year "a man-o-pause reaction to life". On the day of the signing, our business vehicle was already travelling to PEI for individual sessions, so it was necessary for me to take the Mustang. Although November, there was no sign of bad weather when I left home, however there was a fair amount of snow from days before. Leaving Saint John later in the evening was another matter.

Rain came down heavily most of the day and by the time I was to drive home, had frozen on the ground. Even though the tires were fairly new, the Mustang did not act great on ice. It took over two hours to drive half the distance home so I stopped in Moncton for a break and a little Christmas shopping and purchased a karaoke machine for my husband as a gift. The trunk of a Mustang is not meant to carry large purchases, as well as with only two doors it was not possible to place the gift in the back seat. I then put it in the front on the passenger seat. One can imagine my thoughts at this point, if not before, of the impracticality of this vehicle as a second car for someone who had to travel like I do.

I tried to adjust the vehicle's seat, and hit the button for taking the top down. Whoops! I could not put the windows in the back up. At this point, I basically cursed the vehicle; a double whammy by now. I got help from a staff member at Costco and without clearing any negativity, left the parking lot. Remember, nothing in life is an accident; they are created by negative thoughts.

As I left the ramp to enter the highway, the vehicle took on a mind of its own. As I reached the highway, I lost control on the ice. The car leaped ahead then turned in circles a few times and proceeded across the road into a deep ditch. No cars were on the highway, so no one had noticed that I went into the ditch. The snow covered the front end and up to the windows on the driver side. The karaoke machine was heavy and I was unable to move it to get to the passenger door.

To complete this scenario, my cell phone had no power and I was wearing a long skirt. The only way out was through the window and the snow came up almost to my waist. The deep snow created a slow climb to the road and once there a car stopped to help. The driver called the police and had me wait in the car with his wife. I was quite distraught at this point so let him take charge of the situation. Once in the vehicle, I called my husband with their cell phone to arrange for him to come and get me as I was quite emotional. A few minutes later, I realized what was happening: my adrenals were off. The stress of the moment as well as the additional hormones to get me out of the vehicle to the road depleted energy to my adrenals.

I apologized to the lady in the car and explained that what I was going to do might seem strange. I proceeded to place my hand over my belly button (adrenal energy area) and tap my head, breathing in and out while panting: Energy Balance Harmony. Repeating this a few times helped regain my composure, so I called James and asked him not to come. I explained that I would get a ride with the tow truck driver and then left the vehicle to talk with the police. No more tears. Common sense was back, low back pain was gone. The tow truck driver and I discussed natural medicine on the way home as I gave him some information to help a few relatives. Amazing! It is as simple as that.

Hawthorne berries produce natural adrenalin. Low adrenalin can weaken the Body and support hernia manifestation. Hawthorne is a wonderful support for this. Black licorice is a great supplement to the adrenals (except for people with high blood pressure). About every five hours, the adrenals need some sort of nourishment in order to continue supplying strength to the Body. If a meal or some other nourishment is not forthcoming, black licorice can supply the adrenals.

Hypoglycemia and hyperglycemia involve the breakdown of the adrenal glands as well as the pancreas. The pancreas doesn't work alone; it is assisted by the pituitary, thyroid and adrenal glands as well as the spleen, liver plus kidneys.

Dr. John Christopher has a formula he used for years, with success in all age groups from children to elderly patients. The formula is as follows: Cedar berries sixteen parts to one part of each of the following: golden seal root, uva ursi, cayenne, licorice root and mullein.

A simple release of blocked energy and work on the resentment that has occurred in one's life adds to the balance. Passion flower tincture or tea will help as well and is a good product to have when one wishes to diminish the adrenal tire around the belly as is vitamin C and omegas. This should take sixty days if one is working daily to resolve emotional feelings, toxins as well as nourish the adrenals. Root vegetables support the adrenals as well.

Lower back ache may also be adrenal related. When the adrenals are stressed with positive or negative experiences, they can dry out and twist, creating lower back pain. A number of years ago, one of my students had gone to a chiropractor at least thirty times to no avail. After Energy Response Testing, an indication of blocked energy was located in the adrenals and released with Energy Balance Harmony *(see Appendix C)*. It took less than five minutes for the whole process from Energy Response Testing to release, and the back pain stopped. Believe: it is simple.

Bladder

The bladder starts energetically at the third eye (between the eyebrows) and governs the nervous system. A bright future along with hope is the positive aspects of this organ being in balance. Being distressed at someone or something (pissed off) affects this organ negatively. When an individual is genuinely in anguish about a situation, the feeling will affect the bladder and weaken its ability to hold on to fluid. Basically, if a person questions the fact that he or she will eventually be okay, his or her bladder function will be affected.

Symptoms include incontinence, the need for urination yet only a small amount will occur, or bladder infections. Too little water consumption can also create incontinence as the Body tries to flush toxins that have accumulated due to dehydration. Kidney stones can contribute as well, so fear or shame may play a part. Stones are sharp and can scratch the urinary tract while leaving the Body creating an opportunity for infection. This can also create small amounts of blood in the urine and pressure to urinate often.

Spleen

The spleen is found on the left side of the Body; opposite the liver, and is involved with the production of blood, as well as the transportation plus transformation of blood. The spleen is a partner with the stomach and supports the liver; therefore, symptoms in these parts of the Body can be related to anger. Minor incidents can be related to worry as well, due to the relationship with the stomach and process of nutrients.

The main emotional feelings connected to the spleen are abandonment and loneliness. These feelings are predominant in adopted or fostered children as well as adults. They also affect children of a divorce or someone who has lost a loved one through death, whether an aging parent or younger sibling, etc. Living in a household with an alcoholic parent or partner can also facilitate feelings of abandonment or loneliness. Feelings affecting both the heart and spleen in combination will affect the brain.

Thickening in the hip and upper thigh area is one symptom indicating the spleen needs nurturing. Deficiency of B12 or symptoms of not digesting protein is also an indicator of a weakened spleen. All individuals with cancer have a spleen issue to resolve.

The spleen is situated at the center of the five organ networks. As soon as there is an irregular intake of food and drink or overexertion of any kind, the spleen qi (energy) will be harmed. It is most important to consume food at the appropriate time, to drink fluids in regular intervals, as well as to avoid both overeating and hunger pains. Then not only the spleen/stomach network will remain unspoiled and function perfectly, the organ networks will also all be in harmony. The spleen likes room temperature food and beverage, not cold.

Tenderness, approximately one hand width under the armpit, can indicate spleen stress. Red areas that are tender on the upper diaphragm, face or ear can be related to spleen with lung deficiency as well. When the lungs are energetically blocked by emotional or physical toxins, they stop working in conjunction with other organs such as the spleen and the kidneys.

A bunion is related to spleen stress, as a bunion sits on the meridians for spleen two and three. To understand symptoms, a person needs to realize that it takes more than one symptom to project the cause as in this case. The bunion could have started due to a weakness in that meridian or the spleen could be weak due to the bunion. Other factors need to be looked at, that is why it is important to look at the whole Body.

For example, I have two bunions, one on each foot with the left being more predominant. I have had one for at least twenty years. I recognize when they must have started and when they take spurts in growth. In 1998, James wanted to start his own business and in my own mind I had wanted to start one a number of years prior. We both could have, yet I stopped moving forward to let him step up. In life, supporting another is important, however not at the expense of one's self. One cannot live life through another. Each person is unique and here for a reason. The time is now to step up to life.

While writing this book, I am currently focusing on the spleen, liver, kidney, and parathyroid to reverse the past in the form of bunions. It will take about six months to dissolve if I put myself first on a daily basis. This will be the test. My goal is to wear high heels again.

A bunion is basically congealed phlegm and excess calcium that has hardened along the spleen meridian in the foot, applying pressure over time. A combination of emotional feelings and various physical circumstances can lead to this. A gallstone that has blocked a bile duct will reduce liver function. Add to this consumption of high concentrations of sugar, which create dampness in the Body. The spleen is depleted of energy trying to resolve this. With the spleen being compromised, transportation and transformation of fluid is diminished in the Body, which affects the lymphatic system as well as the flow of toxins leaving the Body. The parathyroid, which is part of the Endocrine System, can be blocked energetically from the toxins, thus stopping absorption of calcium in the bones leaving it free to form with the congealed phlegm caused due to the dampness. This combination can cause unstable insulin, diabetes, pancreatic cancer, allergies, and more along with a bunion.

The kidney can play a part too, as the spleen helps the kidney. When fear or shame are present, magnesium absorption creates further excess calcium. Joint pain and arthritic symptoms thus become a part of the package of symptoms. Once all these aspects have been checked via Energy Response Testing, TCM or Bio-meridian machine, or simply by the symptoms available, it is easy to reverse.

Surgery for the bunion weakens the spleen and only resolves the symptom. The cause will over time re-produce another bunion (symptom). See the next chapter for a bunion protocol.

Every symptom has a purpose. What would the Soul be telling a person with bunions? The feet have to do with standing for who one is and what one does, in other words, standing on one's own two feet. Fear of the future has a part to play in that, so the kidneys take a part.

Varicose veins are also spleen related. Strengthen the spleen and one strengthens arteries along with veins, thus reversing this disfiguring reaction on the legs.

"Tumors are phlegm and undigested dead cells (protein) within the Body that have hardened over time due to a weak spleen as well as lack of communication (energy) between the spleen and the liver." Susan Manion MacDonald

The spleen, heart and brain work together in combination to shut down the memory process, creating diseases such as Alzheimer. A move away from home can also cause issues with the spleen if an attachment was negatively developed. Love of one's family and home are important, yet when a person or place becomes an attachment then it hinders growth and possibilities. Releasing the attachment does not reduce love, instead it strengthens it. Again, the written or spoken word will release this negative response.

Stomach

To worry can become obsessive. A person may then become clingy to anything out of desperation and will exhaust Spirit over time, as well as a relationship. Candida (yeast) is emotionally connected to an obsessive behavior. Worry can facilitate low hydrochloric acid (HCl) which is necessary to mulch food particles. Food held in the stomach longer than normal, ferments creating a rising of acid causing acid reflux, heartburn, gas, and bloating. Medications reduce the fermentation; however they do not resolve the low HCl and over time the stomach along with the small intestine produce more negative symptoms.

The opposite of worry is trust; once trust is established calm will occur in the stomach creating digestive harmony. The spleen also works in conjunction with the stomach and if the spleen is impaired will lower production of mucous necessary for lining the stomach and protecting it from acids. When this happens the stomach is open to ulcers and h-plori. The removal of emotional and environmental toxins for both organs will bring back balance.

As with all the organs, there are many illnesses and diseases that can be attached. Again, remember that each illness as well as disease is a name given to symptoms plus are a message from the Soul. Do not be fearful of the name. Understand the pathway it follows to resolve it and BE healthy.

Let's take nausea, for example. There are many reasons that nausea can occur. Too many stones in the gall bladder can create this, and so can a deficiency of zinc in the Body. Calcium deposits in the ears from an imbalance in the parathyroid can result in nausea. Low amylase, an enzyme used in the Body to digest carbohydrates, can also create this feeling. Lack of good bacteria in the sinus cavity can cause an imbalance in the mouth, changing the moisture and creating many issues including Meniere's disease, burning tongue, and nausea.

Emotional feelings create eighty percent of all illness and disease. What is currently going on in one's life? Does one reject an experience or idea, or feel unsafe on some level? Helpful hints: A stone in the gall bladder is a hardened thought, thus anger and worry are also present due to the symptom of nausea so trust needs to be recognized as part of this equation. Zinc not being absorbed indicates the stomach, so worry as well as what is not being absorbed is creating the symptoms. Low amylase is an enzyme produced in the mouth, so what might one not be saying that needs to be said?

There are many resources in the reference area at the back of this book that can assist people in connecting. Each one is unique yet the basics are similar.

"The mind is the projection of our life, one needs to work on the projection, not the screen." Gary Renaud

Heart

The heart affects the tongue, circulation of blood, complexion and the ability to sweat. The heart is the first entry for all emotional feelings in the Body. The heart is connected to the Soul. The heart also plays a part in the brain functioning, working with the spleen, therefore the relationship with Alzheimer's, Schizophrenia, ADHD, Bi-Polar, manias and memory as well as coma. This is in relationship to the Soul and Spirit in combination. The heart is a Yin organ plus is in partnership with the small intestine, which is the Yang organ.

Loving one's self is first and foremost a recipe to wellness. The Soul needs to believe, so harmony and joy in the heart can be achieved. Loving self includes non-judgment, forgiveness, faith that one is worthy and always was, that work does not define one's worth, conception does.

Guilt is the feeling that can bring pain and fear when the heart is out of balance. All pain is guilt, no matter where it is in the Body. Most people do not feel the emotion, as they have put it away for so long. It is not until the dots are connected that it is realized and resolved. The process is not a hard one to experience, as well as can lead to great joy.

A red face, tongue issues, agitation, insomnia, sweating, lack of joy, dizziness, chest pain radiating down the arm, sense of taste are also symptoms that represent the heart.

Ground hot peppers are known to cauterize a wound and taken in the mouth has been indicated to possibly stop a heart attack in progress.

The heart also relies on electrolytes to keep it in harmony. Humans are unique in all aspects and designed to heal themselves at all levels. Sodium and potassium are partners as are magnesium and calcium. The toxic world one lives in has reduced these minerals in people's diets with chemicals used to grow or process foods. Then take into allowance that the Body daily accumulates toxins. The first area noted when guiding a student is the Endocrine System and many blocks of energy are discovered. The thymus works in harmony with the heart and when blocked can create a reaction similar to a heart attack: pressure on the chest that radiates down the arm. Simple tapping on the breast bone will alleviate this symptom while one works on the cause. Toxins can be affecting the production of bone marrow, blocking lymph, definitely reducing immune response plus an emotional feeling of disappointment is the trigger in regard to thymus function.

When the parathyroid is blocked energetically, it stops the absorption of calcium, thus unbalancing the ratio of magnesium. This combination then creates a symptom named Arthritis and over time affects many functions creating plaque, kidney stones, cataracts, bone spurs, Rheumatoid Arthritis, dowager hump, etc. *(See Chapter 6 for a protocol)*

A low ratio of vitamin C will weaken the arteries and allow plaque to build rapidly. A stroke occurs when the arteries can no longer support blood flow at the proper ratio, in combination with the weight applied to the arteries of the plaque. Smokers are more susceptible, as the consumption of chemicals involved with smoking kills vitamin C in the Body.

A story I love to tell is when a gentleman came to see me with emphysema and blocked arteries. He wasn't a smoker, however had worked in the coal mines for years. This gentleman was told he could not be a candidate for open heart surgery as he would die on the table. One of his legs was dragging and he could not walk without breathing heavily. I put him on a protocol to remove toxins as well as build cells with essential fatty acids. He started drinking enough water for his Body size and taking a supplement called RTRE to remove plaque from the arteries. It is recommended to work with a practitioner familiar with the specific dosage. This was also while he worked on his liver with castor oil packs, milk thistle combo in a ratio and time frame as to not cause disharmony. The RTRE and chelating reaction creates gas, so the student stopped the supplement between visits for this reason. Once given knowledge of duration plus possible benefits afterward, he reapplied himself to this protocol. The results still amaze me, as powerful events like this one, happen everyday in this wonderful life I have chosen.

The first thing I noticed was that this gentleman no longer dragged his leg. He did not recognize this had occurred until I spoke and congratulated him on getting the movement back. He looked down and realized the difference. The leg movement had returned so slowly that he was not even aware of it.

He walks miles now, digs clams, built a deck and is enjoying a greater quality of life. The symptoms of what is said to be emphysema are now all gone. One has the ability to heal one's self. Although I gave him knowledge, guidance and support, he healed himself by taking responsibility and action.

Small Intestine

Mental clarity and sound judgment are related to the small intestine as are suppressed feelings; a sense of denial. Denial includes denying one's self the life that is meant to BE. Relationships that are not working or others that are meant to happen can be held in denial for a long time. Yet inaction prevents one from moving forward. The proper relationship with self is a vital part of wellness and foundation for one's authentic self.

The small intestine transforms food, separates clean from dirty and ensures nutrients are being received. The pancreas plays a major role with production of natural enzymes to help break down protein, fat and carbohydrates, along with bile from the liver. If anger is present or sweetness of life has been lost, it can and will disturb this process, creating constipation, IBS, polyps, etc. affecting both large and small intestines.

Candida (yeast) or parasite infestation in the small intestine can also relate to diseases such as Colitis or Crohns. Yeast can block the nutritional process of the small intestine in two ways: first, with the attachment of rhizoids (strings of yeast) to the wall of the intestine. This process at times creates holes in the colon and makes a pathway for food particles to escape into the blood stream. It facilitates immune response also the development then of autoimmune disease such as Lupus and/or food allergies. Secondly, the loss of good bacteria that enabled the process of yeast to escalate causes irritation, mal-absorption and infections. This is emancipated by the presence of parasites as this whole process depletes nutrients and lowers the immune system.

Chronic sadness (loss of joy in life) can affect the heart, arteries plus veins and can impair the absorption of food as well as emotional feelings through the small intestine. The stomach is another variable in this process.

Relate the emotional feeling to the organ so it makes it easier to understand the symptoms and resolve the illness or disease.

Lungs

The nose, breathing, skin, Body hair, opening plus closing of pores as well as transporting and transforming fluids in the Body are the job of the lungs. Grief is directly linked to the lung. When one thinks of grief, one immediately thinks of the loss of another person. Sometimes, though, grief is also linked to the loss of a negative friend in life, such as smoking after it has been given up or during the process of doing a protocol for wellness. The heart also plays a part in the lungs' reaction to feelings. Guilt is the main emotional feeling that affects the heart. The lungs and emotional feelings of the heart play a part in the activity of the large intestine as well. Forgiveness resides in the large intestine, hence IBS, Crohns, Diverticulitis, etc. There is a need to let go and move on.

For sinus issues or sinus headaches, use acupressure on the web point between the thumb and the index finger. Massage for about three minutes. This can also relieve dizziness. Remember, the emotional feeling is easier and lasts longer at relieving the symptom as it is attached to the cause. In this case, grief felt in either the left or right lung, depending on the gender of the one who is being grieved: left for female, right for male. Faith is the opposite of grief. Having faith another breath will follow is imperative to life.

Skin

Skin is the largest organ in the Body. It surrounds one as a protective barrier. When individuals let others cross boundaries that have been made consciously or subconsciously, the Soul will respond via the skin. Having values, standards and boundaries are important in creating an authentic self. Protecting them is vital to life. Anger plays a part as well in psoriasis and eczema as do parasites and yeast.

Large Intestine

The large intestine needs forgiveness of self and others to perform at optimum levels. Letting go of the past and moving on is important at all levels, especially for the process of waste and movement to leave the Body once nutrients are distributed.

Sexual Organs

Sexual organs complete the mix of organs. For males, both the prostrate and the testicles are affected by the kidneys as well as adrenals in their functions. Therefore, fear, shame and resentment play a part. Inadequacy is the feeling which pertains to them directly. When fear blocks energy to the kidneys, and magnesium is reduced in the Body, calcium excess will occur and will irritate the prostrate. If the feelings of inadequacy in life achievements, physical toxins, a combination of low water consumption, as well as high caffeine intake are present, the prostrate will be open to enlargement and cancer. Anger affects the liver also will reduce the blood flow to the penis which creates erection issues. When the kidneys are involved sustaining an erection is difficult.

The female organs of uterus and ovaries involve feeling safe plus secure. If a situation arises that invokes a feeling of insecurity or being unsafe, a female will disconnect emotionally from physical response. A form of this is drying up, so to speak, when it can become painful to have sex. Guilt and the heart are a part of this disconnect. The uterus is the seat of creativity, while the ovaries the seeds. Low libido is due in part to anger held in the liver, while toxins which affect the Endocrine System. Fibroids are physically created due to excess estrogen (soya and hormones added to food products, etc.) and via emotional feelings to nurture and create.

Brain

The brain is a key to the process of emotional feelings, and is affected by all the other connecting organs. The brain works on the level of the feeling of trust and works directly with the Spirit and not the Soul. The heart and spleen hold the emotional feelings that can also affect the brain.

"Incurable means curable from within."

Summary of Chapter 5

1. Symptoms are warning signs from one's Soul to BE a present and feeling BEing;

2. Symptoms are the most prominent way to define the manifestation or cause of illness or disease. Other ways include Live Blood Analysis, Hair Analysis, Iridology, Tongue & Pulse Analysis, Bio-meridian testing (many varieties of this), NAET, Energy Response Testing, Blood and Urine tests, pH for urine as well as saliva;

3. Become acquainted with common symptoms: liver function, toxins, vitamin and mineral deficiency, parasites, the Endocrine System, low water consumption;

4. Specific symptoms, causes and ways to reverse: S.A.D., Acid Reflux, Gall Stones, Vitamins and Mineral imbalance-magnesium, calcium, potassium, sodium, vitamin C, vitamin A and zinc;

5. Liver, Kidneys, Adrenals, Spleen, Stomach, Heart and Lungs. The connection: one is more than a physical BEing and emotional feelings play the largest part in dis-ease.

CHAPTER 6

Easy Protocols

It is hard to understand that even though it's so easy to shift an illness or disease, this information is not given to all those responsible for health care. Believe that one can make a difference, start with self and then help others. BE the bridge.

Chemotherapy is not a solution to cancer; it is a toxin that blocks the function of the liver and other vital organs in the Body as well as bad plus good cells. Nutrients are unable to be held in cells, as well as oxygen is reduced in the Body. Cancer already steals ten percent and Chemotherapy has the ability to steal another fifteen percent or more. Anemia occurs as the liver and spleen malfunction, thus weakening the Body's ability to fight for life.

Natural healing promotes the building and strengthening of cells. It also clears away physical toxins along with emotional feelings buried from the past. It adds oxygen as well as energy supplied by nutrients reacting with healthy cells. Take ownership, BE and empower self as part of the healing process. Juicing plus enemas are therapeutic, as well as a means to let go of control of others while concentrating on self. People who do not make it in the natural process of wellness are ones who want others to heal them rather than just guide them, and others to show love by doing for them, rather than loving one's self enough to BE. It is within one to heal!

A person can heal in one day from terminal cancer if he or she chooses. It takes longer to reduce the tumors and expel them from the Body: anywhere from one day to eighteen months if the practitioner guiding has wisdom, knowledge as well as the protocol is followed, including the inner work. It is the inner work that can heal the cancer in one day if one chooses.

I met a lady during my journey that had the same diagnosis as I, and was cured spontaneously without a protocol of natural or conventional treatment. When I asked her what happened, she stated, "I left a job that no longer related to me and started working in the garden (something I love); forgave individuals from the past while giving gratitude to God for what I have." She started to BE and feel!

Loving and having a relationship with self was part of her journey. Therein lays the secret of life! Some might have difficulty doing this process. I was one who needed guidance from others. Protocols in the natural realm are not that difficult. The dramatic are famous clinics in Mexico where individuals go to find guidance; use regiments to build the Body quickly; the process involves time to work on self, thus if one was controlling others, this tends to stop that behavior. Anger and resentment can form in those not willing to let go of control also can precipitate further deterioration rather than wellness. Once identified and taken care of energetically, the emotional feelings will shift if one chooses.

The bottom line is to BE self and to feel life. Let go as well as BE vulnerable. Is life worth it? I truly believe so! In the meantime, while working on BEing and feeling, here are some protocols to make life easier.

Acne—Pimples

Teenagers are usually afflicted with this issue, although some adults are also. Zinc plus vitamin A deficiency in general are the imbalance taking place physically, while little spurts of anger or rage are the emotional feelings affecting the individual.

A wonderful support would be to juice three carrots and a granny smith apple daily as well as add zinc lozenges to one's diet. When the lozenge tastes sweet the Body is low, and when it tastes sour it has had enough for now.

The medications and creams recommended normally by specialists along with doctors contain toxins that can affect the liver. The liver is the organ that this process has stemmed from due to anger or rage. Applying additional burdens to an already toxic liver can create further loss of the liver's five hundred functions, and is like asking whether the chicken or the egg came first, it will increase anger.

Essential Fatty Acids (flax, omegas, fish oils) are also a positive addition to strengthen cells. The lungs play a major role in skin issues and the necessity for the proper amount of water for the Body size is also a plus to optimize skin. Toxin removal would be recommended to support the liver both environmental and emotional. Apple cider vinegar (organic with a mother) can be applied to the pimple to alkaline the area, stop itching and help the skin to heal.

The skin represents one's boundaries, so a suggestion also would be to meditate and try to understand a subconscious boundary that might have been crossed. Boundaries are put in place for safety by one's Soul and meant to be followed. Now is the time to learn who one really is! That is what the teen years are all about.

Anxiety and Panic Attacks

Anxiety plus panic attacks indicate that the liver is in stress. The liver has five hundred functions, and is a power organ within one's Body. One of the liver's functions is to break down hormones after they have served their purpose. When the liver is congested with toxins, this does not occur properly therefore the hormones are forced back into the system. In turn the results can be depression, anxiety and panic attacks. The severity depends on the toxins accumulated, water intake as well as emotional feelings attached.

Severe hormone imbalance can facilitate chronic fatigue syndrome as well. It is all in the liver to perform its steps in balance with the Body.

My husband, James, had anxiety and panic attacks for over forty-five years. In 2005, James was able to resolve this when he removed toxins via ionic footbaths along with coffee enemas, as well as past emotional feelings James had buried for years. For awhile he still looked for the attacks to appear, as this had been a regular occurrence since he was five years old.

Some might wonder how a five or six year old could collect that much toxicity. His family was poor and James would go with his father to collect coal off the side of the train tracks to burn for heat. The emotional feeling welled up when James saw a young boy get run over by a vehicle just outside of school and die. James felt anger at himself for not telling the teacher that this boy often attached to the back of a vehicle to slide on the snow, and the anger became instilled within. When a child is so young it is easy to feel deeply and take those emotional feelings on. Most times the fault is not that of the child, however, because children take on emotional feelings so easily, in some situations they are unable to release them. Loving self, feeling not good enough and low self-worth also play a part.

When the liver needs cleansing, coffee enemas, ionic footbaths, and far infrared saunas are a start. During the process chosen, castor oil packs followed by milk thistle combo should be added to support regeneration of the liver. Enough water for the Body size and essential fatty acids also play a part. As well, the emotional feelings of anger or frustration need to be addressed from the past or present to finish the process. It is also recommend having a liver cleanse once a year to move stagnant bile and stones from the gall bladder as well as liver passages. (*See Appendix E for this popular cleanse.*)

Arthritis-Bone Spurs-Cataracts-Dowager Hump-Kidney Stones-Rheumatoid Arthritis-Vertigo

The emotional feelings involved in this protocol have to do with the parathyroid plus kidney. First and foremost, the Body is not absorbing calcium. Calcium with magnesium act in the Body as brother and sister in balance. Calcium hardens and tightens the arteries while magnesium relaxes them. Together they work with other electrolytes so the heart functions at optimum and blood flows throughout the Body.

Toxin builds up in the Body and affects the parathyroid, a part of the Endocrine System, which in turn stops the absorption of calcium into bones as well as teeth. When this occurs, depending on emotional feelings or genetic weakness, the free floating calcium may attach outside of the bone, cover an optical lens or form a stone in the kidney, ear duct or gallbladder. The excess calcium can also irritate certain areas of the Body, specifically joints or the prostrate, as well as block arteries.

A simple Energy Balance Harmony tap process *(see Appendix D)* done hourly for thirty to sixty days, depending on the severity of the issue, can be followed. It works in combination with removing the emotional feeling attached: fear for someone, fear of someone, or fear of something. This is in conjunction with the feeling of not speaking one's truth. Rubaplex, an herbal spray by Herbsanté used under the tongue is a great enhancer to dissolve the calcium build up at a faster rate while using the above protocol.

The first time I realized this was possible was with a student who had a hard lump on the back of her neck and shoulder area the size of a human fist. Not only did the lump dissolve; her Osteoporosis disappeared as the excess calcium went into the bones. It simply excites me that we have this power within!

Another plus moment was when a lady set for cataract surgery returned to her specialist to ask them to retest her eyes as she could now see clearly. The specialist refused, stating it was impossible to have this occur. The lady thus cancelled her surgery and is living happily with her sight restored. I thank her for having the authenticity to still refuse surgery, since some individuals would still choose the operation due to a sense of needing approval from the specialist.

Similarly, I have seen kidney stones, vertigo, rheumatoid arthritis attached to fingers, all dissolve and functions return. God simply amazes me on how each one of us is designed. Try this protocol to dissolve excess calcium. There is no harm and what does one have to lose?

Autoimmune Disease-Burning Tongue-Food Allergies-Sinus-Headaches

Candida (yeast infection) is related to ninety-nine point nine percent of food allergies. Some doctors believe that a female would only have yeast infection if she had a vaginal discharge, and that males do not get yeast issues.

When yeast has proliferated in the colon, it does not create a vaginal discharge. Instead it causes rhizoids: a root-like structure which adheres to the colon. In some cases over time, a small hole is made by the attachment of the rhizoid, and fragmented undigested food particles leave the colon into the blood stream. The immune system thus attacks this foreign Body creating an instant allergic reaction. In other cases the foreign object will cause an autoimmune disease such as Lupus.

Kroeger makes the best Candida kits by far. If rhizoids are present, after anywhere from one week to four, a bowel movement can contain as much as a cupful of these white strings (roots). The herbs destroy the yeast and repair the damage while food allergies disappear in most cases. The kit also contains a natural supplement to rebuild good bacteria in the Body. Lupus, as other autoimmune diseases, can be reversed as well, when adding toxin removal, emotional work, as well as support for the spleen and kidneys.

Males also are affected. In an active sexual relationship, Candida can be passed back and forth through sex. A thirty day cleanse with the use of a Kroeger kit needs to take place by both partners to prevent passing it back and forth. Besides food allergies or autoimmune diseases, males may have athlete's foot or jock itch which can proliferate to Wegener's Disease.

"Disease" and "Illnesses" are names given to symptoms in the Body by conventional medicine. Once a person knows all the symptoms which are involved, then breaks those down by using the information given, he or she is able to determine the cause. This gives more complete information on balancing the Body. Along with detoxification methods along with interpretation of the Soul via Energy Response Testing, a person is able to resolve any emotional attachment or blocked energy. Every individual can learn to do this on his or her own with training.

The Body needs good bacteria to balance. Things that can destroy good bacteria in the Body include birth control, certain medications, antibiotics, chemotherapy, radiation, and chlorine in the water when bathing or swimming. Once good bacteria are no longer present, yeast becomes active in the Body. It can cause vaginal discharge, colon issues such as Colitis or Crohn's disease, food allergies, autoimmune disease such as Wegener's disease, athlete's foot, and jock itch. Yeast infection can also affect the sinuses, tongue, mouth, ears and head, as well as cause psoriasis or eczema.

When good bacteria are not present in the sinuses, a fluid tends to drip down the back of the nasal passages onto the tongue, creating burning tongue syndrome. The moisture variance in the mouth then can cause a different vibration connecting to the ear channel, leading to tinnitus and other ear issues. Sinuses feel stuffy and headaches can occur. This can be resolved in most cases with a simple method of opening a probiotic capsule into warm water in a Neti pot and flushing the sinuses with this once daily for two weeks. The first time it can be a little painful.

Again, buried emotions need to be resolved. Affirmations, personal or ones from Louise Hay's books can be used for those not willing to forgive and release. However, affirmations are to be repeated three times, once daily as well as they take thirty days of repetition. Energy Balance Harmony (EBH) resolves the immediate symptoms, and writing letters can resolve the emotional cause within the same day if one feels the emotion while they forgive the individual, not for the incident, as a human and then flush or burns the letter.

When one is on birth control or swimming regularly, ensure that a good yogurt with lots of bacteria and very little sugar is taken daily. Kefir is a good organic product that tastes like yogurt as well as can be taken by tablespoon once a day or at each meal. This product is also easy to make.

Take care of children; too many are being affected by a reduction in good bacteria. If a mother had thrush, food allergies, vaginal discharge, etc. while pregnant most often the child is born with a yeast issue. That is why so many children have food allergies today. When yeast is present in the Body, it causes a low immune response so ear infections and even Autism can occur. A child with a low immune response once given a vaccination, has lost the Body's ability to fight the chemicals in the vaccine therefore, it can affect the Body as disease. Candida (yeast) cleanses taken with the support of a natural practitioner and a detoxification therapy designed for the weight of the child would be the first choices in finding balance.

Bunions

As mentioned in a former chapter, bunions are created due to excess calcium plus hardened phlegm. The spleen, parathyroid and kidneys can all play a part. A bunion sits on the spleen meridian specifically. An overabundance of sugar in the diet can create dampness in the spleen as well as usually a large portion of individuals with bunions will state they crave sugar or did during the building of the bunion.

Toxins affecting the parathyroid, both emotional and physical, can also facilitate a bunion. Hardening is always about hard thoughts and most often this is of self. Self judgement is common with individuals with low self worth.

Getting rid of a bunion takes time, approximately one to six months. Edgar Cayce recommended castor oil and baking soda mixed to form a gum like paste covered with a binding or bandage, twice daily. To increase the results at a faster pace I recommend adding a capsule of magnesium as well. There will be discomfort as the bunion breaks down, similarly, relief when accomplished.

A diet of seventy-five percent vegetables, half ones Body weight in water, juice or herbal teas will also help facilitate this. A glass of pop can reverse the healing affect as the Body will try to compensate and draw further calcium from the bones to alkaline the Body while it neutralize the pop. The excess calcium will gravitate to an already weakened area and increase the size of the bunion.

Castor oil should always be hexane free. Hexane is what is used in the process of the oil by some manufacturers. Drugstores generally sell it with the hexane as natural health food stores without. The best baking soda is aluminum free and found in some grocery or natural food stores. Canadian brands are aluminum free according to health standards. Magnesium citrate is sufficient to work with this combination.

Cachexia

Cachexia is a fat and muscle wasting disease contracted by individuals with chronic or end stage diseases such as Cancer, AIDS, or Cystic Fibrosis. Ninety percent of individuals with end stage cancer acquire cachexia while fifty percent of those die from it. Specifically, it is toxin related to the liver. Removal of toxins will facilitate wellness. The issue is that in the weakened state, toxin removal is difficult. Therefore, a wonderful product that works within twenty-four hours to stop this devastating issue is green algae named Spirulina.

Spirulina has the ability to enter the cell at a fast pace as well as provide nutrients necessary to rebuild the Body and stop the starvation process of Cachexia. One to two teaspoons daily depending on the individual are required. Due to the distinct, often unpleasant taste, putting Spirulina in apple sauce or mashed potatoes helps, a smoothie or smaller amounts in juice over the period of the day.

Spirulina is considered a complete protein. It is also a particularly rich source of other nutrients including various B vitamins, beta-carotene, vitamin E, carotenoids, chlorophyll, manganese, zinc, copper, iron, selenium, and gamma linolenic acid.

Ensure: a product widely recommended by conventional practitioners, is full of sugar and dairy, which in turn grows cancer cells plus contributes further to Cachexia. Coconut water has all the electrolytes one needs. The addition of desiccated liver supplement as well as a daily smoothie with hemp protein powder will support the liver and protect the Body from weight loss.

Symptoms of Cachexia include:

- Loss of weight.
- Loss of appetite including fluid intake.
- Loss of drastic amounts of Body mass.
- Loss of electrolyte balance creating numbness, fatigue and weakness.

The emotional feeling to get in touch with as well as forgive is anger and/or unhappiness.

Cancer

Fungus is related to virus as well as to cancer. It is the progression of symptoms. Earlier, a connection was indicated by an Oncologist named Dr. Tullio Simincini who has a ninety percent success rate with cancer when injecting sodium bicarbonate directly into the tumor.

A mixture of castor oil and baking soda made into a paste then applied to the visible tumor will help to soften and dissolve it. The flesh of a papaya may also be used in this fashion. The skin absorbs what is in contact with it. The Body also needs to BE alkaline as per urine as well as saliva pH tests. Alkaline Therapy protocol can be found in Appendix E. Point five less on the pH scale is not good enough. Disease will not grow in an alkaline Body. BE alkaline!

Emotional and physical toxins need to be removed from the Body, not the symptom covered up. Bottom line "Cancer is a virus" created by fungus due to a weak spleen/liver communication in the Body. The spleen and liver are holding buried emotional feelings such as abandonment along with anger, and are energetically blocked by these along with environmental toxins. Completing the triangle is a blocked hypothalamus due to a feeling of lack of nurturing by a male or a female (right or left temple). This blockage supports the growth of a tumor. A reminder, when pregnant this gland will also block to support the growth of a baby.

Imagine a child lying on the floor that is kicking and screaming as they are upset with someone or something. Individuals who have low self worth, a feeling of not good enough or lack a strong sense of self love, will do this from the inside, shutting down detoxification pathways, organ function and nutritional support.

The organ, structure or gland the cancer has adapted to represents that emotional feeling as well. The breasts would be liver related as meridians pass through the breast from the liver however the emotional feeling would also involve nurturing; the skin boundaries as well as lungs which is grief; non-Hodgkin's lymphoma is not flowing with life: in this case it can't flow as the liver is clogged with toxins and anger. All cancer is about not living life.

The measurement of protein used by Oncologists is what test indicates and they named cancer; however, it is undigested cells (protein) since the spleen is not working at sufficient capacity. Once one works with the spleen, protein, platelets and plasma—issues resolve and the Body will test negative. Again, the liver has to be detoxified as well as emotional feelings in these two organs and attaching organ with the name cancer resolved. Blocked energy in the hypothalamus is an indicator one is still nurturing the cancer or other disease. Energy Response Testing is a simple while invasive way to check.

Cancer is being beaten naturally everyday. The type of cancer is connected to the emotional feeling-eighty percent of the diagnosis. Cells need to be strengthened, toxins removed, nutrients absorbed.

Carpal Tunnel

One of the many reasons for writing this book was to identify ways to save North America's healthcare system. Unless it is required due to an emergency, gallbladder surgery is not necessary, nor is a visit to the doctor for numerous symptoms mentioned in this and other chapters. Leave the services of a doctor to regulate medication for those not ready for the natural realm or to reduce medications for those who have shifted. Doctors can also be supportive for yearly check-ups, lab requisitions, prenatal observation, child growth and development, as well as injuries from accidents or sports.

Carpal Tunnel surgery is unnecessary. In fact cutting the band (carpal ligament) in the wrist area and letting scar tissue form can create a weakness, as well as pain, as one gets older. One needs all the individual Body parts intact. When the pectoral muscle on either side of the chest is massaged or a castor oil pack applied with heat to the pectoral area, the symptoms of what is named "Carpal Tunnel" disappear.

Include strengthening the immune system, which in turn reflects positively on the thymus. The thymus, if not functioning properly, can cause chest pressure and radiate this down the arm. It is also beneficial to note that any blocked energy via the lungs can create like symptoms. There is no need for surgery. Strengthen the liver with toxin removal and the muscles, tendons plus sinews will stay strong and supportive of the Body. Basic stress, whether from working or from suppressed emotional feelings, such as grief or disappointment will tighten these muscles and radiate to the fingers causing numbness or pain depending whether anger or guilt are involved.

Charlie Horse-Cramping Toes & Fingers-Heart Palpitations-High Blood Pressure-Restless Leg Syndrome

The kidneys play a major role in each of these symptoms. The Body is amazing with its connection to organs, glands and simple basics.

When one experiences fear or shame, the kidneys are affected energetically. Blocked energy causes a mal-absorption issue with magnesium, creating the symptoms above in varying degrees and depending on the emotional feeling that is being held. Further symptoms derive from not having enough fluid for the Body size, too much caffeine, red meat consumption, or toxins which affect the kidney, adrenals, spleen and/or parathyroid.

The symptom can disappear in five minutes with Energy Balance Harmony. If the fear or shame is deep within the kidney, it will reoccur. Shame also creates another symptom, which is glaucoma. There can be a gradual closing off of the world around one's (peripheral vision), basically the subconscious suggesting that if one can't see them; they can't see one.

Fear is either *from* someone or something or *for* someone, such as a parent or sibling who has taken ill. It is not uncommon for partners of students who have cancer to end up with high blood pressure or the other symptoms stated above. In some cases the partner can become ill and pass away due to symptoms derived from the fear they are holding for another. It is recommended the partner set up an appointment as well to check their symptoms.

Magnesium and calcium are meant to be in balance, working together to relax or tighten arteries and muscles. Blocked energy from fear or shame stops absorption of magnesium. Thus the relaxer is no longer present, and instead the calcium, which tightens arteries as well as muscles, is predominant. These minerals are a part of the electrolyte system, working with the function of the heart's pump. Therefore, palpitations can arise when an imbalance occurs. A blood test to determine magnesium levels does not indicate the imbalance. It takes a urine magnesium lode test to confirm, if one is prone to conventional tests. Otherwise, Energy Response Testing and symptoms is a great indicator, i.e. lines in the ear lobe. The lines will disappear once magnesium level has been maintained over time.

Enlarged Prostate

Recently a new student intuitively led me to bring this protocol forward. Nothing in life is by accident. Past history of students has identified three important combinations that create this issue: caffeine, water, and toxins.

Too much caffeine dehydrates the Body, making it difficult for toxins to leave. The nutrients, hormones, and necessary chemicals are unable to be transported to the proper parts of the Body.

Add to this dehydration, not enough water for the Body size to begin with, and one has created a pathway for irritation and inflammation to occur. With an accumulation of toxins present, the parathyroid is unable to perform, and calcium is not deposited in the bones. This free floating calcium will add irritation, and with the right emotional feeling trapped from the past, will create an enlarged prostate, the emotional feeling has to do with a feeling of inadequacy. It can stem simply from believing that when a person retires, he is not supporting his family. It's a story created from believing that worth comes through work. It may also be caused by an inability to perform sexually, which can be anger in the liver, reducing the flow of blood, or fear causing a kidney issue reducing energy. Fear for the health of a loved one can also block energy to the kidney. Doubt as well as decision making can play a part and the gallbladder can become involved.

Work on the emotional feelings, increase water consumption, and reduce caffeine intake. Add essential fatty acids to protect the cells of the Body if one is not already doing so plus remove toxins. In the majority of cases, that is all it takes. If there is difficulty in releasing the fear for another, add a magnesium citrate supplement between supper and bedtime to relax the Body plus balance calcium levels.

Diverticulitis

Many people have small pouches in the lining of the large intestine (colon) that bulge outward through weak spots. Each pouch is called a diverticulum. Multiple pouches are called diverticula. The condition of having diverticula is called diverticulitis. About ten percent of Americans older than forty have diverticulosis; the condition becomes more common as people age. About half of all people older than sixty have diverticulitis! www.acq.qi.org / www.gastro.org

Constipation can impact the colon, creating these pockets from the bulk. The extent depends again on the liver as well as the stomach. Once pockets are formed, food can become lodged, causing inflammation and infections. Colonics is helpful when working with this illness.

Simply put, colonics is a process of water being forced into the colon through the anus, expanding and cleansing the colon wall. Once released, the colon acts as a giant rubber band that stretches then contracts. When this is repeated approximately three times, in most cases the pockets disappear as the colon contracts.

To enhance the results, the constipation, which was created by a stomach/ liver imbalance, needs to be resolved before colonics is performed. To do it the opposite way would require more colonics and three times is sufficient. The stomach relates to worry, the liver relates to anger, while the colon relates to not letting go of the past. Toxin removal, castor oil packs, milk thistle combo as well as other liver support are essential. A digestive or simple use of apple cider vinegar (organic with the mother) at the start of meals will help the stomach. Vitamin C in high doses creates diarrhoea therefore a beneficial supplement to take while constipated. Half a lemon squeezed in warm water is also an aid to constipation as one works with the liver.

Fibroids

A fibroid is a ball of fibrous muscle tissue related to the liver function. It can also be manifested as a benign tumor created by a malfunctioning spleen. An overabundance of estrogen in the Body can create a fibroid, whether in the breast, uterus, ovaries or gastrointestinal tract. This is usually a liver/spleen issue. The food that is in the market place can have added estrogen, as levels are added to produce dairy as well as meat at a higher quantity. Birth control medication also involves estrogen, as do some medications as well as soy products.

When the liver and spleen become overworked trying to resolve an overabundance in the Body, fibroids can become the resulting symptom.

Pancreatin or Wobenzym are two product brands that can help to resolve this issue. The first line of defense is to switch to organic dairy or use of local products which are known to contain no additional estrogen. Stop using soy and switch to rice or almond milk products. Taking either of the above enzymes between meals to help break down the fibroid as well as to build the immune system will help the Body take care of the rest. Support the liver plus spleen by removing toxins both emotional and physical.

Acupuncture is a good way to strengthen both of these organs as well, once toxins have been removed. The Key Company in the U.S.A. has a good quality pancreatic enzyme (Pancreatin) for a reasonable price. Wobenzym is quite an expensive supplement, although easier to find in the stores. One can eat pineapple and papaya between meals as well.

Unless health is deteriorating, the suggestion is not to opt for surgery to remove a part of the Body that is meant to be there such as the uterus. Removal will weaken the support of the bladder over time. Over a three month period, even a large fibroid can dissolve and be replaced with healthy tissue. Bleeding is related to the liver needing support and has a relationship with the heart, as guilt plus anger can be buried from the past.

Hiatus Hernia

A hiatus hernia or hiatal hernia is the protrusion (or herniation) of the upper part of the stomach into the thorax through a tear or weakness in the diaphragm.

Start by drinking four eight-ounce glasses of water in the morning before breakfast. The purpose is to weigh down the stomach.

Go up on one's toes and then come down hard on one's heels. Do this three to five times in a row. The purpose is to utilize the weight of the water to force the removal of the upper part of the stomach from the thorax.

Repeat this procedure daily for up to three weeks.

Then start a protocol of one quarter of a glass of aloe vera juice daily for one week to enable the Body to heal the tear.

Once the Body has healed, it is a good idea to work with the diaphragm in tightening the muscle while supporting the liver. The liver is the organ that is involved with the muscles of the Body, and supporting it will help prevent this problem from occurring in the future. Muscle, tendons and sinew issues are related to a weak liver, while bones and joint issues involve the kidneys. It is simple.

Without a hernia it is quite upsetting for the stomach area. So please do not try this unless necessary.

High Cholesterol

As mentioned in an earlier chapter, cholesterol is the responsibility of the liver in the Body; one of the liver's 500 functions.

Removal of the gallbladder increases the chances of having a cholesterol issue in the future. Since the gallbladder supports the liver in its functions, there is an increase in liver stress when it is gone. Strengthening the liver becomes more vital in these cases.

Eggs are not the issue with high cholesterol. If they are free range eggs, they actually help the liver. When chemicals have been added to the chickens' diet, those chemicals are transformed in the Body through the liver and can create cholesterol issues. In the packaging of eggs, ensure that they are free range, no chemicals or preservatives. Adding omegas to eggs that are not free range does not resolve the issue.

The medications given to individuals with high cholesterol deplete the functions of the liver and apply stress to the kidneys. Individuals on cholesterol medication have a seventy percent chance of creating diabetes. The liver works with the muscles, tendons and sinews. Most individuals, when taking cholesterol medications, start having muscle pain. Some cannot even walk and do not realize it is the side-effect of the medication. The symptoms for taking cholesterol medication far outnumber the resolve of high cholesterol. Also understand that the heart is a muscle which can directly be involved in the effect of cholesterol medication over time. Add to this more functions of the liver being affected by the medication, and imbalance becomes predominant in the Body.

It is not old age or genetics: it is toxin related. Resolve the toxin issue, unblocking energy necessary for the Body to function at optimum capacity and support the liver. In the meantime, there are wonderful supplements to help with the symptoms, while one is working at the cause. A supplement should not be required the rest of one's life. Hibiscus tea is an excellent source of nutrients that work with the liver to balance cholesterol. Non-flushing niacin at five hundred mgs daily is a great balancing supplement. It is that simple!

Hot Flashes and/or Night Sweats

The Endocrine System plays a major role in this, as the Body exceeds its toxin limit and each gland has to be at optimum to function efficiently within the Body. When either or both the thyroid as well as the adrenals are affected by emotional and/or physical toxins, one or both of the above can occur.

The emotional feeling necessary to feel and release is speaking one's truth in reference to the thyroid, while resentment in conjunction with the adrenals. Energy Balance Harmony can be done while lying in bed and can stop the inner heat within a minute. The hand in this case is on the base of the neck for the thyroid and belly button for the adrenals.

PMS is only the name given to symptoms in relationship to age. Toxins are prevalent at that age and once removed, the PMS symptoms also disappear, including anger.

Incontinence

The major reason that this occurs is the lack of water in the Body. One is made up of seventy-five percent water and the brain is eighty-five percent. Every joint in the Body requires fluid in order to move smoothly. The discs in the back require fluid to support the upper diaphragm. Organs need fluid to function at optimum. When water is limited the Body will react to preserve its stores of minerals and balance chemicals as well as hormones. Flushing constantly is one of these reactions while the Body works to protect the kidneys.

An emotional feeling involved here can be offended (pissed off) at self, another or a moment in time. The lungs and kidney can also play a joint part with grief plus fear as the emotional attachments.

Lymph Drainage

It is important to understand the basics of the lymph system. It does not have a valve to pump the fluid through the Body while cleansing. The breath acts as the pump. With shallow breathing, this does not occur properly. The lymph node gobbles up debris to prepare it to leave the Body, and if the liver is full of toxins, it reacts like a backed up sink. Debris in the lymph creates enlarged lymph plus issues in the Body.

When one has breast cancer, it is obvious that the nodes will have cancer cells, as that is one way they leave the Body. During cancer surgery to remove a tumor or the breast, nodes are also usually removed. When one has a substantial amount of lymph nodes removed, it is possible that a build-up of lymph fluid can accumulate, causing lymph edema (swelling, pain and pressure).

If unable to have a lymph drainage massage, one can relieve pressure by placing the left hand under the right armpit with the fingers spread open, while the right hand and arm are raised and positioned down the back of the neck area. The hand under the armpit gently pumps that area for ten to twelve minutes daily to clear lymph fluid that may be blocked. A massage by a professional in this field produces a greater effect for a longer period of time.

Please understand the Body can heal itself. When the liver has cleared toxins and the immune system is repaired, the nodes will expel the accumulated cancer cells. Removing nodes is not necessary and in fact dangerous, as removal disengages the pathway for toxins to leave the Body naturally. When the Body is alkaline, and emotional as well as physical toxins removed, the nodes will return to normal size.

Nausea during or after Chemotherapy or Radiation

Chemotherapy and radiation kill the mineral zinc. Zinc is necessary for a healthy immune system, as well as it is also used in fighting skin problems such as acne, boils and sore throats. It is further needed for cell division and for the development of tissue of the hair, nails plus skin to be in top form. Zinc is further used in the growth and maintenance of muscles, as well as the sexual development and normal growth of children.

Zinc helps control the oil glands and is required for the synthesis of protein and collagen, which is great for wound healing along with healthy skin.

When zinc is not available in the Body, and protein is unable to be digested, nausea occurs. At this point zinc tablets daily for a one week period is recommended and then zinc lozenges as needed. The Body will identify when the zinc is needed, as a lozenge will remain sweet. When not required, the taste will shift to sour. Too much zinc can also create nausea.

Other symptoms of zinc shortage:

- Under-performing immune system opens the Body to infections
- Allergies
- Night blindness
- Loss of smell and taste
- Hair loss
- White spots on fingernails
- Skin problems
- Irregular periods
- Sleep disturbances etc.

While building zinc in the Body, ginger supplements daily will help with nausea and produce results usually within twenty minutes. Ensure no other chemical is added to the supplement.

Peppermint tea is also helpful in nausea relief, as is a weakened oatmeal substance called gruel.

Chemotherapy will also destroy good bacteria in the Body; therefore, it is beneficial to include a probiotic daily to prevent yeast growth.

Radiation, specifically in the face or pancreas area can diminish the enzyme amylase and thus create nausea. Amylase breaks starch (carbohydrates) into sugar which is present in human saliva, where it begins the chemical process of digestion. Foods that contain much starch, however, little sugar, such as rice and potato, taste slightly sweet as they are chewed since amylase turns some of their starch into sugar in the mouth. The pancreas also makes amylase (alpha amylase) to hydrolyze dietary starch into disaccharides as well as trisaccharides which are converted by other enzymes to glucose to supply the Body with energy.

Amylase is used by white blood cells to digest pathogens and cellular debris. It is needed to protect the cell from cancer plus to dissolve the coating of a cancerous cell along with other pancreatic enzymes.

Pregnancy can also deplete the enzyme amylase as the fetus drains the Body's supply. This in turn causes nausea as well.

Other symptoms of low amylase are:

- Skin rashes
- Hypoglycemia and mood swings
- Depression and fatigue
- Allergies and sinus issues
- PMS and hot flashes
- Poor circulation causing cold hands and feet
- Neck and shoulder aches
- Inflammation in the Body

Radiation can and needs to be removed once the tumor or blockage has shrunk, or it will manifest further tumors plus blockages, as will anger as well as other negative thoughts.

In 2007, my Body took on physical attributes of disease which started when the book I authored, *BALANCE, nature's way to heal your body* was printed. Fear of success and failure was the emotional feelings affecting my kidneys. Obviously, the spleen was involved, yet at that time I was unable to see that perspective. Lymph nodes enlarged blocking the jaw area and kept growing, distorting my face while making it difficult to consume food. Lessons were still not complete on the Soul level and therefore not identifiable at that moment, so I chose to have radiation.

Radiation is a solution for a blockage, and one has to remember that it can destroy more than cells, tissue along with the growth. It can damage organs, bones plus fluid pathways. Radiation from therapy, x-rays, or CT scans can be removed from the Body via a Radiation Bath. It needs to be removed after the time allotted by the Specialist or the radiation will keep destroying the Body's ability to heal. (*See recipe in Appendix A.*)

Neuropathy

Damage to one's Body occurs in many forms, including damage to a sheath that is meant to protect the nerve end in different parts of the Body. Chemotherapy is a major factor in damaged nerve endings, creating pain or numbness of the extremities. The sheath has the ability to heal, when an individual takes a supplement called Benfotiamine, a fat-soluble form of vitamin B1 (thiamine). Benfotiamine as a fat-soluble is able to stay in the Body for the time needed to repair nerve damage. It supports nerves, kidneys, retinas, blood vessels as well as the heart, and in some cases can keep blood sugar levels at optimum.

Alpha lipoic acid is another important supplement to restore dead nerves as well as circulation. It is an antioxidant that also helps the Body use glucose; hence it is useful in lowering blood sugar levels.

Toxin removal again is an essential part of this protocol, along with essential fatty acids to support strong cells and water consumption according to Body weight. The sinews (nerves) are supported by the liver, so liver support such as toxin removal, castor oil packs as well as followed up with milk thistle combo would be the path to follow. The emotional feeling of anger, frustration or irritation is what is held in the liver, even if one does not feel it. If one has put the anger away years ago, there is no feeling. That is what the Soul is trying to address with the symptoms. Pain again is related to guilt. Depending on which side of the Body and which part is affected, also tells the story.

Planters Wart—Planters Fascia

Planters Warts are created by a virus and appear on the sole or close of the foot. A simple application of three drops of tea tree oil on the wart while covering it with a Band-Aid twice daily usually resolves this issue within thirty days or less.

My sister, Margaret, had a Planters Wart and was scheduled to have it removed by her doctor. She gladly did the above protocol and thirty days later, when the doctor went to examine her foot, the wart came off, root and all in his hand.

When a wart is removed and not simply taken care of with tea tree oil, the virus is still in the Body as well as most likely will return over time and may become cancer. Oil of oregano is a good product to dissolve a virus. It is taken under the tongue daily for two weeks. Stop for two weeks then repeat, to protect one from a virus returning. Three drops a day is sufficient for adults, five drops if in a major symptom. If an individual is unable to tolerate the taste the drops may be applied to the fat part at the bottom of the foot by the toes. Individuals who have had Chicken Pox as a child should all try this process. The Chicken pox virus will stay in the Body otherwise and create warts, cold sores, mononucleosis, shingles, herpes, Epstein Barr plus non-Hodgkin's lymphoma.

Plantar fasciitis is a painful inflammatory process of the plantar fascia. An incidental finding associated with this condition is a heel spur, a small bony calcification, on the heel bone, in which case it is the underlying condition, and not the spur itself which produces the pain. When the parathyroid is energetically blocked, calcium is not absorbed into the bones and can enable the Body to form heel spurs. The excess also creates irritation, particularly in that area, specifically if one is not drinking sufficient water or chooses to drink too much caffeine.

To help with inflammation anywhere in the Body, almond milk warmed on the stove with a teaspoon of turmeric works well. Add magnesium once a day after supper or before bedtime to one's diet. Administer Energy Balance Harmony once hourly, daily for thirty days on the parathyroid area energetically located under the jaw. This protocol helps to ensure the calcium is absorbing from the spur and blood stream into the bone. Remember also that to ensure spurs do not re-appear it is recommended to remove toxins to ensure the parathyroid is functioning at optimum. As for the emotional feeling, *"What is one not standing for?"* would be predominant in this case. Which foot is affected would represent male or female person that one might be falling for instead of standing up for one's own ideals, while not being authentic to self.

The protocol of oil of oregano for chicken pox virus is recommended as well.

Virus—Cold Sore

A virus is an infectious microbe that invades the Body and stays, unless something is done to destroy it. It can show up as a cold sore, vertigo, infection, flu, mono, herpes, etc. Most common infectious diseases are viral.

When a cold sore seems to be gone, most often it is just lying dormant until the immune system is low from overwork, stress or toxins and then reappears. As said earlier, Chicken Pox virus earlier in life can lie dormant and come back later under the right circumstances, as can mono. It can reappear ten years later as Epstein Barr virus or become non-Hodgkin's lymphoma, a form of cancer.

As mentioned above, oil of oregano tincture (drops) is an herb recommended to protect the Body from a virus, as well as clearing viruses in the Body. The procedure is to take this tincture under the tongue for two weeks, then take two weeks off and finally repeat for two weeks. When a symptom is already present, such as herpes, mono, Epstein Barr or non-Hodgkin's lymphoma take five drops daily and repeat the process three times. A cold sore virus seems to do fine with three drops daily for two weeks on, two weeks off, and then two weeks on again. Hedd Wynn is a good brand though there are other great brands. It should be pretty potent. If it brings tears to the eyes, it is strong and one drop would be fine instead of three.

If one finds one can't tolerate the drops, place them on the fleshy under part of the foot by the toes before bed. This is the way to give it to children as well, however children would receive only one drop for three days.

During the hype last year about H1N1 virus, many students used the oil of oregano and not one of them ended up with the flu. My daughter-in-law Stacy was worried for their three little children. She asked their family doctor if he would give the H1N1 shot to his own children. The response was no. That made up her mind, and instead she used one drop of oil of oregano for three days on each child's foot and they were fine.

Herpes as well as genital warts seem to take a bit more to release from the Body. Wonderful results in just over a week have occurred in students taking Fungafect, a tincture by St. Francis Herb Farm: twenty drops twice daily in water. It contains pau d'arco tincture, paracress, oreganum, usnea, and nettle spring tops.

Protocols

Everything in the Body is connected. Each symptom is a result of imbalance due to emotional feelings and of toxins accumulated over time. How is one aware if something is working? The measuring stick one can use is: *"Symptoms" "None!"*

Certain protocols need a little more tweaking than others, depending on how far the individual has let the Body deteriorate. Two examples would be: cancer and diabetes

Cancer is a symptom not a cause. It took four years for my own Body to shut down and acquire the symptom of cancer. *BALANCE, nature's way to heal your body* takes one through that process. Symptoms give the big picture. The only two differences from one cancer to another are the extent of deterioration and the area to identify the emotional feelings that need to be worked on.

Other chapters in this book identify the emotional feelings trapped in each organ. To BE who one authentically is supposed to BE is vital. Doing is living, while BEing is living life. Cancer is a definite symptom of not BEing. The person with cancer should look back at when he or she stopped living life. Was work a story about worth? Each person is worthy to be here on Earth as he or she was born. No other reason is necessary.

The inner child can act out, internalizing the way one feels. Imagine a child who realizes that he or she has never gotten what he or she wants in life. This is not about material wants. Now see this inner child kicking and screaming from the inside out, blocking the flow of blood, lymph, and detoxification pathways. All of those emotional feelings create excess phlegm that hardens and creates tumors out of internal anger. That child is you! One can turn cancer around today from the inside out. First, let go of the control it is giving one over others. Let go, BE vulnerable. A detoxification and nutritional protocol may be necessary to release the attachment to others while focusing on self. Protocols are a way of doing that.

If one really "gets it" and let's go of control; accepts one's worth; loves self one hundred percent; starts to feel the emotional feelings one has tucked away, and BE; then a protocol of any type is not necessary to destroy cancer. One has the ability to do that within self: now! If the symptoms disappear, one has found the answer. If the cancer grows, one has not yet resolved the emotional feeling, strengthened self love, found value in self, or accepted the feeling of being good enough.

Diabetes is created via the adrenals, kidneys and liver, as well as the spleen. The pancreas is part of the lymph system and the spleen plays an important part in transformation plus transportation of fluids. A combination of emotional feelings play a role in the creation of this disease, as it does in cancer. Loss of the sweetness of life, resentment, fear, anger, frustration as well as abandonment and loneliness can all play a part in diabetes.

The combination of symptoms depends on the path of reversal as in all illness and disease. One should not judge when one realizes these symptoms have played the major role in this disease. A gift of transformation is what has occurred. Allow life to flow and ebb, release control and BE.

<u>To remove all of the symptoms</u>: Toxin removal, the addition of essential fatty acids, and enough water for one's Body size are necessary as well as strengthening the liver, kidney, spleen, heart, and lungs.

Each disease is a name given of specific symptoms, all of which have a cause and are connected to one's inner child.

On the TV news tonight, there was a report about weight issues. Research now has suggested that protein and non-glycemic vegetables eaten regularly will reduce weight. One piece of information not noted is that toxins, both emotional and physical, stop the absorption of protein in the Body. To increase protein without resolving this issue will cause further disease and illness.

Live Blood Analysis has noted lack of protein absorption numerous times with individuals. Once proteins are digested, weight loss does take place as well as other syntheses required by the Body. Unprocessed dead cells are also protein that is necessary to have the Body digest.

The obesity in North America starts with toxins affecting the liver and stomach, not enough water, too much sugar depleting the spleen, as well as no essential fatty acids to break down the fat. Removing toxins, strengthening the liver plus spleen, drinking enough water for individual Body size, while adding essential fatty acids, (EFAs) is a great path to follow.

There are four parts to a large belly:

1. A liver ledge from a weakened liver;
2. Weight issues from toxins, sugars, lack of water and lack of essential fatty acids;
3. Adrenal fatigue and the presence of an adrenal tire;

4. Spleen function deficiency, usually identified by large thighs and hips.

A weakened liver will cause other muscle and tendon issues as well, including sciatica, hernias, etc.

BE present to one's life! Understand how unique and special one is! Realize every day one creates one's world from the inside out and have the ability to shift it in the direction of one's choice. Illness plus disease is created by the real you, the one that wants to come out to play and BE, to live life in peace, love while in harmony. Listen to one's Soul intuitively, BE who one chooses to BE.

Summary of Chapter 6

1. Natural healing promotes the building and strengthening of cells, the clearing of emotional as well as physical toxins, with the addition of oxygen plus energy supplied by nutrients reacting with healthy cells;

2. The bottom line is to BE self and to feel life;

3. Chemotherapy and radiation kill the mineral zinc. When zinc is not available in the Body and protein is not able to be digested, nausea occurs;

4. Radiation, specifically in the face or pancreas area, can also diminish the enzyme amylase and create nausea;

5. Spirulina has the ability to enter the cell at a fast pace and provide the nutrients necessary to rebuild the Body while it can stop the starvation process of Cachexia;

6. A toxin build-up in the Body affects the parathyroid: part of the Endocrine System, which in turn stops the absorption of calcium into bones and teeth;

7. The Body needs good bacteria to balance. Birth control pills, certain medications, antibiotics, chemotherapy, radiation, and chlorine in the water when bathing or swimming destroy the good bacteria in the Body;

8. The emotions of fear or shame affect the kidneys energetically. This blocked energy creates an absorption issue with magnesium in the Body, blood pressure irregularities, along with pancreas issues;

9. An overabundance of estrogen in the Body can create a fibroid, whether in the breast, uterus, ovaries or gastrointestinal tract. This is usually a liver and/or spleen issue;

10. Strengthen the liver with toxin removal, and the muscles, tendons as well as sinews will stay strong while supportive of the Body;

11. Everything in the Body is connected. Each symptom is a result of imbalance due to emotional feelings and/or toxins accumulated over time;

12. Stop, look and listen to the real you: one's heart/Soul connection;

13. Cancer is being resolved naturally every day!

CHAPTER 7

Free Will

Illness and disease are not forms of free will; they are acts of control. They are also meant to guide one back to the Soul because one has not listened intuitively. Intuition is a part of free will, and as stated in earlier chapters, is also one's internal GPS system. The Soul is our authentic self, which one is meant to BE. An intuitively healthy six-year-old has already recognized his or her purpose in life. What did one want to be at six years of age?

God does not intervene in free will. Therefore, living life is totally one's choice, to live or not. It's a choice made of free will. Understanding how it works involves following the lessons in life while observing symptoms, which are the language of the Soul. Once one learns the connection, a simple path is created and shifting can occur instantly.

Hope

A young father with cancer started to work naturally to bring his physical Body back to health. To do this takes work within all realms. Emotional feelings affect the Energy Field: the Soul creates symptoms to help move one forward; hope, faith and love bring forth the Spirit to energize the life one has. One cannot sit and wait until one feels better to live life. The Soul is anxious for that to happen now or cancer would not be a part of one's life. Fear of life, not death, is the common denominator. Fear of not being good enough or valued freezes one's ability to move forward in time. Life then can become death!

This father had trouble swallowing. He was fearful, even though he had the basic knowledge of how things worked in his Body. He knew that the liver is responsible for the contracting and expanding of the esophagus via the muscles plus tendons, as well as sinews. He also knew that the emotional feeling of anger was present. This fear: the mind, not the heart, directed his path to have a shunt put in to help him swallow in the future. When a person has surgery of any type, the immune response is to that area. And if cancer is present in the Body, the cancer is given power to grow in other areas. This power is not only physical, it is also emotional; eighty percent in fact. Cancer is a symptom and is precipitated by inaction of one is not being authentic to self. To have the surgery and BE authentically okay with it as a support, while he moved forward would have increased his ability to survive.

This young man passed away recently and through friends I learned he was tired of fighting to live. When a person uses the "Will", it wears down the kidney, which stores the essence of life. Living life is a gentle restoration of energy and living. It dissolves tumors, lets blood flow while swallowing easy. The realization that he was wearing himself down was an indicator that he was still not living life. Even when a person cannot get out of bed he or she can still live life. He chose death. God did not choose that for him. It was not that he did not love his wife or children; instead, it was that he did not love himself enough to let go of the control caused by his subconscious desire to protect his ability to feel good enough.

Does one show one's children they are not good enough? Is nothing good enough? Who does one let take away one's worth or free will? Is it not time to take it back, to realize stepping forward with one's gift in life is scary, yet worth every moment? There was always hope for this young father, until his final choice. I hope his family celebrates his life, not mourns his death.

Does all this seem crazy, yes, and true? We are amazing humans. It takes listening to God and self to put it together while it still thrills me as much as when I first realized how one can orchestrate their life.

Every day is a new beginning, with someone new realizing they have the power within. What a life I live! Thank you, God!!

When a person has been told he or she is terminal or has a disease that will shorten life, it is easy to lose hope. Hope is a quality and an emotional feeling that we are born with. It is a fragile connection linking Soul, Spirit, Body and Energy Field to God. Our existence on earth requires it. To reactivate free will, a spark of hope is a component that is essential.

In December of 2002, when the doctors gave me no hope for life, I dug deep into my Soul and found a spark. With knowledge plus wisdom, the spark ignited into a flame. Past life experiences since I was born, gave me the tenacity to do that or I would not be here today.

Each visit to the oncologist was another opportunity for him to tell me I was going to die. I would tell him he was not God and that it was God as well as one's self that determine death. Still holding on to the feeling of not worth it at that time in my life, I let some of what he said connect as a false truth. I saw him far longer than necessary, out of old habits and not yet being authentically Susan. In 2004, I chose to stop seeing him. We all have the power to BE.

Our Souls do not project terminal cancer on the mind to alter physical existence unless we are sure that we can shift this. Still, we can get caught up in the past, lose hope and faith, and never experience the feeling of true love or worth for self. The result is to die before it is our time.

"To live life, one needs to BE a feeling being. The programs are there to get well naturally, however unless one releases emotional feelings and control from the past, plus feels life again at every level, life will be short." *Susan Manion MacDonald*

A strong emotional feeling can alter a gene, since emotions require a shift in brain chemistry. Life experiences affect the DNA of genes.

DNA is a memory bank of past experiences stored in the cells of one's life. One needs to release the negative charge around the bad memory to flow with positive energy. It is all energy: one is energy.

Hope and belief are both necessary to shift the chemical change as well as to release the negative charged emotional feeling which is affecting the Body. Tune in to what is affecting one emotionally from the past, so then the Body has an amazing capacity to heal itself. Recognize that a cramp in a foot is low magnesium due to fear, either for or from someone, or something. Release the fear, start absorbing again, and instantly reverse that physical distress. Raise one's vibrations (frequency) with positive reactions, words, energy sources. Forgive, release and let go of what is controlling one's life. One can be changed in the twinkle of an eye from illness to wellness. Believe that each one has the ability to transform the world one Soul at a time: our own first.

I had a major experience that in the past would have propelled me to the hospital. I received an email from a friend I rented a space from, asking for an increase in rent. That was fine with me, as I had the thought already in my Energy Field that she deserved more for all she does for me. Suddenly, I got a sharp pain in my left side that bent me over, bringing tears to my eyes. It felt like someone was pulling a piece out of my Body and it hurt. Instantly, I Energy Response Tested and realized it was my pancreas. The emotion for the pancreas is the sweetness of life. How in that instant did I lose some of mine? Pain is guilt, so what was I taking on? Within minutes, it was resolved by tracing steps to less than five minutes prior to having read the email. I read it again, still in violent pain, and realized a sentence attached to my worth had taken me back to my two year old self, thus taking away some sweetness of life. The guilt was caused by my not taking leadership and negotiating rent earlier, when the intuitive self had notified me. Once I released the emotional feeling of guilt, plus took back my worth, the pain completely left within a minute.

There was no need to tell the friend, as we were both in tune. When we talked later that day, I told her I was in agreement with the rental increase. Without a word from me, she stated that she should not have written the email the way she did, and we laughed about our communication flaws. Yet if this had not occurred, I would not have realized there were unresolved issues about worth needing my love and attention. That was a gift from Juli. Awareness can change any energy pattern at will!

Nostradamus lived during the time of "Black Death" in Europe which was created by black fleas in cats (1348 to 1350 A.D.). Thirty to sixty percent of the population of Europe was said to have died from this Bubonic Plague. His recipe to cure the plague was to take a super dose of Rosehips, which is a strong form of vitamin C, cleanse clothes and hang them in the sun. Nostradamus went from village to village to help others get over the plague. It is within each one to heal naturally!

Dr. Jill Bolte Taylor is a Harvard-trained and published Neuron-anatomist who experienced a severe hemorrhage in the left hemisphere of her brain in 1996. On the afternoon of this rare form of stroke (AVM), she could not walk, talk, read, write, or recall any of her life. It took eight years for Dr. Jill to completely recover all of her functions and thinking ability. It took eight years for her to successfully rebuild her brain: from the inside out. In response to the swelling and trauma of the stroke, which placed pressure on her dominant left hemisphere, the functions of her right hemisphere blossomed. Among other things, she now creates as well as sells unique stained glass brains when commissioned to do so. In addition, she published a book about her recovery from stroke and the insights she gained into the workings of her brain. The New York Times bestselling memoir is titled *My Stroke of Insight: A Brain Scientist's Personal Journey.* It is within each one to heal naturally!

In Eastern medicine, healing is knowledge in tandem with the individual stepping into the responsibility of self. North Americans tend to give their power away; however, a necessary shift to acquire knowledge and empowerment from within is now occurring, one person at a time. Is today one's time?

A person attempts to control feelings, subconsciously allowing illness or disease to shut down life. I ask students to say, "It is safe for me to live life." Then I Energy Response Test the subconscious response. If it's "No", the person is encouraged to clear away that feeling while tapping his or her head, breathing in, out and panting while doing so. The next statement to repeat is, "It is safe for others, for me to live life." If the response is "No", he or she repeats the above action.

Sometimes a person subconsciously feels that others do not want him or her to live life, due to a childhood hurt that has led to that conclusion. Having that thought can stop lymph, blood and Body fluids from flowing. Past experiences can also shut down energy pathways or create other negative symptoms. The Soul, you on a deeper level, uses these symptoms to get our attention and to correct this wrongful connection to self. We are the creators of our lives. Let's release all emotional feelings buried from the past, feel life again, connect to our Souls and BE!

Another incident might clarify this even more. The kidneys affect the joints of the knee, specifically when climbing stairs, creating pain or discomfort. The severity depends on the fear that has occurred to create the symptom in the Body.

At our center, there is a long staircase. On some days, I have to travel it many times, and if I am in fear, it is with great difficulty. I had come to terms with the fear in my life as mentioned in previous chapters and could run up plus down them like a twenty year old. Charlene, my middle child, decided to let us use her as a subject for our new weight loss program. She is five foot three weighing two hundred and ten pounds. Part of the process is to access the emotional feelings buried. Charlene's fear that was affecting her subconscious reason for not losing weight was of not having a baby to love and nurture. I took that on myself, while it wasn't even my own issue. Because I took it on emotionally, within five minutes I could not climb the stairs without severe pain and a lot of extra time. My daughter, who understands this process, laughed and said "Mom, get over it, let it go. This is about me, not you." It took a few moments to clear so I again could run up and down the stairs. If this knowledge was not present in my life, I could be using a walker today while taking medication, and would likely be on dialysis some time in the future. Charlene's issue was not even my own. I simply took it on over a false sense of it being my issue, and an unhealthy attachment to my child. Charlene now weighs one hundred and fifty pounds.

Feelings and emotions are different. Emotions are surface reactions to moments in time, such as weeping. Feelings have the ability to touch one's Soul.

Lack of self-worth is a diminished quality, yet the feeling one has with or without it is what makes it powerful and effective to the human being. Self-worth is found through achievements that are useful plus have value. Action is important to self-worth, while inaction can deplete it. Yet, fear of success or failure can facilitate this response. Look into one's life and see when action was not taken. Was a path shifted and then followed by less abundance, joy, or other positive qualities? Clear away any fear that is diminishing self-worth with prayer or energy work such as breathing while tapping. Feelings of "not good enough" are derived from a lack of self-worth. What does one value about self?

Faith

Generally, one has a global life purpose that can be summed up in one or two words: love, peace, teacher, healer, writer, leader, warrior, parenting, and so much more . . .

What is one constantly drawn to do in one form or other, whether in one's personal life or work setting? What makes one feel good to BE?

Life purpose is easy to locate if the person is present, authentic and has faith in self as well as God. Have faith, ask one's angels for help. Archangel Michael's role is to help one discover and lead one's life purpose in all aspects. To ask is to receive! Surrender to a higher power and ask God, "What would one have me do and BE?"

Be humble along with realize that success is available to all who choose to look within. Recognize ego and choose to dissolve it before it comes up.

Have faith in others by allowing them to share their thoughts about the path they see for themselves, and then offer praise. Parents are not there to lean upon, rather to make leaning unnecessary. Great or enlightened leaders do not actually lead anyone. They create an environment where others feel they have a personal responsibility too, and are a part of the process.

When a person's children or partner do not clean up after themselves, even when told to do so, or an attitude of annoyance is present from the parent, what reasons could be present? They may not have faith in themselves due to a controlling parent or partner. To be told repeatedly that they did not do something right creates a feeling of failure: not being good enough and creates a path for inaction. It is safer subconsciously for some to not do the action than to fail continuously in the action. Always use mirroring to resolve issues. The answer is within the beholder. Have faith one will be okay, let go of control and empower those around to let go of fear. Ask why one needs perfection from others. Where is one feeling less perfect?

Three questions to ask ourselves:

1. What am I trying to manifest in life?
2. What tools or practices do I have or use to achieve this? (goal setting; affirmations; law of attraction; vision boards; mediation; prayer; etc)

3. Am I confident I'm doing everything I can, or is there DOUBT? *(Doubt is a feeling held in the gall bladder and may need to be strengthened along with the belief in self.)*

If we postpone life, waiting for a gift to come, it may never happen. It takes many steps to occur before the "AHA!" moment will appear in one's life. Those steps are the wondrous journey that sets the pace while it enhances the path so the "AHA!" moment happens. Be present in all of life!

To postpone life, while waiting to have more energy or wellness, also needs to be recognized as a path to the end of life. When I had cancer in 4th stage, I lost a lot of weight: going from a size fourteen to a size zero. I did not wait for life to shift me back to my wardrobe. Instead I purchased new clothing in the size I had become. Most of it was from Guy Frenchy's, a second hand store in our area. I have met many students who are waiting for that weight to come back on before they start to BE, as nothing fits. That alone is a symptom of not BEing self, not feeling valued for who we are. If being thin during the process to illness bothers us, it is time to take stock of why. It is the inner self that is the compass of life. Have faith that we are exactly where we need to be to learn and love self. Be okay with which one is. Life is not about what one looks like. [To lose weight daily is another issue and talked about in an earlier chapter on ways to stop and reverse this.]

The knowledge to learn and strengthen ourselves can be found in many places. Jerry and Esther Hicks have a wonderful collection about Abraham, a Spirit that is channeled via Esther. *The Law of Attraction* is their work as well. In August, 2008, I came across these four affirmations or "Mantra" from a book I read. *(See Resource list at back)*

1. Life is supposed to feel good, and my overall well-being is natural.
2. No matter how good my life is now, it can always get better.
3. The choice and the power to improve every aspect of my life experience are within my personal control <u>now.</u>
4. Wealth, health, and happiness are my natural birthright.

This phrase brings up another visionary author, Josie Varga who wrote the book *Make up Your Mind to be Happy.* Josie talks about happiness being one's true nature and how it comes from the inside, not the outside. In this book she notes that is up to one to define who one is before others do that for one. Journal and train one's mind to think positively, while seeking out others that make one feel good. Accept who one is. Make self happy.

To have Hope, one needs to feel life, resurface past hurts, forgive and release as mentioned in other chapters. Feeling those moments can hurt; however holding them within the Body takes away hope, faith and love. Most importantly, it takes away the ability to live life to the fullest. Dissolve grief with laughter.

The Dali Lama exemplifies integrity, spiritual awareness, compassion to service, calm, peace, with laughter and joy. He remembers who he is. BE present to that which one is! BE at home wherever one is.

I believe that we are here on earth to live life not just to live. To BE the ones we really are, in peace and harmony; inwardly as well as outwardly, personally plus professionally. Profession is not just a job; it is a purpose, whether that is guiding family or a major corporation. I believe it has become easier spiritually to give power away and that the Soul requires us to BE. To BE means to stand for self, not lean on others, listen to the heart, search for knowledge and let the heart guide. It is time to use our own power and stop giving it away.

We can give power away for many reasons, all of which are defined by a loss of a quality during the lifelong learning process. We can give it to doctors, lawyers, spouses, parents, and so on due to a lack of self worth, or a "not good enough" part of who we have become. We are meant to take the knowledge given and use our free will to take a course of action that is best for each of us, using the heart to guide. Doctors have knowledge of the physical Body; however, what most doctors do not have is the knowledge of oneness. They may lack the understanding that each of us is different, that emotional feelings buried from the past can disrupt the energy of the Body and damage cells while holding memory. Toxins are a part of this society and shift the functions of the liver with other organs plus glands in the Body. Disease is created inwardly as a way of letting go of a control has been held internally for many years, sometimes for a lifetime. This control was used to protect our vulnerability out of fear.

I believe that every person desires nurturing, approval, and love. Therefore, we can subconsciously choose death rather than to live life. We can choose those five minutes, days, weeks or months of risking someone seeing us vulnerable and real, rather than having to keep control of our own life anymore. I believe that each of us is still a child inside; looking for what we did not have for many years while putting up a stiff front pretending all is well, until the Soul calls for us to live life now or be gone.

I believe that no one needs to die prematurely, and that "terminal" is a word devised by lack of complete knowledge. Palliative care is a last place to understand that we can still live life without fear of being discovered that we are not good enough or belief of not being worth it. BECAUSE we are good enough and always have been!!! Believe one is valued for self! To take the power back within self is fearful to someone who believes the story of "not being good enough". How could a person heal self, if he or she feels deep inside that this part of life was only a performance? Most of us are not awake to the possibility enough to heal ourselves, even with guidance. Or we may feel that someone else needs the healing, as they are better than we are. By having these thoughts, we are not living life. Instead, we are controlling life by holding anger, worry, guilt, grief, sadness, fear, and more . . .

So now there is a conflict. On one hand, the disease is being offered as a gift from the Soul to see that life is not being lived fully. Now is the time to BE present, and BE, while loving self as well as believing that one is and always has been good enough. On the other hand, the nurturing, approval plus love given to someone who is ill feels good to the internally sad inner child. The fear of letting go of control and

BEing, is strong enough that one can succumb to the life presented while choose not to stand up for our real self. It may be easier for some to let go of life for those brief moments when they believe that's all there is.

How does a person know that he or she is getting close to letting go and BEing? The fear becomes greater and the symptoms can re-occur. It is not helpful to keep punishing or judging one self for wrong choices. The story is one's to shift, with forgiveness, love and gratitude for the lesson.

Good Enough

While working with a student, I was reminded again of how important this topic is. The student is a wonderful person and others would think immediately that she was good at what she does. Yet when Energy Response Tested, she believed she was only fifty percent good enough subconsciously. As we talked, it became apparent the cancer was not going to go away until she recognized that she was good enough. According to my testing methods, the hypothalamus was still nurturing illness. Part of the conversation stemmed on the student feeling, "How dare I get well when others in my community are not?" Subconsciously, the student felt others were better than she was, and it would not be right for her to let go of control and live life. Needless to say, the student left with mirroring homework plus bought a number of my books; *"BALANCE nature's way to heal your body"*, to pass on to others in the community as her way of planting healthy seeds of life.

Working in a family business with only a grade twelve education, the student had always felt not good enough and had to fight many battles to prove self over the years. The cancer became a retirement package brought on by the Soul in an attempt to have the student listen, BE grateful and understand she has always been good enough; always had value. This thought came from someone else treating the student as though she was "less" while growing up as a child. She encompassed that thought and carried it for many years. The time is now to release it along with to believe she is good enough and always has been.

We are all good enough to BE on this earth, to love and BE loved, to live our purpose while we follow our dreams. It's time to look at what we tell ourselves about situations and immediately reverse any negative thought. There are no accidents in life. They are created in sequence of our thoughts while in total connection with life and our perception of our ability to BE.

Letting Go of Control

Although I talked about this in an earlier chapter, I'm inclined to explain further how this comes about and why it is hard to shift, especially if a person is ill.

A few examples of this are from students, one person in particular, who was a nurse before being diagnosed with terminal cancer. I think that nurses in particular have difficulty feeling good enough, due to the concept of "The doctor knows everything". This concept is present both with patients and in the hospital. In our area, this is shifting somewhat with the use of nurse practitioners. After the consultation process, it was determined by the student that she would detoxify with the use of coffee enemas. A few days later, I received a phone call from her, stating in an indignant voice that a friend believed it was necessary to also have ionic footbaths. She wanted to know what I thought. I thought there should be no question. If a person has terminal cancer and has identified that toxin removal will help lengthen life, an ionic footbath, when available, is favorable to a faster path to wellness. If kept to one or two a week while doing the enemas, and juicing after each, the footbaths indeed help. The student did not want that answer: she is not ready to live life; there is more inner work to do.

Several other students wanted their partner to do the setup and installation of the enema for them, even though they were capable of getting down on the floor, bending, and functioning properly. This is not the partner's illness, it is their own. The illness or disease can become the way to control what is falsely perceived as nurturing, which one missed out on as a child.

Another case which exemplifies this further involves a student who came dressed each time in large baggy shirts and pants. I asked what the student would wear if she was being self and she described quite a different outfit than today. I asked why she wasn't doing that now and she answered that with the illness plus severe weight loss nothing fit. Besides that, the other clothes were upstairs and due to weakness, it was not possible to climb the stairs. Yet, the student has a partner, friends, and other family members who could help. There were closets downstairs, money available, the ability to walk, and someone nearby who could take her to the store. The student has subconsciously chosen illness rather than life: to give rather than to receive, to keep the cancer because subconsciously it gives the student control. A person should not wait until he or she is better to live life. The illness appeared because one was not living life. The energy for life comes as one starts to live it.

First, one has to identify that he or she is controlling something in their life. There are five basic questions one can ask self to define if there is controlling behavior.

1. Does one believe someone one loves is not good enough at something around the house or work and it upsets one?
2. Does one answer for someone else, whether they are there or not? For example, offering a partner to pick up a friend or family member without consulting them first.
3. Is there a portion of life that is in clutter or disrepair-photos, paperwork, ironing, painting, house repair, etc?
4. Is one enabling someone, resolving their issues rather than giving knowledge so they can resolve it themselves or not?
5. Does one have an illness or disease?

Illness and disease involve control without responsibility. It is freedom from inner concern about whether one will be good enough. The biggest obstacle in life, which is driven by fear, is the inner control one has set up as an illness or disease. Catholics brought up going to Catholic schools have a greater issue with this. There were no gray areas in past Catholic school systems. It was either right or wrong, no excuses were allowed and teachers entrenched in this concept convey the mindset one is not good enough when a student has low marks. Great teachers work with the students more than the curriculum and do not create this void in children.

So, one tends to not take action rather than face the chance that what they do is not good enough.

Love

Love has a powerful energy. To be in love with, and share the love of a Soul mate, is energy in motion. I have been married to my Soul mate for thirty-three years, and it has only been the last three years that we have both realized that our coming together was at the Soul level.

We have also learned that to love self is more important than loving another. Transformation to authentic self requires love of self. In the April, 2009 edition of *O Magazine*, Oprah had an interview with Michelle Obama. I kept the article Oprah presents on *"What I know for sure!"* The profoundness of what Oprah said about Michelle excited me. "When she looks at you, you know you've been seen. When she listens, you know you've been heard." Oprah also feels and stands for the same thing. Both of these ladies are fully authentic, and have the confidence to be open to all people.

When one loves self, the Universe lines up to empower and authenticate that Soul. Money is not on these ladies' minds. Their profound service to others attracts money and positive experiences into their lives, as we all can do. It is not about hair, clothes, jewelry, etc. It is about being the best one can be in service to others; to self first. One tends to use others to measure self; a sense of true self can replace this.

One needs to love self, accept love from others, and be able to love another. This combination is wholeness and oneness.

To BE authentic and love self, one has to feel and BE in this world. The Soul's language is spoken through symptoms. When not feeling, or if one has lost connection with the Universe, illness and disease will occur. This book is not saying that traditional medicine is not helpful; however, it is saying that knowledge is power and the impact of emotional feelings and physical toxins is vital to shifting illness and disease. Understanding that it is within self to change the direction of cancer, diabetes, arthritis, heart disease, etc. by feeling and BEing, is a lesson of life that brings joy, peace, hope, faith and love.

The opposite of fear along with self-doubt is joy. Courage is being afraid and going ahead anyway with faith in self. It takes awareness to understand the depth of this. Today, BE present, notice a symptom: do not negate with old age, genetics, etc. Love self enough to realize it is a message from the Soul. Listen to what it has to say. Recognize that one is good enough. Approval of self is all that matters. Worth is feeling and BEing. A workaholic is not buying worth that way, he or she is doing, not BEing, and eventually will be spoken to by the Soul through symptoms.

Prayer is talking and meditation is listening. Both are required to connect with one's real self. One needs to be responsible for one's own life as well as for the illness or disease that one has created. One is a Spiritual being having a human experience. Negative thoughts create plus take away energy: the vibrations of which one is. Thoughts are connected to emotional feelings and magnetize the thought, creating a positive or negative result depending on the message sent out to the Universe.

One needs a clear energetic direction. Energy surrounds and protects the human Body if negative feelings have been released. Remove toxins, strengthen cells, as well as supply the Body with proper nutrients at a higher level. Love self, find freedom, and illness or disease will disappear.

I remember that when my Body became alkaline, and I had removed the toxins, strengthened my cells, and added nutrients through juicing and eating healthier, the tumors in my groin and shoulders melted like butter. My energy level soared. It took a number of years after that to learn how to work with the depth of the Soul. I also learned how to release and feel the remaining emotional feelings that were holding me back from being authentic.

Feeling worthy or valued takes time. Looking for approval still occurs occasionally, as old habits reappear. Once any symptom shows up in my life, I stop and listen. Each symptom is connected to a gland, organ or part of the Body, and with practice, I can decipher the message, release the feeling and BE energized again as one with the Universe.

Being in a coma is an extreme example of Soul loss. Love of self has diminished to a severe level. The modality of Body Talk combined with The Fourth Principle has the ability to speak to the unconscious mind while someone is in a coma. The goal is to connect to their Soul and use energy in hope of guiding them back to life.

While writing this book, I have learned more about who I am and why I am here. As well, I have learned what has been holding me back from greatness, not only success. Recently, James and I worked together to connect some of these dots. I have always felt the need to be loved. When any of us do not love our self, we look for approval and love from others. As Byron Katie would say *"Is that true?"*

My story was that my mother and father never loved me after Patsy, my older sister, died at the age of five. I was two at that time. They chose alcohol and medications to help them forget plus to numb both their pain, at a level that they could function, yet not feel. While doing that, they were not present to the rest of their children. I chose to excel rather than regress from that process, and looked for approval from my parents. I never seemed to get it, or at least that's the story I have told myself subconsciously for years. On the Christmas of my sixteenth year at home, they bought me a pair of cocktail boots that I loved. The next day, the boots had to be returned, as they needed that money to pay a bill. As a result, I felt strongly that I was "not good enough or valued." This created permission in my mind for me to leave home at New Year's. That experience has added to who I am today, and gives understanding that we do not need to be a victim to excel in life. We just need to BE.

"The bottom line for everyone is, 'I'm not good enough'."
Louise Hay

When any of us feel that we are "not good enough or worth it", the story we tell ourselves comes from judgment and comparisons. That gives a false sense of self. One false story I carried around for a long time was about education. Even up until recently, I thought I was not worth it compared to conventional medicine or a Naturopath since they went to school for years and got a diploma. In reality, I go to school everyday, read books weekly, take courses yearly, and ensure regularly that I am around people who can give me increased knowledge. I also make it a point to BE present to opportunity that will enhance what I now have. I am good enough, worth it and having several diplomas does not change that.

Recently, I was at a seminar where the speakers were Clare Hughes, Kevin O'Leary, Frank McKenna and Richard Branson. What I learned from that day was that attitude and action are success in motion, not credentials. Commit to setting goals, keeping on with study, and asking questions. Reconnecting every day with one's goals is the key! Ultimately, all education is self education.

One needs to give self permission to dream, with space to expand that dream. Live it. Feel the passion. Sometimes it can come out of frustration. Richard Branson built an airline because he was frustrated with delivery times for other airlines to take him to his destination.

Clare Hughes did not win the medal because that was her goal. Her goal was to be a great skater for Canada, to BE and feel that while racing. The medal was the gift awarded to her for succeeding in BEing who she really is.

Know who one is with no need to hold back. BE authentic and speak one's truth.

Necessary for Wellness

Emotional Feelings

- Love of self.
- Have a feeling of worth.
- Have a feeling of good enough.
- BE authentic and present to life.
- Feel and Live Life.
- Freedom from the need for control.

Physical Support

- BE alkaline with a pH of 7.4 urine and 7.0 saliva, with an increase in saliva reading after eating.
- BE flexible. Drink water: half one's weight in ounces or milliliters, for mobility, detoxifying, functions of the Body.
- Be energy in motion. Take essential fatty acids for strong cells and to break down fat.
- BE supportive of one's liver. Detoxify for a minimum of ten sessions; ionic footbaths, infrared sauna or coffee enemas. During that process use castor oil packs; later milk thistle combo and a liver plus gallbladder flush yearly. Switch from cold foods and beverages to room temperature.

Symptoms

- A symptom is the language of the Soul: listen!
- Identify what part or parts of the Body are affected.
- What is the emotional feeling attached?
- Clear via prayer, letters or Energy Balance Harmony.
- Love self for being present.

Give Gratitude for each thing in life that is present daily. Focus on the positive. You are the gift that the world is waiting for.

To BE

To love self is the main ingredient to BE at the level the Soul requires. To love self means giving permission to say "No" or "Yes", depending on the circumstance. It gives one access to inner gifts while living life via the heart.

I take my dog, Shorty, for a walk sometimes at six in the morning. On a few mornings, I am doing that responsibly, however most days I am BEing. Concentration on my breathe gives me access to Universal energy and the ability to release trapped emotional feelings I am present to breathe and therefore am BEing.

In the car, while driving to one of our natural health satellite offices, which can take two hours, I play music I love. At times during the trip, I sing loudly and dance while behind the wheel. To me, that is BEing self. I dress in what I enjoy and stop when I desire a treat or a break. I am present to birds that fly by and the sky that is always present in its many forms. I am being Susan. Beauty of nature is one of my values in life.

To BE is to let the inner child come out and play! Illness or disease show that there is a trapped inner child kicking and screaming inside, looking for a way out. Instead of giving permission to BE self, old beliefs as well as stories can keep us locked inside. Now in life, I physically beat a drum to release anger that used to be stored in my Body as blocked lymph; hardened nodes. Internally, I used to block my detoxification pathways when I acted like a child where no one could see me-hiding my vulnerability. We are each capable of blocking arteries, glands, organs, etc. when we have difficulty releasing emotional feelings due to past life stories. The Soul is identifying that to us through symptoms.

I bought bowls with colorful polka dots to use when I feel the need to BE a child for that moment in time. I keep bottles of bubbles around, not just for my grandchildren, for me to release into the air when the moment arises. I love to see them float across the sky, shimmering and glowing while carrying my dreams higher and higher.

Four hula hoops are kept in the den for magical moments with my grandchildren and again for self, just for fun. It took me quite awhile to let my inner child out to play, and keeping it there for those special times can still be a challenge.

When we learn to love self, it is easy to forgive ourselves and others, while giving gratitude for what we have. It is easy to feel the connection, the vibration of energy within and around us. Love generates more love.

When Energy Response Testing others, I ask their permission to check whether they love self one hundred percent, value self and feel "good enough" for the same percentage. If not, I ask that they consider mirroring until this has been raised. Past life issues also have to be resolved to hold this feeling of love for self.

Summary of Chapter 7

1. Know what one would live and die for;

2. Focus on why one is here on earth, not the illness;

3. The perception of limitations leads to hopelessness. Know no limits;

4. There is a need to strengthen love of self first, then others. Peace, harmony, courage, trust, faith, worth, abundance, giving and receiving love will connect;

5. One's beliefs and disbeliefs act as filters through which one views life;

6. One always was good enough and is worth it;

7. Illness and disease can lead to the gift of life. Open the package and receive the purpose;

CHAPTER 8

A Simple Connection

James and I had a conversation in bed this morning that brings this title back to the basics of life. Blame is an excuse, as are procrastination, living with clutter, aggressive behavior, as well as other characteristics. James and I had watched a PBS special the previous evening, which featured Wayne Dyer discussing his new book, *Excuses Begone*. It was not an accident that our guests had left and nothing else was on TV to distract our attention from the program.

Dyer quoted the author; Byron Katie, on her revolutionary process called *The Work*, and used the basic questions: Is it true? Can you absolutely know that it's true? How do you react when you think that thought? Who would you be without that thought?

With God all things are possible. **All things are possible**. It is simple! A person can make excuses and feel the stress, or be free to BE him or her self, experiencing peace and harmony instead. Today, dare to let an excuse go!

Last night, five minutes before falling asleep, I allowed my imagination to see the wondrous possibilities for the future and feel how that would encompass me. Thank you, Wayne Dyer, for reminding me of something I had forgotten over the past few years. Nothing in life is an accident: it is simple!

Examining Myths: are they true?

The Sun is a wonderful healer!

The myths are that the sun is not healthy as well as creates disease and illness. Illness and disease are already present, as Vitamin D cannot be absorbed due to toxins. Therefore the Vitamin D becomes a free radical, causing further illness instead of prevention. Fear is the emotional feeling to work with here, connected with the kidney.

The Energy Field surrounding an individual can become weak due to trapped emotional feelings. Thus, an individual can receive stronger rays from the sun, also causing illness and disease. Again, illness was already present or the Energy Field would not have been weak. The Sun is fine: it is the Body that is not absorbing the rays in a healing, healthy way due to emotional and physical toxins.

Acid Reflux is caused by too much acid in the stomach!

The truth is that it is due to not enough acid, causing fermentation instead of proper execution of digestion. Another myth is that as one gets older the stomach no longer produces this digestive acid. Toxins block the natural production of <u>hydrochloric acid</u> in the stomach as it accumulates during the aging process. This however is not due to old age. Detoxification with seniors eighty or older has proven this over and over, as they are able to return to their doctors and stop the medication that is no longer necessary to cover a symptom.

One will probably acquire an illness or disease, due to their parent's genetic make-up!

Many individuals believe this to be true. Yes, there may be a weak point in the emotional and physical connection, however if the Body is strengthened, disease does not need to occur. Let's take the myth that if a mother had breast cancer the daughter will. It is a concern that doctors approve of many women having their breasts removed in a desire to prevent cancer due to a genetic parental weakness. Instead, women should be encouraged to strengthen their Body physically and emotionally while keeping the Body intact. Breasts are a beautiful part of being a woman. Whether small, large, drooping or withered, they are a part of being a female. Breast issues indicate a lack of nurturing sometime in one's life. The side of the Body represents if this was a lack by a male (right breast) or female (left breast). Also look at anger, as the liver plays a large part in the breast. Detoxification is a vital part of prevention. It is simple!

Old age is responsible for cataracts or arthritis!

This was discussed in the chapter on symptoms. As one gets older and toxins are allowed to collect in the Body, it changes the dynamics and shuts down functions of organs or glands, creating an imbalance. Joints require fluid, so water intake is vital as well as essential fatty acids to strengthen cells. Once these three physical items are taken care of, with the addition of the release of trapped emotional feelings, as well as a thirty to sixty day protocol of Energy Balance Harmony for the parathyroid, what had been called cataracts or arthritis is no longer present.

Eggs cause high cholesterol!

This is also a myth. Free range eggs actually help this imbalance in the liver. Other types of eggs burden the liver with additional hormones, antibiotics and other chemicals which are fed to the chickens. These additives can block the liver function and increase cholesterol.

Hot flashes and night sweats are indicative of pre-menstrual syndrome!

A myth again! Toxins regulate the dysfunction of the glands that create this imbalance. When practitioners work with clients to remove physical toxins and release the emotional feeling of not speaking one's truth or the feeling of resentment, these symptoms disappear.

An overactive bladder is a fluid issue!

Continuous running to the washroom or having accidents is a problem among many. Doctors tend to regularly prescribe diuretics for this symptom, believing it is a fluid issue. This also is a myth. Too little fluid in the Body causes the Body to promote flushing in order to maintain homeostasis. The need for chemicals and hormones to move to their proper status to perform functions in the Body facilitates this to occur when one is drinking too much caffeine and not enough fluid in most cases. The myth also coincides with an individual who wakes up between one and three every morning, believing this act is about having to urinate.

I love to excite students with the phenomenon of adding more fluid and seeing their initial reaction as well as their symptoms disappear. As a natural health practitioner, I do not take individuals off medications. Instead I send them back to their doctors to do so in hopes that someday they will identify what I have learned through time and research. To help with the problem of waking up between one and three, the removal of toxins is recommended. These night time hours are the liver's regeneration time, and it is the liver having difficulty that is waking one up and not the urination.

Eighty percent of incontinence can involve the emotional feelings of grief (lungs) and fear (kidney). This emotional combination creates a disconnection in the transportation and transformation of fluid in the Body. Forgiveness and the use of Energy Balance Harmony or Acupuncture will resolve this.

"It is only when one believes it will happen and therefore do next that will bring about a life change." Dr. Bruce H. Wilkinson

The Simple Connection

We live on a planet named Earth, which is surrounded by other planets and circled by the Sun. We are in a Galaxy. Human beings require the sun, nutrients, air, water and a filtration system to sustain us physically. We each have a Spirit to energize and to continually spark our reason for BEing. We have a Soul which is necessary to give us purpose and meaning, while connecting us to God in the Universe. Also an Energy Field to protect the physical Body, as well as align all forms of energy such as Chakras and Meridians and to magnetize us to Earth while allowing us a free will connection to Spirit, Soul, Body and the Universe.

Take that a little simpler to the sun being a reflection of the element of fire; nutrients the element of earth; air is air or the element of metal or minerals in some Chinese acupuncture literature; water is the element of water; and a filtration system is wood. The inner and outer you are present in all aspects. To sustain life, the earth itself is the same, as it requires all five elements. Water systems also require them, such as rivers, lakes, streams and oceans. We are all in balance separately and together in oneness. Emotional feelings in the human Body or turbulence in relationship to earth and water passages affect that balance. It is simple!

The Meridians were designed as entry points for energy into the physical Body and mapped according to the stars in our galaxy. Chakras are entry points of energy in the Energy Field that surrounds each of us separately. Blocked energy is what precipitates symptoms, which then become illness and disease if not resolved.

Meridians operate on a similar pattern as direct current which is coming into one's home. The Body receives direct current from the earth via the Meridians. Meridians can be blocked by both physical toxins and emotional feelings.

Chakras, the energy points for the Energy Field, receive energy via the Universe. Chakras are energized or depleted depending on the harmony of the Soul and Spirit. The depletion is similar to casting a dark cloud over an area of the Body, which can shut down the flow of life proportionately to the disharmony. Energizing is a wonderful enlightenment and is literally light from the Universe. Similar to how the Body achieves this light energy, certain parts of the world have retained it, for example the Grand Canyon. Being at the Grand Canyon can restore energy to the chakras, although if one does not locate the drain it will keep occurring and the energy charge will not last.

The main form of disharmony in the Body is when one believes the recurring story in the mind that one is not good enough or of real value and worth. This belief can hinder their choices to do what they would like to do, to live life, or succeed. Most importantly, it hinders their ability to let go of control and BE vulnerable: BE seen. Lost qualities disable the Soul, while inaction time and time again disables the Spirit.

There is a simple process to become aware of what is occurring. First, if there is a symptom or an accident awakening one up to the symptom, then there is an imbalance in the harmony of which one is. An intuitive person can sit with meditation or prayer and locate this imbalance as well as the reason behind it. A practitioner can as well, if they are intuitive or have the ability to check via symptoms or Energy Response Testing.

It is also possible to learn Energy Response Testing and to facilitate the answers for one's self. *(See Resources)* When performing the testing, it is imperative to ask to address higher self.

A few great questions to ask would be:

1. "Do I want illness and disease more than I want to let go of control?"
2. "Is it safe for me to let go of control?"
3. "Is it safe for others for me to let go of control?"

Clear each of these one at a time if the response is "No." One can facilitate this by using tools such as prayer or modalities such as Energy Harmony Balance which was described in an earlier chapter.

Confirm when one lost control in living life and how this occurred, by using Energy Response Test. One may be surprised at which event in the past has facilitated this occurrence.

The next part of this process is to take action with a list of five goals. Preferably, set small goals that can be completed over a short time frame.

Once those goals are reached, aim for medium goals and then larger ones. Mirror "I'm good enough" when having difficulty. Other types of symptoms are procrastination, clutter build-up, repairs piling up, emails not being deleted, etc. Keep going with this process, with an aim of having at least one large goal completed every month. Each completed set of goals, no matter how small, should be celebrated, and when one has reached the larger goals, then celebrate each accomplishment: feel good enough: BE.

When a wall comes up, look sideways to see if another path should be considered, or if this path is the right direction. Intuitively one will start to notice the answers to all the questions presented. A reminder is the wording of the question. As in Energy Response Testing, the question is imperative, as one word can shift the response the wrong way. If one is having "good enough" or worth issues, this can stop one from even asking the question in the first place! The thought may occur, "What if I ask the wrong question or it's seen as not good enough?" The control continues unless one is able to break free and find free will again. Acknowledging one is good enough and always was, can take one to freedom.

> *"When I stand before God at the end of my life*
> *I would hope that I would have not a single bit of talent left*
> *and could say, 'I used everything you gave me.'"*
> *Erma Bombeck, author & comedian*

I recently purchased a new children's book for my granddaughter Gia. The reason for the purchase was that I noticed she was moody a lot and had started to respond differently to others, not as freely as she had always done. Gia had lost a quality at seven years of age, and was reacting as if she was not good enough. The book, entitled *I Think, I Am* is by Louise Hay and Kristina Tracy. It is great even for adults. Gia told me that because of what she has learned in the book, at ballet class now when the teacher says that it was not good enough, Gia will look in the ballet mirror and say over and over, "I am good enough, plus I can do this." She added, "It will make me stronger inside!"

Wow! It is simple. Thank you, Louise Hay and Kristina Tracy, for writing this book. Thank you self for being present to life; noticing the need and intuitively ordering the book! Thank you Gia for a positive reaction to what was read.

How does one know that the illness or disease is leaving? Look for the symptoms to no longer be present. If they are not disappearing and/ or new ones are coming, then more inner work is necessary. One really is not living life. Go back to Byron Katie's questions if fearful of using one's own. Learn Energy Response Testing to check the meridians and chakras as indicators of what is being depleted. Check the Endocrine System first, then each organ. Find the emotional feeling that is trapped and look at why one is attached to that feeling. Illness or disease gives an individual permission to say yes or no. Why can one not do that without illness or disease?

Take each symptom and work separately, then as a whole. One can live to be one hundred and twenty to one hundred and fifty years of age with a solid mind and limbs, no walker or nursing home necessary. It is not old age taking one there.

Let's take an example of one person's experience:

An individual is waking up between one and three in the morning. Check the Horary Clock for indicators of this time frame, which pertains to the liver. There is a Horary Clock in *BALANCE nature's way to heal your body* or on the internet if one uses a browser such as Google. Emotional feelings are eighty percent of illness or disease. Therefore, the first thing would be to work on the emotional feeling attached to the liver: anger, frustration or irritation. If one has a rash, go with irritation. Without energy testing or intuitive ability, then one has to look for more symptoms. Identify whether the symptom is male (right side) or female (left side) and what is the issue involved. Physically, it is necessary to ensure getting enough fluid for the Body and that detoxification methods are followed to regenerate the liver. Give the liver nutritional support as well by eating less protein; earlier in the day; have no cold food or beverage, and BE alkaline. (*See Appendix E on liver support.*)

Awaken in the morning with cramping in both hands and fingers. This is an indicator of kidney energy blockage, indicating that fear is present, both male and female because both hands are showing signs. A hot flash also occurred when the eyes were opened. Resentment of having the cramping is more than likely. A quick hand to the belly button and tapping, breathing and panting will stop the initial symptom although not the cause. Fear is usually related to someone or something, or the fear of a person or issue. Failure and success are both places to look, as is one's feeling of good enough or valued. Physically, if one has an adrenal tire, look at drinking passion flower tea or tincture; add omegas; one thousand (1,000) units of Vitamin C; cleanse the kidneys with celery seed tea and drink the proper water for one's Body size daily. (*See chapter on symptoms for easy cleanses.*) Reduce work hours if not relaxing, and balance personal as well as professional sides of life. Work does not depict who one is: balance does.

The same individual has fungus on the second, third and fourth toe on the left foot. Left is female, fungus is about dampness and the spleen is an active part. The spleen is about abandonment or loneliness. The toes also give one clues when checking meridians. To help identify the meridians, either use a computer or take a trip to the Acupuncture clinic close by. Stomach and gall bladder meridians are involved and those are both linked to the spleen plus liver as elements. Break that down to earth and wood: nutrients and filtering of the Body. Shift the diet while removing toxins are prevalent to shift the fungus. Worry and doubt are present, as well as abandonment and anger or frustration. A gall bladder flush with a teaspoon of organic apple cider vinegar for digestion at the start of a larger meal would be indicated until the fungus shifts. The anger is female related. Fungus is hard to shift and will take a few months to accomplish. Warm the Body up with food plus drink at room temperature, staying away from sugar. Have a teaspoon of baking soda daily in water as well as soak foot in baking soda in water; vinegar or, use drops of tea tree oil or oil of oregano daily.

A bit of sinus issues which indicates lungs. With the spleen involvement from above, it is more than likely a bit of yeast. Lungs are related to grief. Check which side of the nose is the most active and in this case that is the right. It could indicate a male issue and/or also a creativity issue. Right is creative (heart) while left is logical (mind). In this case the individual was having difficulty with a project not a man. Clearing the grief attached by writing a letter opened the congestion. Taking a chlorophyll drink daily for a couple of weeks, plus staying away from sugar and alcohol completed the process.

It is simple when broken down step by step. *Symptoms: The Language of the Soul* will help one determine the breakdown. One is a work of art, a unique human being with a purpose and the ability to accomplish that purpose when one listens inside and out.

Pay attention to what is stopping one and clear blockages by releasing emotional feelings along with toxins. Basically, move that energy, raise that energy, have fun with it and the possibility.

"Life is like riding a bicycle. To keep your balance you must keep moving." Albert Einstein

When one has a serious disease, there are usually many symptoms present. The process to eliminate symptoms occurs faster when one has an understanding of the emotional feeling connected to illness. Ideally, when one believes and works on the emotional at the same time the physical is being resolved, the disease moves away quickly. The only reason it stays is that internally there needs to be a strengthening of who one is. It is there subconsciously for a reason. The illness or disease is keeping one from feeling new episodes of not being "good enough" or "worth it". That can be so strong it can lead to death rather than life. Cancer, heart disease, diabetes, and other major diseases can be reversed when one chooses. It is one's free will.

Is one connected to God, right now, in this moment in time? If one does not believe in God that is all right, call the connection Source, Universe, Buddha, The Collective or whatever one believes. Simply BE connected to an energy source, because one is electrical. Rub one's feet on a carpet and touch a doorknob to solidify that point.

Conduct electricity efficiently. Drink enough water for half one's Body size, let emotional feelings go once they're processed, and remove toxins so calcium is absorbing and magnesium levels are balanced. Forgive those from the past. Cleanse the liver so potassium and iodine are available, plus again ensure one is drinking enough water so sodium is playing a proper part. These components are one's electrical team physically, as God is the Soulful part, (emotions) as well as mind is the Spiritual aspect.

Intuitively, I am being told to give some more examples so here they are to help one in this quest:

A natural health student of mine was experiencing a major right hip issue and seeing a Chiropractor and Naturopath regularly for relief that lasted only days. This is normal, as the emotional feeling keeps coming up until it is resolved. After consultation and energy testing, the emotional feeling was identified as a decision making issue based on whether to retire. The partner of the student wanted the retirement to occur, while the student loved the position of employment and was not sure this was the right time. The right side was about a male, while the leg and hip about moving forward in life. Once identified that the hip wanted to move forward which was being held back internally with indecision, thus creating physical tightness in that area, the "AHA!" moment came. It was not about going in the partner's direction. It was about making the decision one way or another. The limbo was keeping the symptom active. A date was set for retirement and the hip has been fine ever since. Fear was the emotional feeling. Kidneys have to do with joints in addition to bones, as well as the lack of magnesium absorption.

Two male students need to be mentioned; both of whom experienced the symptom, cancer of the tongue. One man was young, one was older, and both were having guilt issues. The tongue is related to the heart. The young gentleman was openly willing to work with the physical part of natural healing; however, he unfortunately was not as willing to deal with all of his emotional feelings. The other feelings involved are abandonment (spleen) and anger (liver) as is in all cancer cases: hardening of phlegm. He also chose to have a surgeon insert a tracheotomy tube in case his tongue should swell and stop him from breathing. It was in the hospital just a few days after this that he passed away. The step he took identified to his Soul the disconnection in self, while the surgery created the ability for the cancer to grow rapidly. The older gentleman was reluctant to do the physical steps, yet managing the emotional a bit at a time. In the past he remained silent instead of speaking up as a tool to resolve personal conflict. He would feel guilty for doing this, yet kept up this process due to the "not good enough" syndrome and the fear of saying the wrong thing. He felt he would be shot down verbally if he did speak. He started to speak up and each time the reward was fewer symptoms. It is within all to heal: it is one's free will to choose or not and has nothing to do with loving another. It is about loving self.

The Jabez Prayer

And Jabez called on the God of Israel saying,
"Oh, that You would bless me indeed,
And enlarge my territory,
That Your hand would be with me,
And that You would keep me from evil,
that I may not cause pain!"
So God granted him what he requested.
1 Chronicles 4:10 (NKJV)

Strengthening the Powers Within

- The individual with the illness or disease should be asking the initial questions of the doctor or practitioner, rather than the partner, friend, etc. To support the individual, the other person could offer to take notes and follow-up if something is not asked. The initial questions are indicators of how far from living life the individual has come and the work necessary in the present to shift this. Enabling or creating a path for "not good enough" or not feeling of value has the ability to prevent wellness from occurring.

- The only attachment should be to self and God not the doctor or practitioner. This includes not being overly attached to other people or places one came from.
- There will be a sign of wanting to learn and do more to facilitate life. Setting goals, reading books, talking to people or building a collage are all signs that one is moving toward wellness and accepting his or her own power within.
- Showing up for appointments.
  o Be present to the lessons;
  o Look to the doctor or practitioner for knowledge, not healing. Wisdom comes from that knowledge and guidance is available from within.

- Deal with the emotional feelings trapped in a timely manner. There are no excuses that would stop this if one truly wants to live life.
- Understand that one is not alone.
  o God is there: connect with him;
  o Ask God to answer one's questions and BE present to the answers;
  o Give gratitude daily for all one has;
  o Listen to the inner part of which one is.

- Learn and understand the tools to measure wellness.
  o Live Blood Analysis—BE informed;
  o pH strips—BE alkaline;
  o Symptoms: aim for less not more;
  o Judging self or others are signs of "not good enough" or lack of value being present;
  o Move forward instead of waiting for wellness first. Start with baby steps.

"Forgiveness doesn't happen in your head until it happens in your heart." *Debbie Ford*

- Good Enough-Loving Self-Living Life
  - o Believe;
  - o Inspire;
  - o Transform.

- Worth
  - o Respect self;
  - o Connect in the good that one is;
  - o Value self.

The decision to follow one's heart and live life is not easy for some to make. When one has a health issue with the gall bladder, decision making becomes harder. Starting there physically with a flush is a step in the right direction.

Letting the inner child out after years of holding inner control takes faith along with love of self. After all, it may have been the only control that one felt he or she had over life. When one surrenders, there is no need to control. The gift of transformation is one's self: the one who holds the power on earth to, succeed or fail, to live or die, to be happy or sad, to be well or ill, and to be rich or poor. One has the ability to surrender to peace and harmony or to hold on to the control. Illness and disease are symptoms which show that one is still holding a false sense of control; as enabling is a false sense of self-worth.

The message can come from within or from other messengers who have also started with baby steps in this journey of life. Listen to one's heart to guide, and the teacher will come. Every day one is given the answers, whether through the written or spoken word or a visible sign. Test run that today, it is amazing and that simple!

Soul & Spirit

Through insight this past week I was intuitively guided to this response. Certain things in life excite me.

- ❖ Creating projects or programs.
- ❖ Interviews or motivational speaking on radio, TV or to groups.
- ❖ Travelling around the world.
- ❖ Gazing at waterfalls, the ocean, clouds, blue jays and butterflies.
- ❖ Listening to rock 'n roll music and dancing to it.
- ❖ Hula hooping and sending bubbles floating into the air.
- ❖ When family gets together, photos and traditions.
- ❖ Writing books and being an author.
- ❖ To be of service to others.
- ❖ My relationship with James.
- ❖ Financial abundance.

The list could be longer, as so many things in my life excite me. Being excited is a relationship with Spirit. My Soul is attached to all of the above items. I have checked intuitively and via ERT. Yet that alone does not promote having them in abundance, peace, or harmony. It takes an attachment to the Universe for each item to transform into reality and become the gift in one's life.

The Process to Connect

1. We can make a list of all that excites us that we want. The Soul and Spirit need to be in harmony with the items on the list; otherwise it can be ego therefore not attainable.
2. Check to see if we are connected one hundred percent to the Universe.
3. Connect the items to the Universe with prayer, meditation or visualization.
4. Still not connected? Then meditate around the item or items listening to the Soul. There needs to be a purpose surrounding the request that meets the needs of the Soul.

Formerly, I had been looking for abundance in fun, travel, clothes, and philanthropy. The Spirit and Soul were connected, yet I was not being allowed to connect to the Universe. After a five minute meditation connecting with my Soul, I understood. The purpose of giving and receiving knowledge was necessary to provide a harmonic connection.

This knowledge alone excited me and brought up more questions. I knew my physical Body was still not one hundred percent well, albeit no cancer was present, as well as I wanted to find out why. What I learned was that my Soul plus Spirit were not in harmony. It appears my Spirit loved the excitement of being ill and then returning to wellness, like winning a game. Due to the years of not letting my inner child out to play and obviously still not doing this to the extent that created harmony within, the Spirit looked elsewhere for excitement. Basically, I had provided a source and it was using that path. Wow!

I meditated and talked with God, the Archangels as well as other angels of the light. The way to resolve this became known within. First, I needed to shift the emphasis of my story that when I was young I worked hard and was taught to be responsible. I had perceived that to mean I was not allowed to have fun or even knew how to do that today. That obviously is a story that was keeping me a victim, as well as hindering my stepping forward completely in living life. It injured my "worth it." Once I sat and rewrote the story, I was able to shift this old paradigm and move forward.

To completely fulfill the connection to Spirit and Universe took practice as well as having fun and excitement in life. Finding something to create this every second day was a task at first. Soon it became enjoyment, and finally it is excitement.

Food can become a false excitement, similar to what I had created with the illness and wellness. When a person gets as excited about eating a piece of cake or pie as much as they would in riding a carousel, then it can become a wellness issue and a Spirit disconnect from the Soul. I did that in the past without realizing it. I loved those little chocolate cheesecakes, which would be fine if I had only had one or two. I realized it was an issue when I wanted the whole box day after day.

"Nothing happens until something moves"
Albert Einstein

One cannot lie in bed being nothing except ill and expect to get well. There has to be action in the direction of wellness along with living life. Be it baby steps or giant steps, action needs to occur. This action can not be directed by the will or it will eventually wear the Body out, forcing the Soul to leave and death to occur.

One hears all the time how someone fought such a valiant fight for life and lost. One tends to look at life as not being attached. This needs to shift, as life and energy are one. The flow of life returns as one forgives plus connects authentically to self and to God, gives gratitude for what one has, as well as takes those steps to living life.

As mentioned in other chapters, vibrations play an important part in the harmony of the Body. Vibrations increase by strengthening cells, removing toxins, adding healthy food and water, prayer, meditation and working with different modalities. Wisdom is more powerful than knowledge and shows up when one sparks it.

There are three steps to being fully electrically connected as a human being:

Step One

The first of these is being connected to God. With that comes the need to first believe in God or the name one has given, be it Source, etc. Then one must have faith and freedom to ask questions while being open to receive a response via life. As well, it is important to express gratitude for what one has, no matter how small or large that might be.

Step Two

One needs to BE <u>grounded</u>. What does that mean in its fullness? As human beings, one is magnetically connected to the earth. It is the minerals in our Body that maintains this connection and the minerals in the earth that balance this as well. The Root Chakra is the part of one's Energy Field that guides the connection between earth as well as the physical Body. Emotional feelings plus lack of proper nutrients will weaken this connection. The Energy Field surrounding one can be measured at five hundred hertz or higher, depending on the vibrations acquired through food, meditation, teachings, energy work, toxin removal, cellular strength, and more.

When working with self or others, it is necessary to BE present to self along with aware that one is grounded. One way to do this is to visualize that roots are growing from one's feet down into the ground. If one is low in minerals, water for conducting or have vibrations that are low due to attached emotional feelings, it may be difficult to check the Soul, Spirit, Field or Body. Four percent of Body mass is minerals.

One requires less than one hundred milligrams of trace minerals daily and more than one hundred milligrams of major minerals. *(see Appendix H)*

Minerals play three roles in the physical Body:

1. Structure in forming bones and teeth;
2. Normal heart rhythm, muscle contractibility, neural conductivity and acid-base balance;
3. They regulate cellular metabolism by becoming part of enzymes and hormones that modulate cellular activity.

Minerals cannot be made by the Body and must be obtained through diet. Excess can be toxic. Again, balance is needed in all aspects of life.

It takes vitamin D, calcium, phosphorus, magnesium, zinc, fluoride, chloride, manganese, copper and sulphur to build bones. Bone structure may be reversed when the emotional feeling of fear or shame blocks the kidney, or the inability to speak one's truth shuts down the energy of the parathyroid. Removing emotional plus physical toxins as well as applying Energy Balance Harmony will again help to strengthen the bones.

Step Three

The third step is to be aware and facilitate harmony with self, earth as well as the Universe. Being present takes practice. When one slows down it is easier to become aware of moving, listening, communicating, smelling, tasting, thinking, and being present to all of life. Movement with attention is a powerful tool.

"The quality of our movement is a manifestation of the quality of the workings of our brain and will ultimately determine the quality and vitality of our lives." Anat Baniel

Close attention needs to be paid to movements. Any movement will cause the brain to grow new connections. As one learns to move with greater ease, it will improve the sense of individuality, efficiency, ability to think plus feel, and will also improve self-image. To improve movement, it is necessary to understand along with be aware; the mind plus Body must be connected in harmony. Blocked emotional feelings will shift through paying attention to the movement of the emotional feeling. Most people have gone through life in automatic movement (doing). Now is the time to switch to movement with attention (BEing). Good feelings will become richer while bad feelings will lose their energy force.

Moshe Feldenkrais and now Anat Baniel work with nine essentials to grow as well as develop new possibilities in the brain: movement with attention, turning on the "learning switch", reducing force with whatever one does, firing enthusiasm, setting flexible goals, tapping the power of imagination and dreams, while cultivating awareness. The brain has an amazing ability to constantly reorganize, grow and change when movement with attention in addition to the others are incorporated. The language impaired can speak, the paralyzed person can move, chronic pain dissipates, and the Body can become suppler, when incorporating the connection of the Spirit (mind) with the Soul (emotions).

Science has proven that when one combines attention with movement, millions of brain cells are activated. These cells join to form new patterns and create new possibilities. Every area of life can begin to change. Increased vitality is one benefit which a person receives. The ability to feel is another. After the lesson is learned, there is freedom to release. Pay close attention to the emotional feeling and it will change. Good feelings will get richer.

Slow down and see self well. Take a step in that direction, visualize wellness again, plus keep stepping towards it. Build thought up to wellness not illness, as if one was practicing piano, golf or dance. See one's self in it, each movement and possibility. Practice wellness over and over until it is all that one knows. Slow along with attention: in the present and in BEing; not for others or how others would do this. Others were not given this illness or disease; one has been given this moment in time to BE!

The measuring stick is one's individual symptoms. When one considers measuring others, he or she is measuring self with judgment, not love. This also can shift.

The heart/Soul is the connection necessary to activate the powers within. Deepak Chopra was recently on Dr. Oz's television program, and had a wonderful meditation that shows the way to do this. One can simply go online; type in "Dr. Oz and Deepak Chopra Meditation" and it will come up.

Deepak has been presenting the simplicity of the connection for a long time now.

Feel the gentle breeze slightly touching one's cheek, sunlight filtering through the clouds, the patter of rain on the step, the texture and smell of that piece of fruit one is holding. The present moment is the doorway to our Soul and the spark necessary to ignite Spirit.

Today, BE present to self and to others. Have what others say mean something: they matter.

Desire & Timing

Once a connection has been made and a desire found, it takes authenticity along with a feeling of "good enough" as well as value to connect the timing with the desire.

People change when they feel supported and loved. Support self plus others in being whole. Stand in support of healing self first. Know all energy is interconnected, and lifting negative energy to positive energy is a purpose for all to follow. Dis-ease is a whole being not at ease, a being not living life or loving self. Fall in love and have a relationship with self first. One was born, one is of value!

Symptoms are only terrible to have if one is not present to the gift they offer. They will dissolve with self love, awareness, gratitude, forgiveness and the ability to feel life.

Ask for help or what one desires, and BE present to the answer whichever way it arrives. Every thought has a frequency, a vibration one is sending out to the Universe. The Universe has to correspond with the nature of one's song, the harmony that is one authentically.

There are no accidents. They are actually reminders that one is out of harmony at that precise moment in time. Symptoms are on the way or already there and not recognized for what they really are, due to feelings that are creating an inner response from a thought. The thought can facilitate the malfunction of a system in the Body:

- Detoxification via the skin, liver, kidneys, lungs, spleen, large intestine, small intestine and bladder;
- Immune system: thymus or bone marrow in general;
- The hormonal system, basically the blockage of energy to the function of the adrenals, thymus, thyroid, parathyroid, pineal, pituitary or hypothalamus;
- Blood flow to and from the heart: both need to be checked energetically;
- Lymph fluid, specifically the movement, may be blocked via thoughts;

- One or more of the twelve meridian channels;
- Chakras: the seven basic.

The system would depend on the thought. I was frequently shutting down a number of these: detoxification, lymph, bone marrow, and flow of blood back to the heart in particular. I learned to recognize the symptom rapidly after presenting it a number of times. I tended to put off fixing the cause until another time. And of course, I repeatedly experienced the above until I took the time, forgave myself, as well as stopped letting inner self punish me through the false judgments I had set into play years ago.

Is one experiencing shoulder pain? Look for the guilt that is affecting the heart and blood flow. Relieve the grief, as the lung is also in play; specifically the one on the same side as the shoulder, thus a detoxification pathway. Recognize if it is left shoulder that is in discomfort. If so, there is anger and the liver is creating this. If the problem is with the right shoulder, then the gall bladder and indecision or doubt is present. Strengthen one's "good enough". Feel one's worth, cleanse the gall bladder. It is that simple!

The other day, the Universe sent an opportunity to guide another student and a fellow Acupuncture colleague. A client of hers had a frozen left shoulder for the past four months plus had been recently receiving acupuncture. The Acupuncture had worked each time, only to have it return after a number of days. With Energy Response Testing; grief, guilt and anger were identified; resulting from something that had taken place at work approximately four months prior. Writing a few letters, if done timely, preferably that very day, the Acupuncture should be enough to support the full release of the shoulder. Experience has shown this to be the case in guidance given in the past.

Each day one is sent what one needs to move forward in grace and harmony. Whether that comes in sound through people or media, vision, or even a taste that brings back memories, each moment in time one has the opportunity to BE present to the gifts in life. Take a moment today to BE present to the gifts, and transform one's life one moment at a time. One is unique as a human being, a special person meant to be here on earth. One is good enough and always has been. One is of value (Worth). One is not alone if one chooses to connect to what is!

"As you move through your day, let in what you learn of others by how their being passes you." Mark Nepo

Inconvenient moments such as traffic delays are actual opportunities to slow down, BE present to the moment and the day. The very issues one often tries to avoid return sometimes with different faces, until one takes courage to go through and resolve them.

Too often, one wants another to hold one's sadness or pain because one won't take the risk of asking them to be held while one is hurting. Being vulnerable is part of the lesson one requires in life.

Supplements are no longer needed once the connection has been made between life and BEing. Sometimes this can occur instantly. One day one could need zinc and co-enzyme Q10. On the next day, after the connection is made emotionally the light will come on and soon one is absorbing nutrients as well as expelling what is not necessary in one's Body at maximum again. No more need for the supplements. Totally amazing!!

One has moved into life and stopped living illness. It is necessary to ask the question: "What does life look like to self?"

- Write down the response.
- Take the response deeper with further questions.

I love to study; knowledge empowers me, excites me, gives me approval of self and builds my good enough.

I look at what I love and if my life was on a path connected to that. In some cases, the answer was "Yes," and in some instances, "No." Then I would take the "No" deeper and chunked it down to find out why. A few reasons were related to making mistakes in life. Now that I had read *Move into Life* and *The Talent Code*, I understood they were never mistakes, only lessons on how to make life better in the future. I took each moment and listed the positive events from them. An example is when I married my first husband. The marriage was difficult plus at times unsafe. We had met and married in Ontario. It is through that marriage that I ended up in Amherst, Nova Scotia, met James and have had a wonderful thirty plus years. Knowing what it was like to be unsafe led me to understanding what safe really is, and the feeling that it brings to my life. Tammy, my eldest child, came from the relationship with my first husband, as well as I have two wonderful grandchildren due to that link. Instead of being lost in a large city, I am a part of this community and belong to different organizations. All of these were positive events.

One needs to shift from being stuck to being involved in the solution. One has the answers to every question one has ever had in one's life. Believe it! Wisdom is power. Knowledge is not, though knowledge is necessary for wisdom to occur. Being present to the knowledge gives opportunity for solutions to happen as wisdom moves energy. When one changes the way one thinks about things, the things one thinks about change.

Cancer is a message one gives self when one has lost one's way in life as a BEing, a reminder from the Soul of one's purpose yet to be fulfilled.

If one is still living and breathing, one has the ability to let go of control. As one shifts into natural harmony with self and the Universe, it's possible to use free will to dissolve the tumors.

It is time one realizes this Body that carries Soul plus Spirit is theirs to care for and stop giving that responsibility away to others. If one feels not good enough or not of value to do this, then that is the lesson one needs to learn-now!

A student of mine came to see me for a follow-up lesson. This person had been diagnosed with cancer that had metastasized. After being transformed through dealing with emotional feelings and clearing toxins, she was radiant with life and personal power. Excitedly, she talked about plans to bring positive light to cancer, and has even taken action to establish a group.

There was one issue left that we had to understand; why her left shoulder had grown a lump a number of weeks prior. The lump had not grown since; however, neither had it gone away.

I performed Energy Response Testing and it took a slowing down while breathing to recognize that she had felt a burden with having to take on healing self, even with the lessons learned and support given. The shoulders represent burdens in life, the left an issue concerning a female. The hard lump is a hardened thought projected by anger or frustration from the liver. It's combined with not speaking up, via the parathyroid not absorbing calcium into the bones and instead attaching outside the shoulder bone. The student will see a doctor to have tests to confirm, as well as will also work on the liver along with the parathyroid, emotionally and energetically with tapping plus breathing. A castor oil pack with baking soda and magnesium will also be added to help dissolve the calcium back into the bone. If cancer cells are present, once the emotional and physical toxins have been released transforming to wellness is achievable. Whatever choice she makes is hers alone to make: free will.

Most people are so used to going to a doctor and giving them the responsibility for treatment of the illness or disease. They give away power on a regular basis. It has become such a habit in society that people find it difficult to fathom that we have the power to heal ourselves. One is never alone; there is guidance each day if one chooses. The method is not the issue; it is being present to the choice that will take one to wellness.

Honor life's purpose by letting go of control and choose to live life again. Celebrate the small things. Love and appreciate the shift from doing to BEing, from illness to wellness.

Summary of Chapter 8

1. Write letters to self, God, parents, siblings, ex-partners, friends, employers, or others who may be connected to the emotional feelings trapped within. Feel—forgive—then burn or flush;

2. Identify mirroring. See and listen to what is present to one's life;

3. Express positive affirmations three times daily for thirty days;

4. Strengthen the diaphragm so emotional feelings leave rather than stay;

5. Conduct electricity with a balance of water, calcium, magnesium, potassium, iodine, and sodium;

6. Recharge-sharpen the saw-take time to meditate and exercise;

7. Be alkaline;

8. Be authentic to who one is;

9. Connect to earth and nature to energize one's meridians;

10. Connect to the Universe to energize one's chakras;

11. Identify one's values, standards and boundaries. Each person has his or her own!

12. Be responsible for self;

13. Nurture self and celebrate life;

14. Listen to the Soul intuitively now, rather than later when symptoms begin to appear;

15. Know what sparks one's Spirit so it's ready if one needs it;

16. Build a relationship with self first, then with others;

17. Give gratitude for all one has;

18. Direct one's thoughts to wellness not illness;

19. Slow down-BE present;

20. Live life.

Radiation Bath

1 cup (500ml) of sea salt   1 cup (500ml) of hydrogen peroxide
1 cup (500ml) of baking soda   1 cup (500ml) of aloe vera juice
1 cup epsom salts

<u>Notes:</u>

- Place ingredients in bath with hot water: as hot as one can handle and soak in the tub for approximately thirty minutes.
- Take this bath every three days for a <u>maximum</u> of four times.
- If one is frail, please ensure that someone is close by during this process as the hot water can make one weak. This process raises oxygen, immune response and promotes healing properties.
- Sea salt promotes pain relief, reduces infections, rejuvenates cells, and induces a healthy exchange of minerals & toxins. Combined with baking soda, it reduces the negative effects of radiation.
- Aloe Vera Juice stimulates the immune system, is high in minerals and amino acids, is anti-inflammatory and has high detoxifying powers.
- Hydrogen Peroxide adds oxygen which revitalizes normal cells while enhancing the immune system and transporting toxins from the Body.
- Baking Soda neutralizes acids and is an anti-inflammatory as well. It reduces fungus in the Body, normalizes cells. When combined with the above, it reduces the negative effects of radiation.
- Epsom salts is a bath salt high in mineral content.

APPENDIX B

Soulful Qualities

Acceptance	Harmony	Relationship
Action	Healing	Responsibility
Assimilation	Honesty	Reverence
Awareness	Hope	Rhythm
Clarity	Humility	Security
Compassion	Humor	Self-worth
Confidence	Integrity	Serenity
Consciousness	Inner Connectedness	Service
Contentment	Inspiration	Silence
Courage	Intuition	Simplicity
Creativity	Joyfulness	Sincerity
Empathy	Kindness	Stillness
Enthusiasm	Laughter	Strength
Expression	Learning	Success
Faith	Listening	Surrender
Forgiveness	Love	Sweetness
Free Will	Mercy	Tenderness
Friendship	Oneness	Thoughtfulness
Fun	Openness	Trust
Generosity	Patience	Unconditional love
Gentleness	Peace	Understanding
Giving	Positive thinking	Unity
Gratitude	Purity	Wisdom

APPENDIX C

Energy Balance Harmony

This is an easy protocol that when administered works immediately for some symptoms and takes thirty to sixty days in others. Deep emotional feelings need to be released via forgiveness or they can return.

1. Place either hand over the gland or organ that requires assistance.
2. With the other hand, tap the head front to back and then front again, with hand extended using palm or finger tips.
3. Breathe in and out while tapping.
4. Pant three short breathes while tapping.

Notes:

- This simple procedure is similar to starting a car with a battery charger. Tapping releases electrodes in the head that are connected to all organs and glands. The breathing and panting forces these electrodes to move at a faster pace to the position of the hand placement, thus opening blocked energy in the gland or organ.
- When working with the parathyroid gland; energetically under the jaw, however physically on top of the thyroid. The necessity for ten times daily; hourly is to ensure that the parathyroid functions at optimum level so as too absorb calcium; diminishing a build-up in other parts of the Body.
- Once toxins; both physical and emotional are removed as well as the symptom resolved, this practice can stop.

APPENDIX D

Alkaline Therapy

1. Mix one part baking soda with three parts maple syrup in a small saucepan, i.e. 1 Tablespoon (15ml) baking soda and 3 Tablespoons (45ml) maple syrup.
2. Stir briskly.
3. Heat for five minutes.
4. Take one teaspoon (5.0 ml) daily, as needed. (maximum 3 teaspoons)

Notes:

- Check pH urine and saliva before starting this program to ensure the pH does not exceed 7.4 urine and 7.0 saliva for more than two days;
- Use aluminum free baking soda only. (Canadian brands are aluminum free);
- Do not boil;
- Do not heat in a microwave;
- Store in a glass container (i.e. Mason jar) on the counter.

The purpose of this protocol is too alkaline the Body. Cancer students will benefit as the cancer cell takes in the maple syrup (cancer loves sugar) and the baking soda that is bound to it by heat is able to integrate the cell and create an alkaline base destroying the cancer in the cell. Cancer is in part a fungus.

Liver Support

Keep a journal of feelings or symptoms. This includes emotions; food eating; bowel elimination (color, length, solid or diarrhea, food particles not digested, etc.); nausea; and so on . . . .

- learn to stop, look and listen to one's Body
- know what to look for when guidance is necessary

Support the liver:

- 2 Tablespoons (30ml) castor oil (processed without hexane) on a white cotton folded cloth, placed on the liver in the early evening for one hour. Place a hot water bottle on top.
  - o to absorb into the liver and soften as well as help to eliminate toxins;
  - o alleviates pain and energizes a hard, weak liver;

- A gentle massage of the liver will help the elimination process when in discomfort.
- May need desiccated liver pills to strengthen the liver. Check via Energy Response Testing.
- Carrot juice with apple and/or pear will help the liver's detoxification process.
- Need to remove toxins ASAP from the Body via Ionic Footbaths; organic coffee enemas or infrared sauna. Drink juice following these to replace any nutrients that may have also been removed.
- Daily drink water/fresh squeezed juice/herbal teas for a total of half body weight in ounces per day.

o by noon the urine will be pale unless taking a vitamin B supplement which causes deeper color.

- If eating almonds, nut butters or large amounts of protein do so before two in the afternoon as they are harder to process in the Body and therefore harder on the liver after this time of day.
- Sleep seven to eight hours nightly; nine or ten until five or six in the morning is ideal and gives the liver a better opportunity to rejuvenate.
- May need extra potassium from apples, potatoes, or bananas.
- Digestives may be necessary.
- No cold foods or beverages.
- Milk Thistle Combo tincture is a great addition to a protocol to help with repair.

Gall Bladder Flush

1. Juice: half an organic lemon and mix vigorously in a jar with 2 teaspoons (10ml) virgin olive oil and a little water.
2. Drink down on an empty stomach at bedtime. At least two hours after a meal.
3. Do this for ten evenings and repeat series once more if necessary. This would be necessary if in pain or jaundiced.
4. Drink two glasses of apple juice daily during this routine to widen the bile ducts. Ensure the juice contains no added sugar. For diabetics, sip rather than drink over a period of the day.

IT IS IMPORTANT TO LIE ON <u>RIGHT</u> SIDE IN BED AND TO PLACE A HOT WATER BOTTLE OVER LIVER/GALL BLADDER AREA (right side at edge of rib)

Note:

- A hot water bottle is necessary because an electric heating pad will create a change in Body frequency due to electrical magnetic fields.
- It may be noted that during this flush some thirty to four hundred stones may be found in the feces. They can be black, white, brown, red or turquoise.
- This simple flush also has the ability to alkaline the Body.
- The apple juice helps release the stones by widening the bile ducts, and apples are also a great detoxifier.

- Once completed, it is recommended to follow the instructions in Appendix C on Energy Balance Harmony to balance the pituitary gland.
- If one has stopped for more that three days then the ten days need to start over, as the stones have hardened again over this period.

APPENDIX G

Liver & Gallbladder Cleanse

<u>Items & Ingredients:</u>

1. Apple juice with no added sugar. Amount: require thirty two ounces daily (six liters) to be taken at room temperature. Organic is preferred. Cranberry can also be used although apple juice works the best.
2. Epsom salts: four tablespoons (60 ml) dissolved in twenty-four ounces (750ml) of water to be taken in four equal portions of six ounces. Fresh lemon can be added for taste.
3. Extra virgin olive oil, cold pressed: one half glass (four ounces=125ml).
4. Either fresh grapefruit (pink is best) or fresh lemon and/or orange combined
5. One pint jar with lid to be used for the olive oil & fruit juice.
6. One quart jar to be used for the Epsom salt & water mixture.

Instructions for days one to five:

Drink one thirty-two ounces (one liter) organic apple juice; regular if no organic available; can be watered down if too sweet. Drink at room temperature slowly throughout each day.

Note:

- The malic acid in the apple juice dissolves stagnant bile accumulated in the liver and helps to soften the gallstones, while expanding the bile ducts and creating a cleansing effect.

- Diarrhea may occur as stagnant bile leaves the liver. The apple juice can be diluted with water if necessary.
- **Do not drink or eat cold or chilled food or beverage** during this period as it cools the liver and prevents full flushing.
- Try to avoid animal, dairy or fried foods. Otherwise eat normally: avoid overeating.
- Avoid taking medication or supplements that are not absolutely necessary while on this regimen.
- The seventh day requires rest so please adjust one's schedule to accommodate this.

Day six

- Slowly drink all the thirty-two ounces (one litre) of apple juice between waking-up until noon. Eat a light breakfast such as oatmeal. Avoid sugar or other sweeteners, oils, dairy, and cold cereals. **No protein, butter or oil on this day unless one is diabetic.**
- **Do not eat or drink anything except room temperature water after one thirty in the afternoon other than the remaining protocol unless diabetic, then protein as required. Spirulina would be the appropriate choice as a powder mixed in warm water.**
- Mix in a container: four tablespoons (60ml) of Epsom salts with twenty-four ounces (750ml) of filtered water. Add sliced lemons to reduce taste.

6 P.M. Drink six ounces of the Epsom Salt mixture

8 P.M. Drink another six ounces of Epsom Salt mixture

9:30 P.M.
If no bowel movement has occurred in the past twenty-four hours, it is recommended to have a room temperature water enema. This will trigger a series of bowel movements.

9:45 P.M.
Use room temperature grapefruits, lemons and/or orange: about six.

- Squeeze and remove pulp. **Need three quarters of a cup of this juice**.
- Pour juice and half glass of olive oil into a pint jar.
- Shake about twenty times. Drink this at ten in the evening.

Lie down **immediately** on <u>right side</u> and lie still without even speaking for twenty minutes. Lying on one's back will also work with this. Use a pillow or two to prop one's head up. The head needs to be higher than the abdomen. If one does not have a gallbladder, it may be necessary to go to the bathroom before the twenty minutes are up. Just go back and lie down when done.

Day seven

6 A.M.
Drink the third glass of Epsom salts. If very thirsty, have a drink of warm water first. **Stay in an upright position: in or out of bed.**

8 A.M.
Drink the fourth and last glass of Epsom salts

10 A.M.
Drink freshly pressed fruit juice. Half an hour later, may eat one or two pieces of fresh fruit. One hour later may eat regular, light foods. Eating should be back to normal by evening. Continue to eat light meals during the next two to three days.

Drink water when thirsty.

Note:

- Try to rest for two days following this procedure. This process affects the Body in similar ways as minor surgery.
- Large or small stones may pass in a variety of colors from turquoise to black. Due to the softening process they are like soft putty. However, if removed from the toilet and placed in a jar the stones will harden.
- If nausea occurs during this process, drink peppermint tea.

- Do not proceed with any of this process if there is known allergic reactions to any of the items being used.
- If diabetic, slowly sip the apple juice mixed with water or use cranberry instead, with no sugar added. Diabetics should have a room temperature protein shake when necessary or Spirulina in warm water.

APPENDIX H

Minerals

Trace Minerals

- **Boron** is necessary for healthy bones, muscle growth, and cognitive function. It is also known to increase the absorption rate of calcium, magnesium, and phosphorus. Boron supplements can become toxic if quantities are greater than six milligrams per day. Food sources of boron include apples, carrots, grapes, dark leafy greens, nuts, and grains.
- **Germanium** enhances cellular oxygenation, which in turn improves total Body health. This essential trace mineral is best when taken from natural, organic food sources. It is found in basically all organic food, with high amounts in shiitake mushrooms, broccoli, celery, milk, and rhubarb.
- **Iodine** is found in iodized salt, seafood, garlic, mushrooms, and asparagus, iodine helps to metabolize excess fat and is necessary for thyroid gland health.
- **Molybdenum** An integral nutrient for the conversion of purines to uric acid and nitrogen metabolism, as well as bone and teeth health, deficiencies of this micro mineral are linked to mouth and gum problems as well as cancer. Molybdenum is found in sufficient quantities in beans, dark leafy greens, and legumes.
- **Selenium** is used primarily as an antioxidant. This mineral works synergistically with vitamin E to protect free radical damage to fatty material. It is found in high quantities in brewer's yeast, broccoli, brown rice, garlic, dairy, meat, grains, seafood and Brazil nuts. **Do not take supplements if one**

is eating Brazil nuts, and do not take supplements or eat Brazil nuts if one is pregnant.

- **Silicon** This essential trace mineral is known as the beauty mineral because it is vital for the production of collagen and connective tissue. It is necessary for the health hair, skin, nails, teeth, and bones. As we age, the amount of silicon decreases in the Body, so supplements should be considered. Also, this mineral is known to help prevent Alzheimer's disease.
- **Vanadium** Used for cellular metabolism, bone and teeth formation, and growth, vanadium is another micro mineral that athletes may need more of. It is also difficult for the Body to absorb. Vanadium is found in fish, olives, meat, radishes, and vegetable oils.

Major Minerals

Calcium

Vitamins and minerals work hand in hand. For example, calcium gives strength to bones and teeth, and also stimulates the contraction of muscle fibers throughout the Body. Vitamin D in its turn helps the Body to absorb the amount of calcium it needs to do its job. A deficiency of vitamin D can result in the Body being subjected to a disease called rickets; which is a softening of the bones, due to the Body's inability to absorb calcium. When calcium is consumed adequately, it will optimize bone mass, and as a result reduce the risk of osteoporosis later in life.

Dairy as well as vegetables provide sources of calcium such as green leafy vegetables, beans, lentils, and the soft bones of salmon and sardines. Too much calcium will deplete magnesium levels as they work together to balance muscles.

Phosphorus

Like calcium, phosphorus also provides strength to bones and teeth. It is also necessary to help us properly metabolize protein, fat and carbohydrate. Phosphorus regulates the use of B vitamins.

Phosphorus occurs widely in foods, and can be found in milk, meats, poultry, fish, eggs, grains, nuts, dried beans, peas, lentils and green leafy vegetables.

Iron

Iron is a mineral which one's Body needs to not only form a part of all one's cells, as well it plays a major role in carrying oxygen from one's lungs. Iron however, belongs to the group of minerals referred to as trace minerals, and one only needs very small amounts of these each day. The liver plays a vital role in the balance of iron in the Body.

- Iron can interfere with one's ability to absorb phosphorus;
- Iron may enhance the absorption of calcium;
- Food sources of iron include meat, poultry, fish, clams, eggs, spinach, asparagus, prunes, raisins and cream of wheat;
- Deficiency of vitamin A reduces the ability to absorb iron

Chromium

Although the Body only needs a small amount, chromium is important for life. Its primary role is in blood sugar regulation (metabolism of glucose). Food sources of chromium include brewer's yeast, wheat germ, liver, meat, fish, turkey, brown rice, cheese, legumes, beans, peas, corn, green beans, whole grains, black pepper, and molasses.

- It is vital in the breakdown of cholesterol, fats and proteins;
- Reduces blood sugar and insulin levels in type 2 diabetes patients;
- Chromium promotes a healthy circulatory system;
- This is one essential trace mineral that many people have trouble getting enough of—one in ten North Americans have become deficient.
- Each person has their own individual needs.

Copper

Copper is a nutrient essential to human health. Copper works together with iron in making red blood cells. Food sources include organ meats such as liver, seafood, nuts, seeds, cherries and cocoa.

- Copper also aids in the formation of bone and hemoglobin;
- It is involved in the healing process and energy production;
- Copper is involved in hair and skin coloring, taste and sensitivity.

Magnesium

Magnesium is essential for the absorption of calcium and vitamin C. It is found in a variety of foods. A deficiency of magnesium includes a depletion of calcium; heart spasms; restless legs; cramping toes and fingers; nervousness and confusion. The kidney plays an important role in balancing levels.

- Magnesium converts blood sugars into energy.
- Magnesium helps to maintain normal heart rhythm.
- The richest food sources are whole seeds (nuts and legumes), wheat germ and other unprocessed grains.
- Other food sources include green vegetables, soybeans, molasses, cornmeal and shellfish.

Potassium

Potassium is a very important electrolyte which is essential for a healthy nervous system. Like magnesium, it is also essential for a healthy heart rhythm. It is actually the major ion in every living cell, and can be found in abundance in fresh foods. Potassium aids in maintaining stable blood pressure. The liver plays an important role in balancing levels.

- Food sources include a variety of fruits such as dried apricots, apples, bananas and cantaloupe, vegetables like broccoli, lima beans.
- Potassium can also be found in liver and dairy products.
- Potassium helps to prevent strokes as doe's magnesium.
- It also helps in proper muscle contraction.

Selenium

- Selenium is an essential mineral which the Body requires daily.
- Food sources of selenium are seafood, kidney, liver, muscle meats, grains and seeds.
- It works along with vitamin E to produce the Body chemical glutathione which works to promote a healthy immune system.

Zinc

- Zinc is necessary for proper growth of skin, hair and nails, and in healing wounds.
- It is an essential mineral vital to all stages of growth and helps transport vitamin A from the liver and acts as an <u>antioxidant</u>.
- Food sources for zinc include beef, liver, chicken, seafood, wheat germ, carrots, peas, bran, oatmeal and nuts.
- Too much iron reduces zinc.

Sources: Balch, Phyllis A. "*Prescription for Nutritional Healing.*" Fourth Edition (Penguin Books, 2006) as well as http://www.brighthub.com/health/diet-nutrition/articles/43671.aspx#ixzz1BUZQSEy1

Castor Oil Protocol

1. Use a good quality castor oil; Hexaine free so as not to create more toxins;
2. Apply 2 Tablespoons on a white cotton cloth that has been folded at least twice;
3. Place over the liver area (right side or offending area) and place a hot water bottle over top;
4. This should stay in place one hour (evenings are the best time);
5. Repeat this procedure for five days, then stop for two and repeat for a cycle of three weeks;
6. Take a two to four week break and repeat if necessary;

Notes:

- Two Tablespoons of castor oil are applied each of the five days.
- The cloth may be kept in a container and re-used. When having a break it can be placed in the refrigerator until the next use.
- White cotton is used to prevent dyes from soaking through to the liver.
- A hot water bottle is used to ensure that electric magnetic fields do not affect the body as would a heating pad.
- May use a piece of a disposable under pad as cloth becomes greasy to touch, to place over cloth (between cloth and water bottle)

Resources

Books

The Path of the Dreamhealer: My Journey Through the Miraculous World of Energy Healing, by Adam, Publisher Dutton Adult, Copyright 2006, ISBN-0525949488

The Emerging Dreamhealer: A Guide to Healing and Self-Empowerment by Adam, Publisher Plume, Copyright 2006, ISBN 0452287308

Dreamhealer: A True Story of Miracle Healings by Adam, Publisher Plume, Copyright 2006, ISBN-0452287294

Move into Life by Anat Baniel. Publisher Harmony Books, New York, Copyright 2009, ISBN-978-0-307-39529-0

Your Body's Many Cries For Water, F. Batmanghelidj, M.D., Global Health Sources Inc, ISBN-0-9629942-3-5 copy write 1992, Falls Church, VA

The Journey: a Practical Guide to Healing Your Life and Setting Yourself Free, by Brandon Bays, Published by Atria, 2002, ISBN-978-0743443937

Why is God Laughing? By Deepak Chopra, Copy Right, 2008, Random House Inc. NY, ISBN-978-0-307-40889-1

The 7 Habits of Highly Effective People, by Stephen Covey, Publisher Free Press, Copyright 1990, ISBN-10: 0671663984

The Talent Code by Daniel Coyle, Publisher Bantam Dell Book, New York, Copyright 2009, ISBN-978-0-553-80684

The Hidden Messages in Water by Masaru Emoto, Publisher Atria, Copyright 2005, ISBN-10: 0743289803

Mindwalking: rewriting your past to create your future, by Nancy L. Eubel, Published by A.R.E. Press, 2010, ISBN-978-0876045916

Canadian Angels by Your Side by Karen Forrest, Published by Pottersfield Press, Copyright 2009, ISBN-10:1897426089 or ISBN-13:9781897426081

Excuse Me Your Life is Waiting, by Lynn Grabhorn, Copy Right 2003, Hampton Roads Publishing Company, Inc., Charlottesville, VA, ISBN-978-1-57174-381-7

Power Vs Force: The Hidden Determinants of Human Behavior, by David R. Hawkins MD, Ph.D., Published by Hay House, 2002, ISBN-9-78-1561709335 or free at www.the-tree-of-life.com/gogscrc.htm

You Can Heal Your Life, by Louise Hay, Publisher Hay House Inc., Carlsbad, CA, ISBN-978-1561706280, Gift Edition, 1999

I Think I Am: Teaching Kids the Power of Affirmation, by Louise L. Hay, Kristina Tracy, Manuela Schwarz-Hay House (2008) ISBN-1401922082 www.louisehay.com

The Law of Attraction: The Basics of the Teachings of Abraham, Esther Hicks and Jerry Hicks contributor Neale Donald Walsch. Publisher Hay House Inc. Copy right 2007 ISBN-1-401912273 and 97814019192277

The Soul's Code by James Hillman, Publisher Warner Books Inc. New York, Copyright 1996, ISBN-0-446-67371-4

Soul Retrieval "mending the fragmented self" by Sandra Ingerman, Copyright 1991, ISBN-0-06-250406-1

Maya Cosmogenesis 2012: The True Meaning of the Maya Calendar End-Date, by J. John Major Jenkins, Published by Bear & Company, 1998, ISBN-13: 978-1879181489

Loving What Is-Four questions that can change your life, by Byron Katie with Stephen Mitchell, Copyright 2002, published by Three Rivers Press, New York, New York trademark of Random House ISBN-1-4000-4537-1

Tiger-Tiger is it True, Byron Katie and Hans Wilhelm, Copyright 2009, published by Hay House, Inc., ISBN-978-1-4019-2560-4

The Biology of Belief, by Bruce H. Lipton, PhD, Published by Hay House, Copyright 2005, ISBN-0-9759914-7-7

BALANCE nature's way to heal your body, by Susan Manion MacDonald, Published by New World Publishing, Copyright 2007, ISBN-13: 978-1895814323

The Amazing Liver & Gallbladder Flush by Andreas Moritz, Copyright 1998-2006, published by Ener-Chi Wellness Press-Ener-chi.com, USA ISBN-0-9765715-0-1

Intuitive Power Live-Your Natural Resource Lecture 4-CD Set by Caroline Myss, Copyright 2004 Caroline Myss and Hay House Inc.

The Book of Awakening, by Mark Nepo, Published by Conari Press, San Francisco, CA, ISBN-1-57324-117-2

Cancer is a Fungus: A Revolution in Tumor Therapy by Dr. Tullio Simoncini, Published by Edizioni, Copyright 2007, ISBN-10: 8887241082

Haven by Bobbi Smith, Published by Dorchester Publishing Co. Inc., 200 Madison Ave., NY NY, 10016, Copyright ISBN-08439-5312-8

My Stroke of Insight: A Brain Scientist's Personal Journey by Dr. Jill Bolte Taylor, Publisher Penguin Group USA, ISBN-10: 0670020745 & ISBN-13: 978-0670020744

Dreams Images and Symbols: A Dictionary by Kevin Todeschi, Publisher A.R.E. Press, Copyright 2004, ISBN-10-0876044887

Make up your Mind to be Happy by Josie Varga, Publisher A.R.E. Press, Copyright 2010, ISBN-13: 978-0876045015

It's Not about the Horse-it's about overcoming fear and self-doubt by Wyatt Webb with Cindy Pearlman, Hay House, Inc. Copy Right 2002, ISBN-1-56170-978-6 Carlsbad, Ca

The Prayer of Jabez by Dr. Bruce H. Wilkinson, Multnomah Publishers Inc., Sister Oregon, Copyright 2000, ISBN-1-57673-733-0

A Return to Love: Reflections on the Principles of "A Course in Miracles." By Marianne Williamson, Harper Collins Publishers Inc., Copyright 1992, ISBN 0-06-092748-8

The Shack, by Wm. Paul Young, Windblown Media, Newbury Park, California, ISBN-978-0-9647292-3-0 Copy Right 2007

A Life that Tickles Your Soul, by Suzanne Zoglio, PhD, Published by Tower Hill Press, 1999, ISBN-13: 978-0941668125

Web or You Tube Sites

www.the-tree-of-life.com/gogscrc.htm-AFT free book-Attraction Field Technique David R. Hawkins MD, Ph.D., author of *Power Vs Force: The Hidden Determinants of Human Behavior*

www.bodytalksystem.com-Body Talk

www.edgarcayce.org/-Edgar Cayce's A.R.E.

Association for Research and Enlightenment

215 67th Street, Virginia Beach, VA 23451

http://healingtools.tripod.com/pancpana. html-Dr. John Christopher and adrenals

www.collegeofacupuncture.com/ College of Acupuncture and Therapeutics Inc. 144 Ann St. Kitchener, ON, N2B 1Y3 [1-866-615-2787or (519)885-6401

http://www.crystalinks.com/pendulum.html

www.YouTube.com-You Tube Videos with Donna Eden-1. The Five Minute Energy Routine; 2. Energy Healing One-15-Training Your Meridian-Part 1 and 3. Energy Healing One-13-Your Aura Part 2

http://www.wikihow.com/Use-Dowsing-or-Divining-Rods#_note-0

http://educate-yourself.org/dow/index.shtml-Dowsing by Ken Adashi

www.lettertorobin.org-Dowsing with Walt Woods

www.123eft.com-*EFT*-Gary Craig-This e-book is also available on line

http://www.itmonline.org/arts/emotions.htm

www.ancienthuna.com/ho-oponopono.htm

www.sacredstewardship.net-Charles Hubbard,
Shinimicas Rogation Centre with Biodynamic
Farming-labyrinth, pyramids, dowsing, circles.

www.jtwellness@ns.sympatico.ca-JTW Natural
Health Guidance Centre, Susan & James MacDonald,
Courses and Services to guide you.

http://www.thekidneydiseasesolution.com/-Vitalchi
Wellness Sancturary; 6 Main Street; Blackburn, Vic
3130; Australia; Duncan Capicchiano, N.D.

http://www.buyamag.com/kirlian_camera_photography.php

http://www.peacefulmeadowretreat.com/ louise-white.
php-Cached-Hanna Kroeger-her daughter Gisela
Kroeger Hoffman-and Reverand Louise White

www.drmercola.net-natural health articles

http://maryanneradmacher.net-Mary Anne Radmacher

www.800herbdoc.com-Dr. Richard Schultz American Botanical
Pharmacy at and The School of Natural Healing at www.snh.cc

http://www.thewayoftheheart.com/way.html-Kimberly
Herkert & Daniel Goodenough

http://www.youngliving.com/en_US/wellness/about-essential-oils/

www.kristijn.com/
Tijn Touber-musician, writer, teacher

www.biomedx.org
Microscopic Courses

www.creativecommunication.com
Church Resource

www.transformationandcourage.org

www.columbuspolarity.com
Mary Jo Ruggeri, PhD. RPP

http:/.marthabeck.com

Contributors to my life resources for this book

Rick Adshade, Creative Lifestyle Solutions via Hypnotherapy, www. completebalance.ca, Certified Hypnotist. 10345 Rte. 204. Oxford, N.S. B0M 1P0 Email: rickadshade@me.com. Phone: 902-664-8892

Stephanie Allen, BSc., RMT, Lac, Dip.Ac, 2009 Gateway Development Ltd., PO Box 818 Amherst, NS, Canada, www.gatewaydevelopment.ca

Rose Devine, DNM, D. Ac.-Devine Meditations, Allergy & Naturotherapy Clinic,_10 Greenwood Drive Quispamsis, NB E2E 2T4, rdevine@nbnet.nb.ca

Connie Fisher, B.A. Communications, M. A. Psychology, The Way of The Heart™ Area Coordinator

902-660-2026, connie@thewayoftheheart.com

GOD, prayer, meditation, intuitive response, a heart connections

Dr. Bruce Hayhoe, DC, ND; 123 Hazen St; Saint John, New Brunswick, E2L 3L2

Ruth Hoyt, Saint John, N.B., rahoyt@nbnet.nb.ca

Sharon Joseph, Intuitive Life Counsellor, www.TheBookMaster.ca or www.SharonsGift.com

Kim Lake, Energy Healer and Entrepreneur, owner of Arabella Natural Cosmetics, kimlake@eastlink.ca

Karen Lees, Content Editor; kslawrence@gmail.com

James MacDonald, C.H., n.d. Microscopic Technician, Body Talk Practitioner, Reiki Master, Hypnotherapist www.jtwnaturalhealth.ca

Thelma McCullough, Natural Health Practitioner, 59 Gray Rd, Penobsquis, N.B. E4E 5S7, 506-433-8039

Kateri Meyer, Vibrational Healing/Flower Essence Practitioner and Nature Consultant, wisdom of Akashi Records, www.naturesnotion.com

Juli Oxford, P.A.U.S.E. Wellness Centre, 12335 Highway 224, Middle Musquodoboit, NS; Pathways to Wellness, 2219 Quinn Street, Halifax, N.S.

Gloria Penney, R.N.B.N., DiHom, R.Ac., n.d. The Wellness Centre, St. John's, Newfoundland www.remedyforwellness.com

D. Paul Reilly, Ph.D.-President, Corporate Motivation.org

North American Office: TYG Media Center

6525 Babcock St., Malabar, FL 32950 | Tel: (321) 220-1550

Bahamas & Caribbean Office: P.O. Box N-7121

Nassau, Bahamas | Tel: (242) 327-0312

www.corporatemotivation.org

Kim Ripley, Social Media Marketing, kim.rip@hotmail.com

Al Rodee, EFT and Ho'oponopono, www.alrodee.com

Gretchen Smith-Primal Heart Healing Arts Studio, Reiki master; Holistic practitioner, Educator, Creative Visioning, Intuitive Guidance, The Way of the Heart, Women's Retreats, gretchen.smith@seaside. ns.ca

Kimberly Smith, RMT, Raindrop Therapy & Massage Therapist, kd_smith11@hotmail.com

Eagle Spirit, Contemporary Shaman, Energetic Balancing, Soul Attunements, Soul Journey, EagleSpirit Journeys, www. eaglespiritjourneys.com

Dianna Stewart, Intuitive Counselor, diannastewart@ns.sympatico.ca

Laurie-Anne White, RMT, Awakenings, Massage Therapist, Reconnective Practitioner, harmony4@live.ca

Joanne Works, Avalon Natural Health Therapies, Saint Johns Newfoundland; www.avalonnaturalhealththerapy.com